Praise for the Anat B
by Professionals a

"Anat can bring children with special needs
that has to be seen to be believed."

"This accessible, insightful, practica
needs will profoundly deepen the
Following in the footsteps of the rev
krais, the greatest thinker about ho
century, Baniel shows why our main
wrong, and at times damaging, because they train children to 'ape' developmental milestones they are not developmentally ready to meet. The approach here,
far wiser, far more subtle, truly holistic, far more ingenious, far more in accord
with how brain development occurs, shows ways to access the child's *own* brain
plasticity and yields far greater results, so that the children can spontaneously
grow from within. I know because I have observed Baniel's little patients on
multiple visits, and time after time, I have seen children whose parents were told
their brain-damaged children would never walk, or talk, or be able to think well
or regulate themselves, begin to do just that with this gentle technique. I have
seen the peace on the faces of these children as their minds and plastic brains
suddenly begin to integrate what they have learned for the first time, the explosion
of joy at their first steps and watched them grow and become more independent.
Baniel is a master clinician for children with special needs, especially creative
with brain-damaged children. The stories presented here are not exaggerations;
they are triumphs from which most parents of children with special needs will
surely benefit."

—Norman Doidge, MD, author of *The Brain That Changes Itself*; Faculty
University of Toronto Department of Psychiatry, and Research Faculty, Columbia
University Department of Psychiatry, Center for Psychoanalytic Training and Research

"I have observed Anat's work with severely challenged individuals over a period
of more than two decades, and have witnessed transformations that are simply
stunning. My hope is that the Anat Baniel Method will reach the greatest possible audience and that it will become a part of academic teaching, training and
research programs in rehabilitation medicine and in physical therapy, and the
sooner, the better."

—Dr. Daniel Graupe, Professor of Bioengineering and Adjunct Professor of Neurology
and Rehabilitation Medicine at the University of Illinois, Chicago

"Anat's work with children is magical. She's their *brain whisperer*. This hugely important work will free special-needs children and their parents from fear and limitation, moving them into a world of new possibilities and joy."

—John Gray, author of *Men Are from Mars, Women Are from Venus*

"Anat's work is wonderful and profound. *Kids Beyond Limits* does a masterful job of helping parents and caregivers help the special child in their lives. This is a book of great wisdom as well as deep appreciation for the great challenges of raising a child who has special needs."

—Jack Canfield, author *of Chicken Soup for the Soul* and *The Success Principles*

"The Anat Baniel Method allows my four-year-old daughter to continuously reach and redefine her potential, physically, cognitively, and emotionally. It is awe-inspiring to watch these transformations unfold. It is my hope that someday all special-needs children and their parents will have access to this work and its benefits."

—Michele Shusterman, mother of child with cerebral palsy

"After my son's first week of sessions with Anat, Teo was paying attention for the first time in his life. At home he became more curious exploring the world around him and more aware of his surroundings. Through this work I gained amazing tools to use with my son."

—Karinna Barlow, mother of child on autism spectrum

"Jack began getting lessons at fifteen months of age. Today, after receiving lessons in the Method for three years, my son is no longer diagnosed with autism. He is highly verbal, affectionate, intelligent, and playful."

—Patty Tobin, mother of child on the autism spectrum

"Today Plum crawled for the first time. Her crawling was just like an everyday thing, and yet the greatest miracle."

—Yeshi Neumann, grandmother of child with undiagnosed developmental delays

"At three months old Joseph was diagnosed with uncontrolled seizure disorder. As a consequence, his development has become extremely delayed. The changes in him since he began getting lessons in the Anat Baniel Method are incredible."

—Fiona and Chris Stewart, parents of child with seizure disorder

**For more testimonials from parents and professionals,
please visit www.anatbanielmethod.com**

Kids
Beyond
Limits

The Anat Baniel Method for Awakening
the Brain and Transforming the Life of
Your Child with Special Needs

ANAT BANIEL

A PERIGEE BOOK

A PERIGEE BOOK
Published by the Penguin Group
Penguin Group (USA) Inc.
375 Hudson Street, New York, New York 10014, USA
Penguin Group (Canada), 90 Eglinton Avenue East, Suite 700, Toronto, Ontario M4P 2Y3, Canada
(a division of Pearson Penguin Canada Inc.) • Penguin Books Ltd., 80 Strand, London WC2R 0RL,
England • Penguin Group Ireland, 25 St. Stephen's Green, Dublin 2, Ireland (a division of Penguin
Books Ltd.) • Penguin Group (Australia), 250 Camberwell Road, Camberwell, Victoria 3124, Australia
(a division of Pearson Australia Group Pty. Ltd.) • Penguin Books India Pvt. Ltd., 11 Community
Centre, Panchsheel Park, New Delhi—110 017, India • Penguin Group (NZ), 67 Apollo Drive,
Rosedale, Auckland 0632, New Zealand (a division of Pearson New Zealand Ltd.) • Penguin Books
(South Africa) (Pty.) Ltd., 24 Sturdee Avenue, Rosebank, Johannesburg 2196, South Africa

Penguin Books Ltd., Registered Offices: 80 Strand, London WC2R 0RL, England

While the author has made every effort to provide accurate telephone numbers and Internet addresses at
the time of publication, neither the publisher nor the author assumes any responsibility for errors or for
changes that occur after publication. Further, the publisher does not have any control over and does not
assume any responsibility for author or third-party websites or their content.

KIDS BEYOND LIMITS

First edition: April 2012

ISBN: 978-0-399-53736-3

An application to register this book for cataloging has been submitted to the Library of Congress.

PRINTED IN THE UNITED STATES OF AMERICA

10   9   8   7   6   5   4   3

The author has changed the names to protect the identities of the people mentioned in this book,
but none of these changes has affected the truthfulness and accuracy of her story.

Most Perigee books are available at special quantity discounts for bulk purchases for sales
promotions, premiums, fund-raising, or educational use. Special books, or book excerpts,
can also be created to fit specific needs. For details, write: Special Markets,
Penguin Group (USA) Inc., 375 Hudson Street, New York, New York 10014.

To all the children I've worked with, whose ability to learn and grow in the face of real challenges is a continuing source of inspiration.

And to all the parents who never give up on their kids.

Our only limitation is our belief that it is so.

—MOSHE FELDENKRAIS, PhD

Contents

Foreword

Kids Beyond Limits is a great gift to every person who loves a child in great need of help. If that describes you, please take the important messages of this book to heart. The author's approach to the child with special needs has evolved from her own rich clinical experiences, which showed her over and over again that the brains of these special children *can* change, often dramatically, to awaken and enable and empower *and transform* their young lives. We humans are all endowed with a plastic brain, that is, a brain that is capable of constantly changing throughout life. Even while they struggle, these children still operate with this great resource, ready to be taken advantage of by them, by the enlightened clinician who is trying so hard to help them, and by the parents and grandparents who love them. Anat Baniel brilliantly explains how the effective engagement of this marvelous, innate human capacity for positive brain change *can* be the stuff of miracles.

I have spent much of my own scientific career trying to understand how we can harness our capacity for brain remodeling for the benefit of children and adults in need of neurological help. From several decades of research, summarized in many thousands of published reports, we scientists have defined the "rules" governing brain plasticity in neurological terms. We now know how to drive brains to change for the better.

It has been a great wonder to me, then, that my friend Anat Baniel, working in parallel along a completely different path, has defined almost exactly the same rules. Moreover, Anat interprets them here in practical and understandable human terms, in ways that should contribute richly to your own more enlightened parenting, grandparenting, or clinical intervention.

As she explains in this book, Anat began her journey of discovery working closely with her mentor, the great Israeli visionary Moshe Feldenkrais. From this platform of understanding, through close observation of the thousands of children whom she has helped, Anat elaborated and crystallized her understanding of how to connect with and then really help children in great need. As her reputation for providing help to the "hopeless child" grew, she began to see children from almost every condition and diagnosis of special needs. From this almost unequalled personal experience, Anat discovered two great truths.

First, the principles that underlie the limitations of the child with special needs—which are the same ones that can lead to real progress for that child—are the principles of brain plasticity. Those principles are beautifully outlined here in practical human terms as Anat Baniel's Nine Essentials.

Second (and this is an even greater truth), most "hopeless child" cases aren't.

This book is an important manifesto expressing important practical implications of what I have called "the brain plasticity revolution." Our brains are subject to continuous change. Each time we acquire or refine a human ability, we physically rewire—*specialize* by remodeling—our brain machinery. Every new or improved ability is a direct product of this kind of physical brain change. How can we make better use of this great human asset in our own lives? How can we assure that this human capacity is most effectively brought into play for the benefit of our own growing children? The child who struggles so hard just to respond, to initiate action, to understand, to move competently, and to have command in his or her world can especially make great use of their brain's plasticity on their path to growing and evolving their capabilities in ways that contribute to a better life for them. If you can really connect with such a child—as the author so beautifully describes—then with appropriate guidance almost every kid with special needs is capable of substantial, continuous, and *sometimes almost unbelievable* personal growth.

Don't underestimate the complexity or difficulty that may be involved in getting a child with such struggles on a positive growth path. Building a more effective and more powerful brain requires us to start where the child is, and where that brain is right now. This can require a highly personalized approach and almost certainly a great deal of very hard work for all concerned. The principles in this book should provide you with a new understanding of how to achieve that personalization in order to begin helping that special child in your life make new and real progress in a positive, empowering direction.

Remember that a little positive neurological change achieved each day can represent great progress over the course of a year, and even more so across the span of a young life. The author provides us with a number of wonderful examples that illustrate how each newly established level of neurobehavioral control opens up a whole new set of possibilities for each child. Anat Baniel explains how the principles that govern the operations of a brain built for change can be practically applied to set up a child for continuous growth. Once the child is on that positive growth path, every little advance can be truly exciting for them, and for you.

I strongly encourage you to take the advice presented in this book seriously so that you have a clearer idea about how you might be able to really help the child that *you* love.

—MICHAEL MERZENICH, PhD,
neuroscientist, professor emeritus at UCSF, and member of the
National Academy of Sciences and the National Academy of Medicine

Introduction

A number of years back, parents and students began urging me to write a book about my work with children with special needs. Even more than their repeated requests, it was the thousands of children, from a few weeks old to teenagers, whose transformations I had witnessed over the years through my work or through the work of practitioners I had trained, that compelled me to write this book. I felt a strong drive, a responsibility, to communicate what I know to parents and caregivers who are trying to help their child move beyond his or her present limitations.

Just yesterday I saw, for the first time, a fourteen-year-old boy who had suffered severe brain damage in infancy. The injury had left him blind, with no language abilities and with no voluntary movement. After just a few days of sessions with my colleagues and just one session with me, for the first time in his life he began vocalizing and moving his legs; his arms were freer, and it was clear that he was engaged in the process—he was even able to follow some simple movement instructions I gave him—and loving it. He was waking up to himself.

At the end of the session this boy's mother, who had dedicated her life to caring for her son, looked at me and we exchanged knowing looks. There were tears in our eyes as we felt the gratitude for these wonderful, albeit modest, changes, even as we dared not declare another thought aloud: *If, at fourteen, he could change and come to life this quickly, and in ways he had never done before, what would his life have been today had he received this same opportunity thirteen years ago?* The closest his mother came to expressing this was when she said what many parents before her had: "I wish we had found out about you and your method sooner."

This boy's breakthrough moment was by no means unique. It is only one of many thousands of lessons where I have felt a deep yearning to reach out to others who are caring for children with special needs, to let them see and know what is possible for their children. When I began this work, some three-plus decades ago, I was surprised when parents labeled my work with children as "miraculous." I knew the changes we were seeing were real, but I had limited understanding of the connection between what I did and the outcomes with the children. Over time it became clear to me that the results we were witnessing were not flukes. Because these outcomes were repeated over and over again, with hundreds of different children with a variety of conditions, it was impossible to explain them away as spontaneous recoveries or misdiagnoses—as physicians sometimes did when they couldn't otherwise explain what was happening.

I have witnessed thousands of stunning transformations over the years but I have never thought of myself as a miracle worker. Rather, I have understood that these transformations always occurred within the child's own brain, and the changes in the children were all well within their brains' capacities.

Every time I witnessed a child's transformation, be it a child diagnosed with autism, sensory integration disorder, cerebral palsy, attention deficit hyperactivity disorder (ADHD), or any other diagnosis, I felt an urgent need to bring the knowledge and tools of this method to as many children as possible. I wanted to provide parents and other caregivers with easy, practical ways for helping their children's brains take advantage of their untapped remarkable capacities and potentials. This is what this book is about.

The materials presented in this book constitute a paradigm shift; they are a game changer. These materials can be invaluable for you in helping your child. Through them your child can experience the remarkable transformations that the brain of virtually every child with special needs is capable of, transformations that he or she might otherwise never be able to access.

Over the years I have formulated an understanding based on a combination of what I had learned from my teacher Dr. Moshe Feldenkrais, from my own experience with thousands of children, and from research in the neurosciences. Every year science brings us more knowledge about the potentials of the human brain, discarding old paradigms, pushing the boundaries of what is believed to be possible, and revealing new options for helping both healthy and injured brains do their job better.

For the remarkable potentials described in this book to manifest, you need to develop an appreciation for the mind-boggling capacities of your child's brain to change itself, given the right conditions, through what has been labeled *brain plasticity*. And then, of course, you need practical, easy, and concrete ways to apply these principles in real life with your child, regardless of his or her specific conditions or unique history. This was my intent and purpose in writing the book you are now holding in your hands.

The first three chapters offer you an understanding of how your child's brain can change to further improve and often transform his or her life. The nine chapters after that describe what I call the Nine Essentials that the brain requires to wake up and make quantum leaps in achieving more of your child's potentials. At the end of each of the Essentials chapters, you will find a section in which I list tools for practicing each Essential. These are concrete, easy-to-use suggestions for applying the Essentials in your daily life with your child, in this way taking advantage of cutting-edge brain plasticity principles. The Essentials and tools move the discourse about the amazing capacities of your child's brain from *great promise* to actual manifestation.

At the back of the book you will find a section of frequently asked questions (FAQs) that I've collected over the years. You will also find references and notes compiled by my associate Neil Sharp, MD. There you will find scientific research related to what's discussed in each chapter. The references are given in full with abbreviated notes; full notes are available online at www.anatbanielmethod.com. Relevant research will be updated regularly as it becomes available.

I recommend that you read the first three chapters because they provide the background for understanding the unique aspects of this work. After reading the foundation chapters, read the first Essential, Movement with Attention, because it is a key for all that follows. After that you can continue reading the Essentials in the order in which they appear in the book or in an order that appeals to you. I suggest you spend a few days with each Essential and its tools to familiarize yourself with them, to master the skills required, and to deepen your understanding. Once you have gone through all the Essentials chapters you may want to go back from time to time and study them further. You can find short videos, parents' testimonials, and samples of lessons with children, online at www .anatbanielmethod.com.

I trust that in these pages you will find powerful new ways to help your child go beyond his or her current limitations on a daily basis. This book is an invitation for you to discover new ways for your child to access and improve the enormous capacities of his or her brain to change itself.

Part I

The Foundation

1   How It All Began

We have more possibilities available in
each moment than we realize.

—THICH NHAT HANH

I am often asked how I became interested in working with children who have special needs. Was there something that drew me to this work early in my life? Was there a child with special needs in my own family or among my friends? Was I simply drawn to working with children? The answer to all three questions is no. My introduction to kids with special needs was not something I had planned for or consciously chosen. It began when I met a baby named Elizabeth.

It was early in September 1980, during the first year of my practice. My teacher and mentor Dr. Moshe Feldenkrais and I had recently arrived in the United States from Europe.

We had made arrangements for him to teach some workshops and see a few students at a friend's place in Manhattan's Upper West Side. I would be assisting him.

When the doorbell rang that first morning, I welcomed in a handsome young couple in their thirties, carrying a crying baby who they were desperately trying to calm down. The baby, Elizabeth, was crying so hard and was in such great distress that it would have been impossible for her to receive the work she had come to do with Dr. Feldenkrais. After a few moments Dr. Feldenkrais asked if I would watch the baby—whom the mother placed in a safe position on the couch—while he took the parents into the next room for a short conference.

At this point I had never worked with children and had never even considered it. In my own practice, back in Israel, I worked primarily with adults involved in high-level physical performance, such as dancers, musicians, and athletes, who were having pain or were bothered with other limitations. As I watched baby Elizabeth, lying there on the couch crying, something happened that I would never have anticipated. She was in a great deal of distress and discomfort, and was unable to move on her own. But I had only one thing in mind at that moment, a deep desire to ease her discomfort and unhappiness. Though I hadn't the vaguest idea of what to do for her I took her into my arms. I knew none of the particulars about her medical diagnosis or condition, nor was I thinking of her as *special*. I knew only that she was very unhappy.

Other than holding her, there was nothing intentional in what I did, but within seconds she stopped crying and calmed down. Suddenly she was peaceful and seemed comfortable. As her crying stopped I dried her tears and gazed into her tiny face. Looking back on it, there was nothing tangible or objective that supported what I was feeling at this moment except that I experienced a deep connection with her. I was also quite certain that she was making a connection with me that was comforting to her. As I gazed into her big brown eyes, which were no longer flooded with tears, I experienced a real person there, a consciousness that was capable of far more than her present diagnosis was suggesting. Her official diagnosis—which I would learn about only later—was indeed quite dire, pointing in the opposite direction of what I was feeling.

The medical explanation was that she had "global brain damage." This was years before MRIs and other brain scans were widely used for diagnosis, so doctors could say little more than that something was terribly wrong. That much was clearly evident in my experience of holding her. For example, there was very little sense of her musculoskeletal system operating in any coherent or purposeful way: The muscles of her left side were very spastic, her eyes were severely crossed, and there was little to indicate that the baby was aware of her own body.

At the time I met Elizabeth and her parents, a traditional physiotherapist had been working with her for approximately six months, with no encouraging results. Similarly, the prognosis of two leading pediatric neurologists was distressing: One had suggested that the baby be institutionalized for life. The medical community offered no hope of her ever enjoying any degree of autonomy. The parents were devastated, but they still clung to the belief that there were happier alternatives; they were unwilling to accept these opinions or recommendations. They were not giving up on her.

I recall Elizabeth's father saying that when he looked into his daughter's face he was certain he detected an intelligence there, trapped and unable to express itself. My experience of holding Elizabeth in my arms and gazing into her face convinced me that he was right. I fully agreed with him. This was when we began our work together. The deep inner knowing that I shared with Elizabeth's parents proved to be both accurate and extraordinarily fruitful.

Elizabeth's First Session

As Dr. Feldenkrais returned to the living room after his talk with the parents that day, all three of them noted how baby Elizabeth was nestling in my arms, quite content, quiet, comfortable, and alert. Dr. Feldenkrais watched with great interest, then asked me if I would come with him and hold the baby while he worked with her. I carried Elizabeth into the next room and held her in my lap as I sat down on the edge of a low table, similar to a massage table, that had been set up there for him. Dr. Feldenkrais took his place in a straight-backed chair, facing us so that he could easily reach out and touch his tiny student.

To an untrained observer, I am sure Dr. Feldenkrais would have appeared to be doing very little. He was not forcing Elizabeth into a supposed correct position or movement. He was not massaging her muscles or adjusting her back. At first an observer might have noticed only his unusual concentration and attentiveness. For a few moments he just watched Elizabeth with a deep, focused attention and presence that was virtually palpable, so characteristic of him when he was conducting what he referred to as a "lesson." After a while he reached out and touched the baby's upper back; later, he gently, and very briefly, moved her legs in various ways, then lightly touched his finger to her hands and arms and face.

As he worked I was acutely attuned with his intense focus and quiet intentionality. I began to experience confirmation of the hidden intelligence that Elizabeth's parents and I felt was there. This first revealed itself almost magically in one hopeful and unmistakable way: Elizabeth was *paying attention*. A connection between her and Dr. Feldenkrais was being established. The changes in how she felt in my hands were ever so subtle, yet profound and definite, confirming that her hidden intelligence—her awareness—was awakening.

That entire first session with Dr. Feldenkrais took less than an hour, including the conference with the parents. It was agreed the parents would return the next day for a second lesson. The next day I met them at the door and, just as before, Elizabeth was crying very hard, a very unhappy baby. Again she quieted down in my arms before I carried her into the next room for her lesson. With her sitting limply in my lap, her back resting against my chest, Dr. Feldenkrais reached out and gently held her head between his hands and began ever so lightly to pull her head up. I noticed that her pelvis was not moving, which was a valuable observation: Normally, when a child's head moves up, the brain "knows" to arch the lower back and roll the pelvis forward. It is a whole pattern that is formed in the brain over time, though quite early in children's lives, as they develop. I placed my hands on either side of her pelvis, pressing it ever so slightly in the forward direction as Dr. Feldenkrais was gently pulling her head up, as if to awaken her brain to these parts of herself so that she could begin synchronizing these two movements. Then I pressed ever so gently on her pelvis, providing her with the feeling that she could roll it backward as Dr. Feldenkrais lowered her head a bit. After doing this for a while, Elizabeth began moving and rocking her pelvis, coordinating it with her head movements. Her brain had figured it out! I felt Elizabeth's whole being awakening in my arms.

At this time, Elizabeth was thirteen months old, an age at which most children would be sitting up by themselves; however, she was not able to do this on her own. Nevertheless, it was *not* our intention here to exercise her sitting abilities or to make her sit up. In fact, getting her to sit up wasn't even a consideration in our minds at the time. What I was acutely aware of was that somehow Elizabeth didn't seem to even know she had a back, a pelvis, or a head; her brain had not yet formed any relationships with these or other parts of her body. She wasn't sitting up because her brain was not creating the rich web of connections to her body, and the interconnections between the different parts of her body, from which her ability to sit up would emerge.

Once her brain had formed this intricate, dynamic web of connections, Elizabeth would have the resources to figure out how to sit up all by herself. Her brain would then be using the background information it received to create patterns that would tell her muscles what to do to sit up. Her brain would also be able to use these same background resources for creating and refining many other future skills.

The whole point of these sessions was for Elizabeth's brain to become a *learning brain*—that is why we call our sessions lessons rather than therapy. The focused attention, intention, and awareness of the teacher, coupled with the focused attention of the child as the flow of new information comes to her brain, is how the remarkable transformations occur.

When this second lesson was over I got up and handed Elizabeth over into her father's arms. He had been watching the whole lesson. Something had changed in Elizabeth's demeanor and it was significant. As her father held her against his chest Elizabeth was now able to control the motions of her head. She began intentionally arching her back, throwing her head back and looking at me upside down, then bringing her head back up, noticeably delighted with the game she'd just discovered. In that moment, she had the experience of controlled, intentional, and pleasurable movement for the first time in her life. She was being *playful*—and playfulness, as we know, requires a feeling, thinking, functioning brain! It requires awareness of one's *self* and the world around her.

As basic as Elizabeth's movements might have seemed to a casual observer, these intentional motions of her head and back, the remarkable change in her demeanor, and her playfulness, were all cause for great celebration, signaling us that Elizabeth's globally damaged brain was capable of learning, capable of organizing itself to produce deliberate and voluntary control of her body and her mind, and ultimately of her own life.

Upon my return to Israel after my introduction to Elizabeth, the focus of my practice began changing almost immediately. Within weeks, Dr. Feldenkrais was referring other special needs children to me. A whole new world, filled with new possibilities, opened up to me. Elizabeth's parents wanted her to continue her work with me, beginning an association that would continue for twenty-plus years. She would face many challenges in the years ahead, but she never stopped progressing; she never stopped working and learning. Over time she gained abilities that defied all the odds.

When I recall our work together, there were many memorable breakthrough moments, but one in particular comes to mind because it beautifully illustrates the dynamics of the process I would come to call the Anat Baniel Method (ABM).

The Little Girl Who Made Tissues Fly

During my sessions with Elizabeth my whole focus was on her, giving my full attention to what she was doing and feeling and thinking. At the same time, I was looking for any opportunity I might use to help her discover her own present abilities, refine these abilities, and learn new ones. I am at one with the child even as I become a resource for her. Often, the opportunities we found together were ones that because of her special needs she might have never otherwise discovered on her own. Here's an example: When Elizabeth was seven years old, she was able to stand up and walk by holding onto something but was unable to walk on her own. Anytime she tried, within a step or two, she'd abruptly lose her balance and, like a drunkard, fly off in any direction and fall flat on the floor. I'd been racking my brain for months, searching for what it was she needed to walk independently. I knew she was very close.

At the time Elizabeth was still unable to catch a ball, an invaluable form of play that contributes to complex coordination, something seven-year-olds usually do quite easily. When a ball was thrown in her direction, Elizabeth would reach out with her hands and hold them in front of her in a fixed position. The moment the ball was thrown her way, her eyes would freeze so that she was unable to track the ball and coordinate her movements to catch it. I had found a large, light-weight inflatable beach ball which moved slower when I threw it, but still she couldn't catch it.

Serendipitously, Elizabeth asked for a tissue during one of these sessions. As I picked one out of the box I thought, aha! The tissue might offer exactly the opportunity I'd been seeking. I held the tissue in front of my face and blew it in Elizabeth's direction. The tissue, being almost weightless, and presenting a fairly large, soft mass, floated toward her like a leaf on a gentle breeze. And it proved to be exactly what she needed. Instead of Elizabeth's eyes becoming frozen, as they usually did when the ball came sailing toward her, she was able to track the slow, wavy, moving tissue and catch it. When I recall this moment, knowing what we now know about the human brain's organizational capacities, I picture a highly active process going on in her brain. Millions of new connections are being formed between various neurons, creating whole new constellations in her brain as she performed the very complex activity of following the tissue and catching it.

The lesson did not stop here. Elizabeth was just delighted with the game and thrilled with her newfound ability to catch the tissue. She laughed as if she'd just discovered the most wonderful game in the whole wide world. She suddenly stopped to catch her breath and held the tissue up in front of her own face. I could see what she now had in mind. She had decided that she was going to blow the tissue back to me!

Elizabeth blew on the tissue but her exhalation of air was not strong enough to propel it all the way to me. The tissue fell on the floor next to her. She bent down, picked it up, and blew on it again. This time, something quite extraordinary occurred: She followed behind the tissue, walking and blowing on it again and again, keeping it in the air until it reached where I was sitting. All this time she was walking independently, blowing the tissue and laughing hilariously. The tissue was very forgiving since it was slow to fall to the floor, so she had time to blow on it repeatedly. At that time I was well aware of the enormity of the moment. Elizabeth had just walked independently for the first time in her life. She'd been so involved in the game with the tissue that she hadn't even realized it. All that she had learned to date, combined with her newfound ability to use her eyes to track the tissue, had somehow come together to give her another new skill—walking.

Through the years that I worked with Elizabeth we always made a point of identifying and building upon *present abilities* rather than focusing on her disabilities, transforming the abilities we had identified into greater abilities, again and again. Over time Elizabeth learned not only how to walk but to talk, read, write, make friends, and socialize. Fast forward to her teenage years—to her Bat Mitzvah celebration where the enormity of Elizabeth's accomplishments suddenly hit me so profoundly that I was moved to tears. I wept joyfully and openly. I was not alone; many others in the audience were crying, too.

....

Through the years that I worked with Elizabeth we always made a point of identifying and building upon *present abilities* rather than focusing on her disabilities, transforming the abilities we had identified into greater abilities, again and again.

....

Some years later, I received an invitation to her wedding. I recall seeing her at the ceremony, radiant in a beautiful white gown and her dark flowing hair, surrounded by admiring and loving guests. Today, in her early thirties, Elizabeth has master's degrees from two excellent universities, is happily married, and runs her own successful business. Recently, in a phone call, she enthusiastically told me about her family and her work.

She said, "Anat, I have found my passion in life. I am happy." Elizabeth's processes and successes have become living benchmarks for me as well as for hundreds of other children and their parents, constant reminders for us all to *go beyond limitation to the miraculous.*

> **Elizabeth's processes and successes have become living benchmarks for me as well as for hundreds of other children and their parents, constant reminders for us all to *go beyond limitation to the miraculous.***

What's Possible for My Child?

At one time or another most parents ask themselves, What's possible for my child? My answer to that question, whether the child has special challenges or not, is always the same: Expect miracles. The nature of change is such that we can't see or accurately predict the future from our present perspective; if we try to, we have a tendency to see a limited picture of the future through the lens of what's there in front of us right now. Thirty years ago, when Elizabeth was a small, severely challenged and very unhappy baby, few could have predicted or imagined her future.

> **The nature of change is such that we can't see or accurately predict the future from our present perspective.**

When we closely examine what we call the miraculous, we often find that it wasn't the result of mere happenstance or luck but that it came about through a series of events—sometimes large, sometimes small, sometimes deliberate and well reasoned, and sometimes through creative efforts that brought about transformational change. The willingness to entertain the impossible becoming possible may very well be where remarkable changes begin. This is true even in science and medicine, which are based on knowledge that we think of as solid and unchangeable, built on exhaustive study and incontestable evidence. And yet, both science and medicine are constantly changing. For instance, even twenty years ago the medical profession did not consider autism real; most people viewed attention deficit conditions (ADD and ADHD) as "bad behavior" rather than as neurological conditions requiring special help. And when a child had a stroke, causing damage to some part of the brain, it wasn't understood that other parts of the brain could take over and organize actions they do not ordinarily do.

Today we know that the brain can change itself. It is the part of us that is, in fact, most capable of change. We are developing an increasingly large and sophisticated body of knowledge about how to make better use of the brain's capacities, thanks in part to the science of *neuroplasticity*— that is, the brain's ability to reorganize itself and gain new skills by forming new neural connections. It is this field of study that supports and helps us explain the practices I describe in this book and that have been so successful with children with special needs over the past three decades.

> **Today we know that the brain can change itself. It is the part of us that is, in fact, most capable of change.**

Because of my formal background in clinical psychology and statistics, I am of a scientific mind. But for many years there was very little in the scientific literature that confirmed both my theory and my repeated experience that under the right conditions the brain can and does change itself very readily. This remarkable ability of the brain has helped explain the results I have continued to get for over thirty years with children who have special needs.

A Significant Departure from More Traditional Modes

The process I describe in this book is a significant departure from traditional systems of teaching, therapy, and medical intervention. For instance, many traditional systems tackle the child's special needs by attempting to force the child to conform to a standardized model or to otherwise try to have her do what she "should" be doing to keep pace with her age group or *developmental stage*. Rather than imposing what the child is not yet able to do on her on, we first look at her present abilities and needs and then seek ways to provide whatever information her brain needs to progress to her own, unique next ability.

> **For the child to change and grow we need to communicate with her brain; neither the problem nor the solution is to be found in the muscles.**

For the child to change and grow we need to communicate with her brain; neither the problem nor the solution is to be found in the muscles. The muscles are doing what the brain tells them to do. The mind—that part of us that forms speech, solves math problems, and thinks—is also organized by the brain. If the leg doesn't move it's because the brain hasn't figured out how to do it; the brain isn't telling it to move because it doesn't yet have the information it requires to be able to form the necessary pattern that would bring about the desired movement. When a child is having difficulties with speech, problem solving, or thinking clearly, the same principle applies. Our brains can change themselves—and there are ways to help the brain of the child with special needs function better—a realization that was revolutionary when I started this work thirty years ago.

The Anat Baniel Method is a proven way of connecting and communicating with the brains of children with special needs to form patterns of movement, thought, and feeling by taking advantage of the children's innate abilities. Through employing these methods we provide experiences that lead children to discover themselves, to learn the next thing they are able to learn, regardless of how large or small, simple or complex it might seem. Our goal is always for children to awaken to themselves and develop their underlying fundamental ability to *learn and grow*. They experience their bodies in new ways, moving in ways they were not previously able to do; they learn to feel what is going on inside them and around them. They wake up to themselves. Through this awakening they become more comfortable and more capable, feeling better about themselves.

> **Our goal is always for children to develop their ability to awaken their brain's fundamental ability to *learn and grow*.**

Parent Power

Never underestimate the power of parental love. This is especially important if your child has special needs. It is your love and your desire to have the best for your child that motivates you to seek the opportunities that will provide him or her with the highest possible quality of life. I see this with all the parents I meet. Their willingness to take a stand for new possibilities for their child as they seek to unlock their child's hidden capabilities takes courage and is inspiring. There's power in this determination and love teaming up with science and skill. It expands the child's opportunities beyond the limits of clinical diagnoses, commonsense reasoning, and past experience. It is often the first step on the pathway to the miraculous.

2 From Fixing to Connecting

There is no surprise more magical than the surprise of being loved. It is God's finger on man's shoulder.

—CHARLES MORGAN

A child is born. It is perfection, a miracle. Without knowing any of the details, and often long before the birth, we have begun creating a vision for that child's future. He will grow up to have a full and satisfying life, independent and whole. Then comes the shock. Something is wrong with my child! Sometimes this moment comes all at once, at birth or even before. At other times the realization unfolds gradually. The diagnosis and cause might be clearly defined, at least in medical terms, or it might remain uncertain.

As the realization that *something is wrong* sinks in, it can bring with it overwhelming fear, confusion, and deep grieving (sometimes unconscious) and often a disquieting sense of guilt. But the overriding part of the experience is a powerful desire to do anything and everything we can to help our child. We want to help him grow up to be "normal," to be able to walk, talk, think, and feel and to have an independent, rewarding life. The questions we must ask ourselves are, How do we get there? How do we go about helping the child grow beyond his present limitations?

....
We must ask ourselves, How do we go about helping the child grow beyond his present limitations?
....

When we learn that something is wrong, whatever it might be, the natural thing to do is to focus on the limitation, on what the child *can't do*, or on what he is doing *wrong*, and then we try to conquer, stop, or otherwise overcome it. We want to *solve the problem*, and *fix* the child so he will sit up, talk, read, write, relate to others, and reason the way he would if it weren't for his special needs.

The desire to fix what is broken or malfunctioning is tremendously important and useful. There are times when fixing is exactly the right approach—for example, when doctors need to surgically repair a hole in the heart, when an antibiotic is used to combat an infection, or when a blood transfusion is needed. When they're necessary and when appropriate treatment is available, those fixes need to be carried out. At the same time it is important to understand that fixing is but one way of approaching problems, one that has great limitations and can at times even be counterproductive. The Nine Essentials presented in these pages are intended to guide us beyond the limits of the fixing approach, providing new opportunities for the child's own brain to create the solutions it requires.

Looking More Closely at the Fixing Model

Most of us have an understanding of fixing as *repairing* what is broken, or *restoring* the way something is supposed to look, function, or be structured. When we're talking about a mechanical object, such as a car or home appliance, we generally know what to do: If we can't fix it ourselves, we hire an expert who does know. When we have a flat tire we have the leak repaired; when the car's engine misfires we have a mechanic replace worn parts and get it running smoothly again. The repair person employs her brain, her experience, and available resources, such as replacement parts, to restore the machine to its original design and functionality.

Unlike the child, a car or other machine can take no active part in the repair process. It has no mind of its own, no self-healing ability, and it doesn't possess the capacity to learn, grow, and evolve. The car mechanic's role in replacing parts and tuning up an engine is the essence of the fixing paradigm. And how natural it is to want to use this same paradigm for a child with special needs! We want to replace any missing parts or parts that aren't working well. We want to find somebody who knows how to adjust this or that so that everything will be working just right.

....

Unlike the cars or kitchen appliances, your child is not a finished product. Children are living, feeling, and experiencing beings; *works in progress*.

....

Unlike the cars or kitchen appliances, your child is not a finished product. Children are living, feeling, and experiencing beings; *works in progress*—growing and evolving; in the process of figuring out and continuously forming the abilities to move, think, understand themselves, and relate to the world around them. At the center of all this unfolding potential is that most remarkable of all organs, the brain. Regardless of his special needs, your child possesses a brain that must be actively involved in creating new connections and patterns for overcoming the limitations and difficulties he may have. This is what every brain is designed to do. And this is where our hope lies.

> **At the center of all this unfolding potential of your child is that most remarkable of all organs, the brain.**

To make full use of the brain's remarkable potentials, we need to make a shift in our thinking, away from the fixing paradigm. To be truly helpful, we need to know how to focus our attention on what we can do to awaken and strengthen the capacities of the child's brain to do its job well. We are not alone in the process of trying to help the child with special needs; our greatest resource and our best partner in helping our child overcome challenges is the child and the powers of his own brain.

Making the Transition from Fixing to Connecting

To be truly helpful to the child with special needs, we need to back off from trying to *make* the child do what he can't do. We need to more fully recognize the fundamental role the child's brain plays in learning and refining new skills. The brain has the ability to figure itself out and, amazingly, to create successful solutions to problems. No matter how much we may want to help, and no matter what our expertise, we are 100 percent dependent on the child's brain to make the necessary changes.

Through the Nine Essentials we move quickly beyond the limitations of the fixing paradigm to help the child's brain do its job better, providing the underlying process by which all skills and all learning emerge. *The*

Nine Essentials will help you to get your child's brain working brilliantly.
Yes, you read that right. In the pages ahead you will discover how your
child's brain can evolve to function in remarkable ways despite the very
real challenges he is facing.

> **The Nine Essentials will help you to get your child's brain working
> brilliantly.**

Whenever we ask the child with special needs to do what he cannot
do, that's the fixing paradigm in action. Let's say he cannot sit up; we put
him sitting up, and we do this again and again, hoping that after repeating
this enough times he will somehow *get it* and do it himself. If he cannot
talk, we ask him to imitate certain words or sounds, over and over again,
hoping that with enough reiterations his speech deficiencies will be fixed.
Sometimes this approach produces the desired results, and sometimes it
completely fails. If we instead focus our attention on awakening and
strengthening the process by which the child's brain can create and discover its own solutions, the results that become possible are of a completely different order.

> **Whenever we ask the child with special needs to do what he cannot
> do, that's the fixing paradigm in action.**

In the pages ahead I describe how to move beyond the fixing paradigm, guided by the Nine Essentials, into a partnership with your child
and the creation of a roadmap for awakening the potentials of his brain.
At the heart of learning how to best help your child is this basic truth: *If
he could, he would; if she could, she would.* If he could sit, he would sit;
if she could talk, she would talk. Discerning and respecting what your
child can or cannot do at any given moment is a key factor in helping them

move beyond their limitations. Accepting the basic truth that if he could, he would; if she could, she would, becomes an exciting and inspiring opening when applied in light of the Nine Essentials.

The Nine Essentials are tools that your child's brain, and every brain, requires to wake up, become a powerful learner, growing and evolving on all levels. The Nine Essentials help you establish the ideal internal environment for your child's brain to do what it must do to develop and grow, creating the unique patterns and solutions that his particular special needs require.

> **At the heart of learning how to best help your child is this basic truth:**
> *If he could, he would; if she could, she would.*

Everything we do—walking, talking, thinking, feeling, relating to others—is made up of the millions of random experiences that we have had since the moment of our conception. All of our activities are made possible because our brains organize our experiences as dynamic, ever-changing patterns that direct those activities, whatever they might be.

> **All of our activities are made possible because our brains organize our experiences as dynamic, ever-changing patterns that direct those activities, whatever they might be.**

The Necessity and Purpose of Randomness

When a child has a special need, that condition itself will limit his opportunities for having certain *experiences*: physical, emotional, and intellectual. For example, when a healthy infant is lying in the crib awake, his arms, his legs, his back, and his belly will twitch and move from time to time. These movements are unintentional; they are what I call *random movements*. When a baby's arms are tight, immobile or spastic, spontaneous and infinitely rich and varied random actions cannot take place. Those random movements of the more typical baby may not seem like much at the time. But for the child's brain, they provide a rich flow of experiences and information that are absolutely necessary for the brain to eventually develop controlled and effective movements and actions. These random experiences would ordinarily be generated through the child's own random actions; they are in fact required for every child's brain to form itself as fully as it might. It thus becomes our challenge to figure out ways for the child with special needs to get those random experiences that his condition otherwise prevents or limits him from getting on his own. Along the way, we need to remember that these experiences will become rich sources of information for his brain.

The good news is that we can create opportunities for children to have these random experiences. When forcing them to do the actions that they are presently unable to do—the fixing paradigm—we deny them the richness of information their brain needs to learn that which we'd like them to learn. By introducing randomness to the process we make it possible for the child's brain to ultimately create better, more organized patterns for moving his arms or doing what he would otherwise not have the information to do. The child can only do this by starting with where his abilities are at the present moment.

....

Those random movements of the more typical baby may not seem like much at the time. But for the child's brain, they provide a rich flow of experiences and information that are absolutely necessary for the brain to eventually develop controlled and effective movements and actions.

....

Moving Beyond the Fixing Paradigm

For a person wanting to help a child who is unable to crawl, it might seem perfectly logical to get down on the floor with him, put him up on his hands and knees, support him in that position, and then try to assist him in making crawling motions. To some extent, we might be successful, but just as often this doesn't work, or at least not well. Why doesn't it work? To put it simply, by focusing on the end result we want the child to achieve, we rob him of opportunities for having the myriad random experiences his brain requires to form the inner patterns to do that activity well; note here that these are experiences that the healthy child *does get*. We are thankful there's an alternative, which I describe as the Nine Essentials in the pages ahead. By using the Nine Essentials we provide the child with the *opportunities* to get the random experiences and wealth of information his brain requires. The rich body of experience that the child then gathers, like a veritable galaxy of knowledge, provides that brain with what it needs not only to figure out and perform certain actions but to refine and enhance them, in short, to become an exquisite learner.

> **By using the Nine Essentials we provide the child with the *opportunities* to get the random experiences and wealth of information his brain requires.**

What we know from the science of neuroplasticity—that is, the brain's ability to reorganize itself by forming new neural connections—is that the brain uses every bit of information that it possesses in an infinite number of ways, surprising and unpredictable in their ingenuity. This underlying galaxy of knowledge, the billions of connections and patterns that the brain creates, will become the source of information to create skills and refine abilities from now into the future. The experience of crawling, of babbling, of listening to music, of catching a ball or recognizing the difference between cold and hot, will come into play in everything we do, be it physical, emotional, or intellectual. It can be helpful, in this respect, to consider everything we think, do, and feel as movements organized by our brains.

From Fixing to Connecting

The Nine Essentials move us quickly beyond the limitations of the fixing paradigm, helping any brain do its job better, and providing the underlying process from which all skills and learning emerge. The Essentials help get your child's brain to work brilliantly, as well as, or even better than, other children's brains, which the child with special needs will require to problem solve and figure out ways to make the impossible possible.

The Nine Essentials are tools for you to feel, see, notice, and create; more important, they will increase your own capacity to connect with and work with your child, whatever his special needs may be. You'll expand your ability to experience the world from your child's point of view, oftentimes lending him the capacities of your own brain to feel, to think, to differentiate, to move, and to listen.

> **The Nine Essentials are tools for you to feel, see, notice, and create; more important, they will increase your own capacity to connect with and work with your child, whatever his special needs may be.**

The purpose of connecting with your child through the Nine Essentials isn't just about being more compassionate. Nor is it about doing for your child what he cannot do himself. On the contrary, it is about providing your child with the greatest opportunity to develop real skills and a strong sense of self, to feel good about himself and to have the ability to continue to learn and grow, with a genuine sense of accomplishment and pride.

Children Learn What They Experience

Connecting in the ways described in the Nine Essentials builds on the knowledge that all children *learn their experience*; they don't necessarily learn what we intend them to learn. When we *drill* a child in our efforts to teach him to do something he can't presently do, the child learns his own experience of those efforts. This may very well include learning to fail at what he is attempting, or acquiring bad habits at what he does learn to do. Added to this are the possible feelings of fear, inadequacy, being bad or wrong, and even anger or resentment and a sense of failing to meet another's expectations. Any skills the child might learn in the process of being drilled include the child's *whole experience* of that effort. Limitations the child experiences in this way may support his belief that he cannot move beyond those limitations.

Every child is a living, feeling, sensing, thinking, and actively learning participant in any and every ability he ever develops in his life. The effectiveness of any help we might offer depends on how successful we are at assisting the child's own brain in creating its own unique solutions. Instead of trying to impose these solutions, as a car mechanic does when she replaces worn parts, we need to provide the child with the richness of experience he needs to feel, and from which he will form every ability, every movement, every action for himself and within his own brain. It is important to remember that these experiences have to begin *where the child is right now* in terms of what he can already do; only then can the child connect with what he is doing, as well as to his own self, if he is to make sense of the experience and progress beyond his present limitations.

....
**The effectiveness of any help we might offer depends on how success-
ful we are at assisting the child's own brain in creating its own unique
solutions.**
....

Any time we try to take the child away from where he currently is in terms of his present abilities, both parent and child will immediately experience the loss of connection with the other. When that connection is lost, it is usually a signal to us that we have slipped into the role of *fixer*; little will be accomplished until we reestablish that connection. For instance, if I see that it is very difficult for the child to sit up, I need to pull back, at least for that moment, and stop trying to force him into a sitting position. I then go back to something that he is actually able to do. Through the Nine Essentials you will be able to better recognize what your child is experiencing and work with his present capacities whatever they may be, even as you are facilitating their next breakthrough.

....
**Any time we try to take the child away from where he currently is in
terms of his present abilities, both parent and child will immediately
experience the loss of connection with the other.**
....

In the pages ahead you will discover how to make this profoundly important shift, from *fixing* to *connecting* with your child. As elusive and challenging as this shift might seem, it will make a huge difference in your child's life and in yours. Parents often remark that the possibilities that open up often border on the miraculous. Through the parents' work with the Nine Essentials a child who seemed oblivious to his surroundings suddenly takes great interest in the people around him; a baby with brachial plexus injury (injury involving nerves to the shoulder, arms, and hands) suddenly begins moving and using his arm; a child who has great difficulty solving math problems begins to understand the meaning of numbers, and to everyone's surprise starts loving his math class. The shift from fixing to connecting, which comes about through the skills of the Nine Essentials, will provide your child with rich new opportunities to feel and connect with himself and for his brain to function more and more effectively.

Through the Nine Essentials, you will learn to focus and awaken the underlying process of your child's discovery and creation of self, which is at the heart of successful growth and development. You will learn to shift your focus away from what your child "should" be doing now according to age and known developmental stages. You will become an astute observer of the smallest changes that occur in your child and develop an increasing appreciation for these changes and how it is that from the smallest of changes the big solutions grow. We'll examine how and why this shift is transformational for you and your child and look into the science that presently supports it.

> **You will become an astute observer of the smallest changes that occur in your child and develop an increasing appreciation for these changes and how it is that from the smallest of changes the big solutions grow.**

As you practice the Nine Essentials with your child, you will find yourself stepping beyond your own fear, shock, confusion, guilt, and myriad other feelings you may have. As you already know, your child's out-of-the-ordinary needs call on your out-of-the-ordinary potentials, beyond your own expectations and aspirations. The Nine Essentials make accessible what might otherwise seem beyond your reach, making the impossible possible for both you and your child, and making your time together more pleasurable and rewarding.

3 Your Child's Amazing Brain

We are in the early stages of a Brain Plasticity revolution.

—MICHAEL MERZENICH, PhD

From the very beginning of my work, thirty years ago, it was clear to me that the problems I was seeing with children who have special needs have to do with the brain. Regardless of the need or disability, whether it is autism or cerebral palsy or some other condition, the issue always comes back to the brain.

Our brains organize all that we do. They create order out of chaos and make sense of the constant flow of stimulation coming our way. But how does the brain do this, and what does this have to do with your child's special needs? The first part of the answer is that everything we do, every action we take, every movement that expresses our lives, every thought and emotion is made possible by our brain's capacity for organizing and bringing coherence to life's endless flow of stimulation and sensation. When a child has special needs, this process is interfered with. It is here, in the brain's capacity for organizing and making sense of itself and its world that we find our greatest opportunities for helping our child grow past her present limitations.

> Our brains organize all that we do. They create order out of chaos and make sense of the constant flow of stimulation coming our way.

Random Movement Feeds the Brain

After a child is born, she is just beginning to discover that she is a separate being in the world, an individual with a body, feelings, desires, and needs. She is flooded with sensations from all of her senses, from various processes going on inside her, and from her own movements and interactions with her environment. This is where creating order out of chaos comes in, transforming her mostly random movements and sensations into actions that are purposeful, intentional, recognizable, and meaningful to her.

As the baby lays in her crib during the first weeks of life, her brain is just beginning to figure out what to do with her sensations and how to organize her movements and perceptions. Watch a newborn baby and what you'll probably see is a lot of twitches, wiggles, and unintentional movements, which I call *random movements*. All this activity may seem aimless. What we don't see is what is going on in the brain. And there's a huge amount going on in there.

With each movement a rich flow of sensations is being sent to the brain, sensations from the baby's arm as she move it across the fluffy blankets, the sensations of pressure on the child's back, the complex of sensations that are sent to the brain by movements of the muscles, joints, and bones. When a little arm reaches out and is caught in Mother's hand, followed by Mother's affectionate squeeze and the soothing sounds of her voice, all of this is experienced by the child. Each sensation experienced has the potential to feel different, one sensation from another. The brain's ability to perceive the distinct differences in these sensations is the source of information from which the brain performs the extraordinary process of organizing itself, the body, and making sense of the world. It is here that we find the greatest opportunity for helping the child who has special needs by facilitating her brain's ability to perceive differences.

In the Beginning: Perception of Differences

The transformation from random to intentional and purposeful movement and action begins with our brain's ability to perceive differences. How easy it is to take this extraordinary ability for granted! It seems like such a simple thing. It is one of those abilities that goes on in the background of everything we do, without our having to think about it or to even know it exists. But without this ability we could do little or nothing in life. All action, all skill, actually our very survival, totally depends on it.

> **The child's ability to notice differences in what she sees, hears, tastes, smells, and feels in her moving body is at the heart of the brain's capacity for creating new neuroconnections and pathways.**

The child's ability to notice differences in what she sees, hears, tastes, smells, and feels in her moving body is at the heart of the brain's capacity for creating new neuroconnections and pathways. It is the source of information for the brain. It is from this ability to perceive differences that all future patterns are formed, be it learning to grasp a toy, learning to say *Mama*, walking, responding to a specific word or name, or expressing delight when Daddy comes home. When we truly understand the profound importance of this capacity, it opens up vast new possibilities for helping the child with special needs.

Thing One, Thing Two: Help Is on the Way

Without exception, the brain of a child with special needs will require help with perceiving differences, at least in those areas relating to his or her present limitations. What might this look like in real life? I'd like to tell you the story about my work with a little girl I'll call Kassi. Her story illustrates the results we can get when we understand what the brain needs for developing a particular movement, skill, or action and how we can provide opportunities for this to occur.

I saw Kassi for the first time when she was three years old. She had suffered brain damage at birth, which left her with severe cerebral palsy. The muscles of her arms, legs, and belly were extremely tight (spastic), and there was very little movement that she could do on her own. Whenever she tried to move, her whole body tightened up even more. When her parents placed her in a sitting position on my table (a wide, padded, very stable table that resembles a massage table) her back got very rounded, and she held her arms even more tightly to her body. It was difficult watching the great effort Kassi was making just to keep herself from falling. It was obviously very scary for her. Her legs were straight in front of her, held tightly together.

After several months of Kassi's regular weekly sessions with me, during which I employed the Nine Essentials (described in detail in the chapters to come), she had improved greatly. She gained more mobility and control in her arms and back. She sat up more comfortably and maintained her balance better. Sitting up was no longer scary. Even her speech improved and so did her ability to think. She no longer repeated the same three or four sentences over and over again, but formed independent thoughts and learned to communicate her desires more clearly.

But there was one thing that seemed out of my or Kassi's reach, one thing that stayed the same no matter what we did. Kassi's legs remained tight and held together all the time, even when she was inactive, as if held together by invisible straps. When I moved her legs very slowly and gently I was able to separate them and move them freely and independently. But the moment Kassi tried to move her legs on her own initiative or move in any other way, both her legs instantly became very spastic. I kept wondering, how could she be learning new ways of moving and gaining greater freedom everywhere in her body except for her legs.

Then one day, it suddenly dawned on me. Kassi did not know she had two legs. She had never felt them as separate because they always moved together as one. She had never perceived the difference between her right leg and her left leg. And difference that is not perceived does not exist. In her experience, and in her brain, she had one leg, not two. There was no "Thing One" and "Thing Two." There was only Thing One. Clearly, anyone looking at Kassi could see that she had two legs, a left one and a right one. But *her* brain did not know this.

....
Difference that is not perceived does not exist.
....

Recently researcher Michael Merzenich and colleagues were able to induce cerebral palsy–like symptoms in the hind legs of rats. They did so by tying the two hind legs together at the time the rats were born so they always moved the two legs together as one. After a while, when the restrictions on the legs were removed, the rats continued moving them together as if they had only one leg, just like Kassi. Their brains had mapped the legs as one, not as two.

My realization that Kassi's brain was mapping her two legs as one was an important breakthrough, profoundly influencing my work thereafter. It opened a vast world of new possibilities for helping children with special needs take advantage of their brains' remarkable flexibility and capacity for remapping and changing itself by providing the conditions for the child to perceive differences where she had not perceived them before.

Let's Play: Kassi Discovers Thing One and Thing Two

Once I had realized that Kassi's brain had mapped her two legs as one, it became clear that she needed to somehow *feel* and recognize that she had two legs. But how could we bring this about? I had gotten her legs to move separately many times, but to no avail; all these exercises and sensations continued to be interpreted by her brain according to its one-leg map. I understood that it was Kassi, not me or her parents, who had to notice her two legs. For that to happen, I needed to somehow get her to take interest in, pay attention to, and perceive the two-ness of her legs.

Like all children, Kassi loved to be playful. I got out my washable nontoxic markers, placed Kassi in a sitting position with her back leaning against my chest, and then I gently brought her right leg up so she could see her knee. I tapped lightly on her right knee and when she looked in that direction I asked if she would like me to draw a picture on this knee. She said yes. Then I asked, "Shall I draw a cat or a dog?" (This is about the limit of my artistic skills.) After thinking about this for a moment Kassi said, "Dog." I asked, "Would you like the dog to be brown or red?" She chose red. These were all questions requiring the brain's perception of differences—exactly what was required for Thing One and Thing Two. I proceeded to draw an image of a red dog. I did this very slowly, naming each part of the image as it emerged: "Here's the dog's nose. Here's one ear, and another ear," and so on.

Kassi was transfixed, listening to my voice, watching my drawing and feeling the marker on her skin. When I was done, I helped her move her leg around to show the picture of the dog to her mom, who was in the room with us, then to show it to me, and then to look at it herself. I then put that leg down and slowly lifted her left leg.

With surprise and mock disappointment in my voice, I playfully said, "Oh, there is no dog or cat on this knee!" In that moment I could tell that for the first time Kassi realized *there is another one of those* over there. There are two legs, not just one. I asked her if she would like a dog or a cat to be drawn on this other knee. This time she selected a cat. So a cat it was. I proceeded to slowly and deliberately draw a cat on this knee.

The fact that there were different pictures on her two legs opened up a vast world of new possibilities for Kassi's brain to begin transforming her *one leg* into two separate legs. Which picture did she want to show and to whom? Did she want the cat and dog to be close to each other, as when she pressed her knees together? Did she want them farther apart, as when I helped her spread her knees apart? How far apart should they be? Just a little bit? More? Far, far apart? The dog could touch her hand and the cat could touch Mommy's hand, and on and on.

Soon she was able, for the first time in her life, to differentiate and move either the cat knee or the dog knee independently and intentionally by herself. She had two legs for the first time in her life. Those initial movements were somewhat stiff and jerky, with a limited range, but they were *her* movements; she was *generating them herself*!

What Kassi's Brain Was Doing

Through our little game, which was fun and playful for her, Kassi's brain was receiving, assembling, and perceiving differences, organizing a growing complement of sensations with finer and finer differentiation. With these changes spasticity of her legs gradually decreased and her ability to control movement improved throughout her body.

It's important to see here that our work together was providing Kassi's brain with opportunities to feel and perceive differences: Thing One and Thing Two—leg one and leg two—as two distinct parts of herself, leading to greater movement and control. Note that we did not exercise her legs. This was not about trying to get her to do what she should have been able to do had she not had cerebral palsy. I didn't try to make her stand or walk. Rather we focused on her brain getting the information it needed to be able to recognize and organize the movements of her legs by helping Kassi perceive differences she had never perceived before. In a very real way, it was *brain* work, not leg work.

Over time Kassi continued to improve. The last I saw her, she had learned to pull herself up to a standing position, cruising slowly, walking sideways, step by step, holding onto furniture. Her thinking got clearer and better all the time. By the time she was five, people were seeing her as a very bright girl, which it turns out she was, though nobody had thought this when she was three years old.

The Making of a Duck

When everything is working well, each difference perceived contributes to an expanding source of information that the brain uses in an extraordinary process of organizing itself and the body, and in making sense of the world. The brain uses information it acquires through perceiving differences to create new connections between different brain cells; this capacity is called *differentiation*. Through differentiation your child's brain grows and changes, creating the complex integrated patterns and mappings that will give her the ability to move and act in ways that are intentional, fluid, accurate, and effective.

In my seminars I often start our discussion about *differentiation* by drawing the outline of a duck on a whiteboard. Then I draw four or five

Acquiring Action Skills Through Increased Differentiation

The desired "shape"—action

Limited differentiation—
few chunky "pieces" in the brain

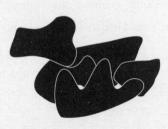

With only a few chunky "pieces"
the brain cannot successfully
organize the "shape"—action

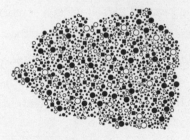

Greater differentiation—
many tiny "pieces" in the brain

With many tiny "pieces" the brain
can successfully organize the
desired "shape"—action

large, bulky, amorphous shapes, and ask people to imagine putting these shapes together, as if they were puzzle pieces, to try to match the outline of that duck. Of course, creating an image that even resembles a duck with only those four or five bulky pieces is virtually impossible.

Next I draw lots of much smaller shapes on the whiteboard: tiny circles, squares, triangles, amorphous shapes, and dots. I point to all these shapes and ask my students to imagine that there are as many of these pieces as they might want for creating the image of the duck. This, of course, is easy for them to do. With all these tiny pieces you can create precisely the image of the duck or create any other image you might like.

This demonstration, I point out, can help us understand the process of differentiation and integration that occurs in the brain, leading to the development of more precise and controlled movement skills. With enough small shapes in the brain we can "draw" the movement we want to make. This same process applies to any thought we want to form or to understand what is said to us. Remember that every movement we make—physical, cognitive, and emotional—is organized by our brains. In essence, our brains create patterns that give order to *all* that we do. And it does so from the many different pieces it has at its disposal; this repertoire of information is generated by the *perceived differences*.

Recall the point in Kassi's story when she first realized she had two legs: Thing One and Thing Two instead of only Thing One. We had found a variety of ways to play with the dog and cat pictures that I'd drawn on her knees, giving Kassi's brain the opportunity for creating a *collection of dots and shapes, a collection of many little pieces*. For the first time in her life she perceived a difference between her two legs, which allowed her brain to begin differentiating the movements of her legs; her brain now had the information it needed to start the process of creating separate maps for moving them voluntarily. She now had millions of more pieces for mapping her two legs, perceiving not only how her two legs were two instead of one but also gaining what her brain would require for moving them more smoothly and more accurately, with greater ease and control.

It is important to note that all the dots and shapes her brain was forming would also serve in differentiating and creating patterns for many other movements she would learn in the future. As the brain gains greater and greater differentiation, it applies that greater collection of dots and shapes to virtually everything that it does.

From a Blur to Clear Focus

Okay, you may be thinking, I can see how this dots and shapes idea works for physical limitations like Kassi's. But what about behavioral, emotional, sensory, and intellectual issues, such as when my child doesn't respond to her name? And how can I make use of this information when my ten-year-old still doesn't read, even though we've spent hours working with her and have tried everything? How can this help when my child gets upset and starts screaming whenever she is in a room with more than three or four people?

....
The brain organizes the mind and body as one whole; it does not separate one from the other.
....

Some of these symptoms will be familiar to you if your child has been diagnosed as being on the autistic spectrum, or having pervasive developmental disorder, or has a sensory integration disorder. If you have noticed emotional and cognitive challenges with your child, you most likely will have also noticed physical and motor challenges. That is because the brain organizes the mind and body as one whole; it does not separate one from the other.

As challenging as it might be to understand the connection between your child's physical limitations and the brain, it can be even more elusive to figure out what the brain needs when the problems are in the areas of thinking, feeling, emotions, and behavioral issues. The good news is that the very same process of perception of differences and differentiation applies in the development of all skills—and this includes thinking, feeling, emotions, and social behavior.

To demonstrate how the power of the perception of differences and differentiation helps children diagnosed with issues involving cognition, emotions, and social behavior, I would like to tell you about Julian. I first met him when he was three years old. His diagnosis: autism. I vividly recall walking down the hallway next to him on our way to my office for the first time. Early on, my attention was drawn to the physical symptoms—that is, how he slouched forward as he walked, his feet dragging slightly on the floor.

From the start, Julian seemed to be comfortable with my presence, so I decided to ask him some simple questions. He responded readily, but his diction was slurred and hard to understand. He drooled excessively. And his sentence structure was incoherent. Everything he said was partially formed, with unfinished thoughts that seemed to hang in midair. Julian's mother told me that he also had problems with fine motor coordination.

Once we were in my office, I noticed that Julian would pick up a toy and then, as if he'd forgotten he was holding it, he would just let it drop out of his hand. His losing track of the toy in his hand and letting it just fall to the floor reminded me of how he began to form thoughts and then let them dissipate into nothingness. My impression was that Julian acted as if someone had placed a foggy lens at the gateway to his brain so that everything coming in appeared blurry, fuzzy, and vague to him. He was unable to perceive differences clearly enough to make sense of himself or the world around him.

Having this idea in mind, I put Julian lying on his belly on my table.

I placed my left hand under his right shoulder and lifted it very gently, just a fraction of an inch or so at first. In fact, his shoulder would only move a small amount. As I lifted in this way I could see that his shoulder and back moved together rigidly as one unit. The same happened when I lifted his left shoulder. It was more like moving a block of wood than it was like moving the live human form with all its flexible joints, soft tissue, and resilient muscles.

As I proceeded to check out how well the movements of his legs, pelvis, and head were organized, it became very clear to me that Julian's brain, for whatever reason, was not differentiating the various parts of his body enough for him to gain any sufficient degree of dexterity, strength, clarity, and control. Similarly, he was unable to differentiate the sounds and sights around him or to make any but the most rudimentary sense of language and ideas. His brain was obviously not very good at perceiving differences; clearly, he did not yet have enough *dots and shapes* to work with. I decided to start our work together by providing Julian with opportunities to notice as many differences as possible, starting with the movements of his body and, whenever appropriate, using words to describe to him portions of his experiences as they were happening.

Though Julian was three years old, the differentiation of his fingers and other parts of his hands was more like what one would expect in a one-month-old. The infant who doesn't yet perceive his hand as having five separate fingers can make only a fist with his hands and let go. Julian still perceived his hand as Thing One. When he grabbed a toy, he was essentially making a fist and letting go; that was about the limit of his control.

Julian's *blur*—his poor perception of differences and his lack of differentiation—wasn't demonstrated only in his hands. It showed up in the way he walked (dragging his feet), in his drooling, in his slurred speech, and in his confused thinking when he tried to express himself. In fact, this lack of differentiation was global, evidenced in every part of his body as well as in his mind.

Through different movements I helped Julian perceive his head as Thing One and his shoulders and back as Thing Two. Then his shoulders as Thing One and his back as Thing Two. As if by magic, Julian was soon moving his back much better. He was able to arch his back with greater strength and twist from one side to the other with greater flexibility, precision, and ease.

I continued this session by lifting one of his arms, holding it at his forearm, and pointing it toward the ceiling. I then gently and playfully shook his arm so that his hand flipped back and forth at the wrist. After a few seconds I stopped. Julian waited, watching his hand expectantly, then said, "Again!" He had noticed that his hand stopped moving—he perceived the difference. I repeated the action and then stopped. After a second or two he once again asked for more and I resumed.

Julian's attention was now palpable. He no longer seemed to be in another world as he had been when he first came in. Now he was right there with me, fully in the here and now, noticing himself and his experiences.

After a few repetitions, I began asking Julian which arm *he* wanted me to move, then followed his direction. Julian was rapidly becoming aware of his arms and this new movement in his wrists. By having him decide which arm to move next, I further empowered him to use his increasing capacity to perceive differences and awaken his awareness of self. We continued with more movement variations in this way for an additional twenty minutes or so, and then finished that lesson for the day.

The next day Julian's mom reported that his drooling was greatly reduced. He had also initiated playing with a game that he had previously avoided because it had required greater hand coordination than he had until then and had been too challenging for him mentally. Now he could do it easily and well. All of this was evidence that his brain was doing a much better job of perceiving differences, differentiating, and organizing his actions.

Each day thereafter I continued to create opportunities for Julian to feel himself in new ways and to perceive new and more refined differences. By the fourth day, to my amazement, Julian looked at me and told me that his father was working in his office today. His diction was much clearer and the sentence complete. I asked Julian, "Do you ever play in your father's office when he is working?" His initial response was somewhat garbled and I couldn't make sense of what he said. It was obvious to me that Julian was doing some thinking but at that moment was unable to turn it into a coherent thought. So I asked the question again, phrasing it a bit differently. This time his response was clear and rather sophisticated. He proceeded to explain to me that his father had one office at home and another office not at home, and that he sometimes played in his father's office at home but not at the office not at home.

I could barely contain my excitement. Julian's ability to express a clear difference between his father's two offices was indeed a significant change. It showed that Julian's brain was becoming better at perceiving Thing One and Thing Two and thus was able to create order out of disorder. To go back to our duck drawing metaphor, Julian's brain was differentiating more and more, developing a larger collection of tiny pieces. His brain was rapidly gaining information to successfully map his movement, his speaking, and his thinking.

> **It showed that Julian's brain was becoming better at perceiving Thing One and Thing Two and thus was able to create order out of disorder.**

Making the Shift

As discussed in Chapter 2, our first impulse when we try to help a child with special needs is often to focus our attention on getting her to do what she can't presently do, be it exercising a spastic arm to try to make it move or by repeatedly trying to make a child have eye contact and respond to language. Most children will do their best to comply, and more often than not we see at least some degree of progress.

We certainly don't want to neglect the child by doing nothing. However, over and over again in my practice, I see children who rather than learning what others were trying to teach them, have learned instead the experience of their limitations—*what they can't do*, or *what they can do only poorly*. And these experiences become *grooved in*, making the child's present limitations and the brain maps associated with those limitations more deeply entrenched. We always learn what we experience—that which is actually happening for us. This is different from learning *from* our experience.

> We always learn what we experience—that which is actually happening for us. This is different from learning *from* our experience.

We are most useful to the child when we focus on helping her brain, through the process of differentiation, create the millions upon millions of Thing Ones and Thing Twos, which healthy children have in great abundance and which the brain requires for creating new, more complete, and well-organized mapping of action.

The shift, from focusing on what is right there in front of us (an arm that is not moving well enough, a child who has trouble understanding what she is told, or a child who is unable to roll over, sit, or walk) to focusing on helping the brain itself create the solutions can be elusive. It is of the utmost importance to make this shift in our own thinking—that is, to think in terms of what the brain needs in order to be able to form the patterns and skills for making those movements. It is the child's brain that has to figure it out; we cannot do it for the child.

Children arrive at the ability to roll over or sit up, or do any of the things they learn to do in life, through an extensive process of differentiation and integration set in motion within the brain. Billions upon billions of Thing Ones and Thing Twos lead to the formation of millions upon millions of different brain connections (called *synapses*). Those connections come together in complex, dynamic, responsive, and continuously evolving patterns that eventually result in the child being able to sit up, stand, walk, and so on.

The child doesn't plan, or know ahead of time, that she is going to sit up, roll over, or stand up, or say *Mama* for the first time. Rather, the first time it happens the child finds herself doing it. From the child's vantage point, achieving such a milestone is a complete surprise, always unexpected. Our job is to help wake up the child's brain and support this process of creation, formation, and discovery. You will learn to provide this support through the Nine Essentials, all of which can be easily incorporated into any activity or interaction you have with your child. It is all very doable, and you will begin witnessing changes right away.

> **Our job is to help wake up the child's brain and support this process of creation, formation, and discovery.**

You can bring the Nine Essentials into any exercise or therapy routines you may be doing with your child at home. You will discover that your child will learn and improve faster and with greater ease and, at the same time, become a happier child.

Part II

The Nine Essentials

4 Essential One
Movement with Attention

Movement is life; without movement life is unthinkable.

—MOSHE FELDENKRAIS

Nothing happens until something moves.

—ALBERT EINSTEIN

In previous chapters we've discussed how all of life, everything we do, think, feel, and learn is movement. However, there are two kinds of movement: movement that we do automatically or mechanically and movement that we do with attention. Understanding the difference between these two kinds of movement is key to helping your child get beyond his special needs or limitations. Both forms of movement—Movement with Attention and automatic movement—are important. Automatic, repetitive movement allows us to reliably perform different functions in our daily lives, like walking, talking, cooking, driving, and certain communications with others. However, when we want or need to learn a new skill or improve an existing one, automatic, repetitious, or mechanical movement won't do. Research shows that movement done automatically creates little or no *new* connections in the brain. What it does do is reinforce or groove in the existing patterns more deeply— *including the patterns we want to change*. On the other hand, when attention is brought to movement, the brain creates new connections and possibilities at an incredibly rapid rate. It is estimated that at such times a young child's brain forms 1.8 million new connections per second! Understanding this can be life changing for you and your child.

> **Research shows that movement done automatically creates little or no *new* connections in the brain.**

The attention the child brings to his own movement—be it physical, emotional, or cognitive movement—is a key ingredient for new learning and development, vastly expanding the brain's ability to form new neuro-connections, transforming what the child is able to do, often in seemingly miraculous ways. This attention factor—specifically the attention to what we *feel* as we move—is not exclusive to children with special needs. It is instrumental in learning and refining abilities for all of us, from the time we are first born to the last days of our lives.

If you carefully watch young children move as they are just beginning to experience themselves and the world around them, you'll notice how deeply involved and often very attentive they are. At such times we can see the phenomenon of Movement with Attention unfolding before our eyes. For example, a two-month-old infant lies in his crib watching in endless fascination as his own hand moves in space.

Or consider a twelve-month-old baby who sees a toy on a sofa a few feet away, gets curious, crawls toward it, pulls himself up to standing position, holding onto the edge of the sofa, then reaches out with his right hand to grab the toy. It is too far to reach. He goes up on his tippy toes but still can't reach the toy. Then he bends his right knee and lifts his leg in an effort to climb up on the sofa. But his knee hits the front of the sofa because he can't lift his leg high enough. His attention shifts from the toy, to himself, to his leg. To climb up and reach the toy he can no longer rely on the movements he already knows how to do automatically. He tries again, but this time he tries to do it differently. He lifts his right leg in a sideways direction in an attempt to bring it to the seat of the sofa. That doesn't work either. He brings his leg back down, fully focused on himself. He takes a few seconds to digest his recent experience, then lifts his leg once again. He goes back to bending his right knee. Lifting his leg sideways had felt uncomfortable. This time he arches his lower back a whole lot more than before. This movement lifts the pelvis higher and the leg feels lighter, too, easier to lift, and he is now lifting it higher. He feels his knee move past the edge of the sofa to rest on the seat of the sofa. Once he feels that, he puts pressure on that knee, simultaneously plants his elbows, pulls on his arms, and successfully climbs up onto the sofa. At that moment his attention shifts back to the toy, which he can now reach.

The moment that something he already knows how to do doesn't work (in this case he can't reach the toy), the little boy has to pay attention to his movements and to what he feels; only then can his brain get the new information it requires for figuring out how to climb up on the sofa. We can't predict all the ways that the child's brain might make use of what it's taking in during this process, but we do know that it is essential. Perhaps the information the brain gains from the experience of figuring out how to bring a knee up high enough to get on the sofa will be used later to balance on one leg, climb up the stairs, jump, ice skate, or solve problems in physics. Maybe his brain will apply the information it has received from this early experience to develop the dexterity for playing the piano, cello, or some other musical instrument.

It is important to note here that we are not talking about you having your child pay attention to *you*, a therapist, or a teacher but rather for you to find ways to help your child do the action of noticing and following the sensations and feelings he is experiencing as he moves himself or is moved by you—what we will call *attentioning*.

Bringing your child's attention to his movements and actions in this way opens up possibilities for learning and transformation that would otherwise not be available for his brain. This is why it is so important to recognize the vast difference between automatic or mechanical movement and Movement with Attention. For example, let's say a child has difficulty grasping objects with his hands. We might put him on the floor with a truck, grasp his hand, put his hand on the truck and mechanically move his hand through the motions of driving the truck, believing that if we do it enough he will be able to do it himself. More often than not this won't work. If the child is already close to being able to do this himself, your assistance might help him learn to do it on his own. However, without the child's participation and close attention to the sensations in his own body as he engages in this activity and if he does not correct himself in response to what he feels, like the boy climbing up on the sofa, very little is going to change in his brain. When the child is able to bring attention to his own movements and feel those sensations, meaningful changes will begin occurring right away.

> **Bringing your child's attention to his movements and actions in this way opens up possibilities for learning and transformation that would otherwise not be available for his brain.**

Often the difficulty or even inability to pay attention is itself your child's special need; at other times the special need interferes with his ability to move or to move with attention. What I've realized working with thousands of children with special needs, and with their parents, is that it's not only imperative we help these children develop their ability to attend to themselves and to what they feel as they move but, without exception, it is possible for them to develop this ability. This is where your understanding of this first Essential—Movement with Attention—comes in. This knowledge, and your *application* of the tools introduced in this chapter, offer great opportunities for you to help your child.

Beware! Your Child Is Learning

Parents' dedication and willingness to spend hours each day taking their child through repetitious exercises trying to help him develop movements or skills he presently lacks is both moving and inspiring. And it is very difficult if after months of such hard work the child gets only limited results. Over the years I have come to recognize what might be holding the child back. When exercises are done mechanically and repetitiously what gets grooved into the child's brain—what your child is learning—is his actual experience. The child is learning that which is really happening for him, not what we would have wanted the child to learn. The patterns formed in his brain will take in everything he experiences while doing exercises—physical or cognitive—including patterns of *not being able to perform* that movement or skill or not being able to do it well. This is what I call the learned *patterns of failure*. And what is so easy to overlook is the child's feelings about succeeding or failing in that process, which will also be incorporated into these patterns. Consider the example of a child with cerebral palsy who is unable to stand by himself. Every time he is helped into a standing position, his knees bend, his legs cross, and the muscles of his legs violently contract or become spastic. If this experience is repeated over and over again in an attempt to teach him how to stand, every time he even thinks about standing, his brain is going to re-create the pattern he experienced in his body. He is learning more about *not standing* than he is about standing.

The patterns formed in his brain will take in everything he experiences while doing exercises—physical or cognitive—including patterns of not being able to perform that movement or skill or not being able to do it well.

Through Movement with Attention—the child's deep absorption in the feelings and sensations of his own movements—his brain, with the millions of new connections that are being formed, gets opportunities to create new solutions and to find better ways to do whatever it is he is learning. Rather than attempt to place him in the standing position, have him be in a position he is comfortable being in so he can be attentioning to what he's feeling. This might be sitting in his wheelchair or even lying down on his back. Then focus on one element from the totality of standing—for example, when he is on his back, slowly lift and bend one of his legs and place the sole of his foot on the floor as it would be if he were standing. Then very slowly assist him in sliding his foot a tiny bit to the right, then to the left. The point is to have him focus on the sensations he is getting from the bottom of his foot. If doing this is too hard for the child, change the approach in this way: With his legs straight, take a book and place it against the sole of one of his feet, then slightly increase the pressure and decrease it, having him tell you when you are doing one or the other. Then ask him to push with a tiny bit of pressure against the flat surface of the book. Have him increase and decrease that pressure. You'll most likely be able to observe a significant reduction in the tonus of the muscles of the legs, which will make it easier for him to move them.

These are just two examples of what you can do to help your child bring attentioning to and feel his own movements. (At the end of the chapter you will find more tools you can use with your child.)

Think of Movement with Attention as bringing about a virtual explosion of activity in the brain, but an explosion that leads to an amazingly high level and complex order. At such times, the quality of information that the brain generates is very high, creating order from disorder by organizing the tiny pieces and shapes that you read about in Chapter 3. At such moments an enormous field of new possibilities opens up for your child. Through this process of increased differentiation you can almost always count on there being some changes for the better. The changes will often surprise you because we cannot know in advance the specific solutions your child will work out at any given moment. You see, there is always more than one way—and usually a great many ways—to do the same thing. And, as discussed in the example of the boy and the sofa, brain connections created through one activity can be applied in infinite and predictable and unpredictable ways in developing other skills.

By now you may be asking yourself, What does bringing Movement with Attention to my child look like? And if this can help my child, what can I do as a parent to employ it? The following story will help illustrate the awakening of a child's attention, showing the positive, measurable results it got with this particular boy.

"He's a Transformed Child!"

I first saw Ryan and his twin brother, Brandon, when they had just turned two. Ryan had been diagnosed as being on the autistic spectrum, while Brandon was developmentally normal. During our first session I immediately saw that Ryan made no eye contact with me or with other people. While Brandon played with the toys in the room, Ryan sat in his father's lap, arching his back forcefully and throwing his head back against his father's chest. He moaned and cried, repeating these movements with his head and back over and over again.

I learned that in addition to Ryan making no eye contact, he was not speaking or relating to adults or other children, nor did he respond to his name. He had difficulty eating and refused most food. When other people were around, he often tried to hide under furniture. During his first visit to my office he attempted to crawl under a stool that was way too small to accommodate him, suggesting that he had very little sense of himself and the size of his body. He was physically weak, with low muscle tone, and was so passive that he had become the object of his brother's bullying, who snatched toys from him and pushed him down.

While his parents conversed with me, telling me about Ryan's birth (the twins were born premature and there were other complications), Ryan continued to arch his back and throw back his head. His father held him firmly, mostly to keep the boy from falling to the floor as he bucked around in his arms. It was clear to me that Ryan's thrashing around was automatic rather than intentional and, despite how it might have seemed, he was not trying to get away from his father. While the parents were externally calm as they spoke, they made it clear that they were definitely overwhelmed by Ryan's condition. They had done everything they could in their efforts to help him, and nothing seemed to work.

I turned my attention to Ryan, as he continued to thrash around on his father's lap. I remained calm inside, watching and wondering what was going on for him. As I observed him in this way, it seemed to me that little Ryan didn't *know* he was thrashing. Even though he was moving his pelvis, head, and back, he was not feeling himself moving and seemed unaware that he had a back and pelvis. It was almost as if Ryan didn't know he existed.

At this point my attention was not focused on trying to change or control Ryan's behavior even though, like most people, I felt an urge to try to stop this disturbing behavior. However, I knew what little good that would do. Instead I observed Ryan closely and wondered how to best help him begin to notice and experience himself and his own movements in a safe and pleasant way, so that he could come home to himself more.

Ryan was moving his pelvis forward every time he arched his back and threw his head back; he then moved his pelvis backward when he stopped. To help Ryan bring attention to, and begin to feel the movements, I gently placed my hands on either side of his pelvis and followed his moving pelvis with my hands. Each time his pelvis moved back I also pressed it lightly against his father. My light yet clear contact with his moving pelvis, and the repeated increased pressure of the back of his pelvis against his father's body, accentuated the sensations coming from this area of his body to his brain, making it easier for Ryan to begin feeling himself moving. Even though he continued to thrash around as he'd been doing, the intensity of the arching and the frequency went way down; this indicated that he was beginning to feel and change.

Next, I very gently took hold of his left foot and leg and began moving his leg slowly in different directions, wondering what it would feel like. It was stiff and tight at first. After a minute or two Ryan stopped thrashing completely for a few seconds and looked down at his foot, as if feeling it and seeing it for the first time in his life. I remember thinking that, judging by the expression on his face, this might have been the very first time he realized that he had that thing we call a foot. This was further indication that he was bringing his attention to his own body and his movement. His flash of recognition lasted for only a few seconds, and then he resumed his occasional thrashing. I then began doing similar movements with his other leg. Once again Ryan stopped thrashing his body, becoming very still, and moved his eyes to look at his legs. He stared at his legs for a long time with great interest as I was moving them. Now both of us were very attentive, me to him, and him to himself and to the movement of his legs. Suddenly the room became very still. The father was trying very hard to hold back his tears. His son was transforming before our eyes.

Now that Ryan was attentioning fully to the movements of his legs and what he was feeling, his brain was changing extremely quickly.

I thought perhaps words could start having some meaning to him. I decided to put into words what he was noticing. "Oh, here is your foot!" I said, with a somewhat high-pitched voice, playing as if I were discovering his foot for the first time. I continued: "And now your foot is moving here, and now it's moving over there," as I moved it a bit to the right and then a bit to the left. All of a sudden he looked me straight in the eye, as if discovering my existence for the very first time. He held that connection for a long time. His eyes widened, sharply focused on me, as if with a flash of recognition. His face relaxed and became still and calm. And then his eyes and his whole face lit up with a beautiful, angelic smile. He never thrashed again through the rest of the session.

....

Now that Ryan was attentioning fully to the movements of his legs and what he was feelinyg, his brain was changing extremely quickly.

....

After that first session the parents reported to us that Ryan began responding to his name, was a lot calmer, had much better eye contact, began saying one or two words, and even his eating got better.

Ryan returned for the next two months and worked with other practitioners at our center, employing the Nine Essentials with a variety of Anat Baniel Method techniques. He continued to improve. All his original symptoms either disappeared or were greatly diminished. He was becoming increasingly aware of himself, no longer hiding under furniture, and quite obviously moving with attention. He became stronger, his muscle tone becoming more balanced and healthy. In his interactions with his brother he pushed back when pushed and no longer let him snatch toys away.

At the end of the two-month period, I saw the family again to evaluate Ryan's progress. The mother was delighted with the changes in her son, reporting that, "Ryan now plays with other children, makes great eye contact, eats better, is talking a lot, and using more words. He takes an interest when we're talking to him and understands what we tell him." She paused, got a big grin on her face, and said, "He is a *transformed child.* He's really just fine!"

Are We There Yet?

After those initial sessions, we did not see Ryan for several months. Then his mother brought him in because his eating was not as good as it had been and he was not making as good eye contact as he had been doing before. He had regressed some. It took only two sessions with us for Ryan to regain those abilities and go forward from there. He mostly needed help in reawakening his attentioning to his movements. It was as if his brain had reverted some to its earlier state, had gotten sluggish, and was tending to function in a compulsive automatic fashion.

At this point Ryan's parents agreed to begin implementing the Nine Essentials at home on their own to ensure that Ryan's brain continued to differentiate and grow in a healthy way rather than being pulled back by his condition. By doing so, the Essentials became more and more integrated into their everyday lives, benefiting Ryan as well as his brother. Parents often tell me that while they may first be motivated to learn the Nine Essentials to help their child, the same skills and practices improve their own lives in ways they hadn't dreamed possible.

What Science Tells Us About Movement with Attention

Daniel Siegel, the author of *The Mindful Brain* and codirector of the Mindful Awareness Research Center at the University of California at

Los Angeles (UCLA) School of Medicine, talks about the "science of mindfulness," a meditative process that makes use of the power of attention for effecting change within our brains. Siegel points out that:

> The practice of intentional, nonjudgmental awareness of moment to moment experience has been practiced since ancient times in both East and West. Wisdom traditions have for thousands of years recommended mindful practice in a variety of forms to cultivate wellbeing in an individual's life. . . . Now science is confirming these benefits.

....
"Wisdom traditions have for thousands of years recommended mindful practice in a variety of forms to cultivate wellbeing in an individual's life. . . . Now science is confirming these benefits."
....

The research Siegel cites looks primarily at a practice called *mindful meditation*, which consists of people developing the skill of paying attention to their breath, their movements as they are walking, etc. His own research studies at UCLA, as well as those of microbiologist Jon Kabat-Zinn at the University of Massachusetts Medical Center, showed that "adults and adolescents with attentional problems achieved more executive function improvements (sustaining attention, diminishing distractibility) than are accomplished with medication for this condition."

In experiments with owl monkeys, Merzenich's group demonstrated a clear correlation between the power of attention and the brain's ability to change itself. When the animals in the experiments had to pay attention to the sensations they were receiving (what they felt in a specific part of their body) sensory cortex connections in their brains that were associated with those parts grew significantly. When they did not pay attention to what they were feeling, there were no significant changes in the brain. The same correlations were noted with movement; that part they *paid attention to*—for example, the movements of the arm—grew real estate in the brain. Conversely, those parts that moved but did so *without attention*, either didn't change at all or actually shrank. Merzenich stated: "Experience coupled with attention leads to physical changes in the structure and functioning of the nervous system."

The good news is that this remarkable power of attention coupled with movement is easy to harness in the daily life of your child.

Movement with Attention in Your Child's Everyday Life

You can start experiencing the extraordinary powers of Movement with Attention to help your child in surprisingly simple and straightforward ways. You needn't add new regimens to your already very busy life. Instead, you will be bringing Movement with Attention to things you are already doing with your child. Whether it's feeding your child, changing diapers, bathing, getting your child dressed, doing any exercises or home therapies that you do, helping your child with homework, or playing with him, look for ways to call your child's attention to himself as he moves. This will become an important part of *the how*—that is, of the way that you do whatever you are already doing with your child. Remember that you are *not trying* to have your child pay attention to you, but rather to have your child bring his own attentioning to himself, to what he is feeling as he moves himself or is moved by you.

How Can I Tell If My Child Is Attentioning?

How do you tell when your child is attentioning in the way I've described? What does it look like? Here are five ways that you can tell if your child is attentioning at any given moment.

The Inner Stare: One way, explored in my description of my lesson with Ryan, may seem counterintuitive at first. When Ryan first began attentioning, he stopped all his wriggling and thrashing, became very still and stared into space for a few seconds. But rather than spacing out or tuning out, he was becoming deeply attentive to his own feelings and sensations generated by the movements we were making. You will see that your child, at such times, stops, goes within and stares, hardly blinking, in some cases, for quite a while. You'll recognize this when it happens; it is almost palpable. These are golden moments. It is very important for you to be aware of such moments and allow your child the time to be attentioning without interrupting him or trying to get him to snap out of it. People often mistake this form of attentioning for its opposite. I always tell parents that these few seconds of their child's attentioning are incredibly valuable. This is the moment when their child's brain is flooded with new activity and possibility. It is the moment of transformation.

Following: Another indication that your child is attentioning is that he is watching and following with his eyes something that is moving—be it his own movements, a ball you have rolled toward him, or your moving his leg or arm. Just as with his eyes, you may also notice him following a sound that he is hearing. You'll notice this as he moves his eyes and perhaps turns his head in the direction of the sound or when he stops something else that he is doing at that moment to listen.

Anticipatory Participation: Another manifestation of your child's attentioning is what I call *anticipatory participation*. When a movement or activity is one that your child has experienced before, whether it's in the last few minutes or in the more distant past, you will notice your child anticipating what is coming next; you will see or feel little anticipatory twitches in his muscles or even more obvious movements that tell you his brain gets what is going on and is trying to execute the anticipated action. Whether your child is fully successful in these efforts or not doesn't matter. What is important is for you to recognize the significance of these movements. Even the tiniest movements with attention that your child initiates in these ways make a difference, building real estate in the brain that is necessary if he is ever to successfully execute whatever the skill you would like him to acquire.

Joy: One of the really fun signs of your child's attentioning is when he is delighted with whatever he is experiencing, doing, or you are doing with or for him. He laughs, becomes happy. Such moments are as delightful for parents as they are for the child.

It's All a Game: Another manifestation of attentioning is when your child becomes playful; whatever it is you are doing, he thinks it's a game. He is creatively participating in whatever activity he is involved in. *It's fun for him!* From his point of view, he is the creator of his world at that moment and that requires close attention to himself and to that which is happening around him as a result of his actions. Scientific research demonstrates the importance of playfulness, joy, and fun for successful growth and learning. These are also manifestations of attentioning that elevate the quality of the functioning of your child's brain and are always associated with an increased sense of well-being. It is in moments such as this that significant changes occur within the brain.

The Full Meaning of Movement

What does the movement part of Movement with Attention look like? What do we mean by *movement*? As we've mentioned before, it is very common to think of movement as only the movement of your child's body that you can see, what is commonly referred to as physical movement. That is the most obvious manifestation, such as the movement of your child's arm, leg, back, or hand. Very often when dealing with issues arising from the child's special needs, the movement focus is narrowed down to repetitive exercises trying to address where movement skills are limited or missing. There are three kinds of movement the child can feel and bring attention to: physical movement, emotional movement, and movement of thoughts.

> There are three kinds of movement the child can feel and bring attention to: physical movement, emotional movement, and movement of thoughts.

Physical Movement: Physical movement is *any* movement of your child's body whether it is done by your child or you are the one moving him. And any such movement is an opportunity for attentioning—that is, for having the child's brain connect with that movement and organize it better. Your child's attentioning to *any* movement that he is doing or that you are doing for him will elevate the quality with which your child's brain functions and organizes that movement and all other movements (see Chapter 3 for details).

Emotions As Movement: Emotions are also movement, and as such, bringing your child's attentioning to the movement of his emotions opens up remarkable possibilities for transformational changes in both brain and behavior.

Thinking As Movement: Perhaps the most elusive form of movement is thinking. Thinking, the creation of ideas and beliefs, recognition of relationships between things, and the process of understanding—*making sense* of ourselves and the world that surrounds us—are all manifestations of movement within our brains. We can feel the outcomes of thinking even though we can't see, touch, smell, or taste it. Even if in the beginning it may feel elusive to you, you can learn to help your child bring his attentioning to his thinking (see the next section). In my practice

I have seen some of the most dramatic transformations when helping a child bring attentioning to his own thinking.

Remember that at the heart of your child's successful development is the process by which his brain becomes better and better at organizing movement, whether that movement is reaching out to grasp a toy, talking, walking, expressing an emotion, or solving a math problem. All of this is accomplished through differentiation and integration, which we've previously discussed. It is an ongoing process of getting better and better at perceiving differences, and movement that requires constant change with attention leads to perception of differences and is at the heart of developing those abilities.

The Tools for Movement with Attention

Your Own Attentioning: The key for helping your child is your own attentioning. By this I mean having nonjudgmental, accepting, open-ended, and deep interest in your child's actions, experiences, and behavior. Think of your brain as being connected with your child's brain through an imaginary cord. Your child's brain can read your brain through that cord. When you are attentioning at a high level, your child's brain, which needs help organizing itself to function better, can take a ride on your own higher quality of organization. As I so often tell parents, the attentional skills that you bring to your interactions with your child serve as the model for his brain to begin *doing attention*, or what we call *attentioning*. I like to emphasize how important it is to think of attention as an action, something the brain does and needs to learn to do more and more, better and better. For that reason I suggest that you add the words *attentioning* and *to attention* to your vocabulary, though using these words this way might seem a little strange at first.

Take Attentioning Moments with Your Child

In Movement of the Body: During your daily activities with your child, attention the movement of the body. For example, as you begin bending down to pick up your young child, pause. Don't complete the action yet. Instead, notice whether he is anticipating being picked up: Is he attentioning to what you are doing? Is he in his own way joining with you in that action? In what ways is he engaged and participating? Perhaps he reaches out with his hands. Maybe he smiles up at you. Is he bending his knees as if to jump up or coming up on his toes? Or maybe all he can do is tighten his muscles and move the upper back just a touch forward. Once you've observed any such attentioning and participation on your child's behalf, slowly complete the action of picking him up. Know that in this moment your child has just practiced his Movement with Attention skills.

If you don't see any evidence of his participating, see if you can call on his attentioning by *not* picking him up. Instead of completing the action, stand up, wait for a few seconds, perhaps say your child's name or make an unusual sound, such as singing out his name or making clicking sounds with your tongue; then restart the action of picking him up to see if he wakes up to himself and to what's going on. Keep working with his attentioning in this way, in different situations and as often as you can, to help your child's brain wake up and be a part of the action.

In Thinking: Bring your child's attentioning to his thinking to help him improve his thinking processes. You do this by bringing your attentioning to what and how he communicates with you and others. One of the simplest ways to do this is by asking him questions. For example, if he can speak but he is difficult to understand because his speech is unclear in diction or meaning—as we frequently witness with children on the autism spectrum, with attention deficit disorder (ADD), or with fragile X chromosome disorder, for example—even if you can guess what he is trying to say, do not understand him too quickly. Don't *fill in the blanks* for him. Also, don't ask him to speak more clearly. (Remember, if he could he would.) Instead, in a friendly voice say, "I don't understand what you just said to me. Is there something you want?" You might find that your child won't answer at first. It is very possible that he has no idea that his speaking is unclear. Don't try to extract an answer from him. Instead, wait until he speaks again. Then if you have some inkling about what he's trying to communicate, ask him: "Are you asking about————?" and here you might fill in the blank with your best guess. Then you ask, "Yes? No?" Wait for an answer. Unless it involves an urgent need, stay with this process until he says yes or no. If he does neither, simply move on to the next thing.

This is a way to call on his attentioning to his speaking so he can begin differentiating between being understood and not and begin realizing that this has something to do with the way he forms sounds. He will experience and begin bringing more of his attention to how some sounds get him what he wants and some don't. When he begins to hear what he is saying, his brain will gradually be able to differentiate his diction and his language so he can be more precise, making speech work better for him. This increased differentiation not only improves his language skills but goes hand in hand with improving the quality and clarity of his thinking.

The Power of Your Touch: Your touch has the power to awaken and increase your child's attentioning ability as you have seen in the story about Ryan. It is a powerful mechanism for communicating with the child's brain. When you touch your child he feels himself and this helps him learn where he starts and where he ends. Lots of loving and attentive touch is central to our successful physical, emotional, and cognitive development; when touch is lacking, it can have serious consequences for the child's development. You have probably heard that when infants are denied enough loving and attentive touch, as sometimes happens in orphanages, they wither, and some of them even die. We all have an intuitive understanding of how important touch is in our lives.

Six Ways of Touching

Gentle touch: Always use the least force necessary.

Attentive touch: Feel and be present in your touch.

Safe touch: Touch and hold your child with full support.

Connected touch: Move your child as if your body and his were one—like ballroom dancers.

Loving touch: Be attentive to your child's response to your touch, and be responsive to his response.

Seeing touch: Touch as if you had eyes in your fingers and the palms of your hands, seeing your child—not trying to change or manipulate him.

Touch calls on our attention. A friend touches you on your shoulder and you turn your head to look at him; we say his touch got your attention. For your touch to help your child's brain do its job better, it is important to realize that not all touch is equal. As we become more skillful with our hands, we become increasingly efficient and automatic in performing routine tasks. This is a good thing. There are times when we need to be efficient and go on auto pilot. In the morning you help dress your child; you have done it hundreds of times. You get all his clothes on, all his buttons buttoned, and his zippers zipped. But when you are not rushed, do not do it automatically. Instead take your time when you dress your child, change his diapers, put him in the high chair, lay him down and do it with lots of attention to the sensations of weight, temperature, or texture and mobility or stiffness in his body you can feel. By attentioning this way you will waken your child's own attentioning to himself and turn these daily mundane moments into golden opportunities for growth for your child.

Early on, I discovered that whenever I slipped into automatic pilot as I worked with a child through movement and touch, there was very little change, and usually the child would begin resisting after a while. On the other hand, when I paid close attention to what I was feeling, along with paying attention to the child's reactions and what he seemed to be feeling, I got very different results. The child began attentioning intensely to my touch and his own movement. There was suddenly a clear connection between the child and me. And what a profound and delightful experience that is! This seemingly simple shift from automatic touch to attentioning touch and connection induces change—often very dramatic and life-altering change. This discovery was a huge turning point in my work, as I'm sure it can be for you in your interactions with your child.

Seeing Hands: In workshops, when an adult participant has difficulty doing a movement such as lifting his arm, perhaps due to injury or maybe from lack of use, I touch his back, shoulder, or some other area of his body where I sense he has a need to wake up to himself; almost always the person finds that he can perform the same movement with greater ease and either less or no pain. The transformation is instantaneous. I touch as if to see the person through my hands not as if to control or manipulate his movements in any way.

When I am demonstrating to parents how to touch their child to awaken his attentioning abilities, I have them imagine that they have eyes in their fingers and the palms of their hands; if it's in a workshop I have them touch a classmate while that person is performing a simple movement. I tell them to touch in order to see the other person through the eyes they imagine they have in their palms and fingers. I remind them that they are touching their classmates in order to see them, not to change them. Anytime you do anything with your child that requires physical manipulation, you are providing another opportunity for you to shift from autopilot to *attentioning touch*.

When you touch your child in this way, you will not only help him feel himself—providing his brains with useful information by which to grow—but you will be infusing your child with the feeling and knowledge that he is cared for and loved just as he is right now.

You'll find that developing this way of connecting with your child with *seeing hands* is easy to do and very gratifying. You are not trying to force your child but are using your touch as a path for him to pay attention to himself and to what he is doing. Through your seeing hands, he will be able to feel himself more clearly, helping his brain make sense of himself and figure things out.

Go with the System: Think of *going with the system* in this way: Instead of trying to change a movement or behavior your child is doing, actually support and even exaggerate those movements or actions as they presently are. This helps your child bring his attentioning to what he is doing, thus gaining greater choice and freedom. Mason was a six-year-old boy diagnosed with severe attention deficit hyperactivity disorder (ADHD). A few moments after his mom brought him to his first lesson, Mason sat down on the floor and pulled off his shoes. His mom commented that they just got the shoes on the way to the session.

My office at the time was on the 40th floor in midtown Manhattan. One of the windows was open a crack. Mason stood up with one shoe in each hand. He scanned the room, saw the open window, and began walking quickly in that direction. His mom told Mason to *not* throw the shoes out of the window. Her voice was understandably tense. What she didn't realize was that Mason was not fully aware of what he was doing, even though he certainly seemed determined to discard the shoes. His movements and actions just "came out of him." While moving quickly toward the window myself, I asked Mason: "Are you walking? Maybe you can come meet me at the window?" He gave me a quick glance and continued his march toward the window. I then said: "I wonder who is going to get there first, you or me?" I made sure to get there first and when I did, I announced: "You are almost here."

I blocked the opening of the window with my body and said: "Do you have anything in your hands? Do you want to hold anything in your hands?" At that point Mason looked at his hands and *saw* the shoes. I then asked his mom to hand me a piece of paper. I tore it into two pieces, showed them to Mason, and asked him if he would rather hold a piece of paper in each hand instead of the shoes. He held on to the shoes. Then I told him that I was going to throw the paper out of the window. He looked at me wide-eyed as I took one of the pieces of paper and demonstratively threw it out. I then asked him: "Do you also want to throw something out the window?" He approached me and nodded yes. At that point I told him, "No problem, but it's not going to be the shoes. It can be the paper."

Mason bent down, put the shoes on the floor, and reached out with his hand to grab the paper. He then slowly and deliberately went closer to the window, put out his little arm, and let the paper fly off. When you help your child do what he is already doing, rather than trying to change him, it helps him recognize what he is doing and how he is doing it; this frees his brain, perhaps for the first time, to do something different, new, and better.

Be an Actor, Dancer, and Mime: Have you ever gone to a theater performance specifically for young children? When you do, you will see the children get so immersed and involved they forget they are in a theater. What they see and hear happening on the stage is just as real to them as anything else in their lives. They will call out a warning to the hero when danger approaches; they will jump up and down with excitement. They might even run up to the stage to help out when the suspense gets intense.

Most parents, even shy ones, become actors and singers and performers with their kids. Without even thinking about it, they awaken their child's attentioning in this way. You can use your theatrical capabilities to intentionally awaken your child's attentioning to himself when he seems disconnected from himself or doesn't know what he is doing, to guide him into possible alternatives. Remember, in my story about Ryan, how I used my voice and said, "And now your foot is moving here, and now it's moving over there." In this way I helped him recognize his own foot and leg, which he had never done before. Similarly, with Mason, my choreography around reaching the window first, then throwing the paper out, helped him awaken to what he was doing.

Think of your child's attentioning like the air that surrounds us all. The opportunity for it is there all the time and you move in and out of it with ease.

It's Easier Than You Think

The transformative powers of Movement with Attention begin with you. You may be worried or perplexed by not knowing what is going on with your child or extremely busy and feeling that you just haven't time to take on anything more. You're not, after all, a Buddhist monk who has hours every day to spend in the practice of *mindful meditation* or focused attentioning. Nor, most likely, are you a therapist or movement expert. The good news is that you needn't be an expert to be of great help to your child. Any increment of improvement in your own and your child's attentioning to movement will make a huge difference in your child's development. And as we discussed earlier in the chapter, movement—physical, emotional, and mental—is everywhere. Any action or interaction you have with your child can be an opportunity to use the tools I describe in this book and help him grow and improve.

Through practice, Movement with Attention quickly becomes second nature, just part of the way you do things. And as so many parents have told me, it turns out to be a real gift, having a tremendous impact not only on their child's ability to move beyond present limitations but on the quality of their own experience of life.

> **Through practice, Movement with Attention quickly becomes second nature, just part of the way you do things.**

5 Essential Two
Slow

To climb steep hills requires slow pace at first.

—WILLIAM SHAKESPEARE

As the parent of a child with special needs, you might feel that the word *slow* has negative connotations. There is no question that being slow to develop can be the first indication that your child has a special need. In addition, the word *slow* can easily bring to mind words like *dull, dim, dumb, obtuse, boring, ho-hum, tedious, sluggish,* and *slothful.*

Given these associations with *slow,* it may seem counterintuitive to be looking at Slow as a powerful way to help your child's brain work better and to reach beyond what you or others might believe possible. In this chapter the word *slow* has a very different connotation and use: to increase your child's brain's opportunities for greater differentiation and to help her brain integrate these into new skills. This could be developing a movement of the hand, figuring out a better way to communicate, solving a math problem, or anything else the child has challenges with. Here you find ways that Slow can be used to increase new neural connections in your child's brain for developing and refining new skills, whatever her special needs may be.

Don't Leave Me Behind

Early on my path of discovering Slow as one of the Nine Essentials, a concept I learned from Dr. Feldenkrais, I had a pivotal experience with a twenty-two-month-old girl with severe cerebral palsy. This was the very first time I had worked with a child with her condition. What I discovered at that time has been invaluable in my more than thirty years of work with children who have a wide variety of special needs.

The first time I met Ali, she was in her father's arms. He carried her into the office and sat down on the edge of my work table, holding his daughter in his lap. Ali's mother sat in a chair facing them. I sat down next to Ali and looked at her. She was very skinny with large, deep brown eyes. One of her eyes was completely turned inward. Both her arms were tightly bent at the elbows, with her hands held in fists and each of her thumbs sticking out between her index and middle fingers. Her legs were clamped tightly together, her knees knocking, and her ankles were turned so that the tops of her feet were rotated inward.

The little girl sat quietly, with no movement in her body except for her one mobile eye which followed me as if she were checking me out. Her parents explained that she was one of twins born prematurely. Each of the twins had been placed in an individual incubator immediately after birth, providing warmth and oxygen. A few days after the girls were born a terrible thing happened: the oxygen supply in Ali's incubator failed, and by the time it was discovered she'd suffered severe brain damage, resulting in the symptoms diagnosed as cerebral palsy. The parents told me that she had been receiving physical therapy, but they were not seeing much progress. She still had no voluntary movement, her legs and arms were always tight, and she wasn't talking yet.

I had no idea what I was going to do. There was no specific technique or prescription for me to follow, no routine to model. Out of necessity more than anything else, I took my time to observe Ali and give her time to get familiar with my presence. This state of *not-yet-knowing* and slowing down turned out to be very fruitful and an important opportunity for discovery. Since then, before I start a lesson with a child, I re-create this I-have-no-idea-what-I-am-going-to-do approach. I very deliberately slow everything down.

At that point, I wondered how her legs would feel to my touch. What would happen if I tried to move them? I had never touched a child like Ali before. As any parent to a child with spastic cerebral palsy knows, the moment you try to move children with this condition or they try to move themselves, their muscles get even tighter, which makes it extremely difficult for them to move all together. Sure enough, when I gently placed my right hand on her left thigh, I felt the incredible tightness of the muscles of her very skinny leg. I was inspired to try to move her leg. When I tried I immediately felt the resistance. Her legs were tightly held together and it felt as if they would *never* move. I then observed that if I held her leg gently, and I slowed my movement of her leg way, way down, moving it in tiny movements that were barely perceptible to outside observers, her leg began moving just a tiny bit.

As I continued with these tiny, very slow movements, Ali seemed to be attentioning—paying close attention to herself and to what she was feeling. To my astonishment, the muscles of her leg suddenly let go! Her left knee opened to the side and even her ankle moved freely. Wondering if this was unusual, I looked up at her mother questioningly. Her jaw was dropped, her eyes opened wide and she exclaimed that this had never happened before.

Surprised and heartened by the outcome, I decided to re-create what I'd just done—what I'd come to call the Essential Slow—and repeat this process with Ali's other leg. I took my time, making sure to move her other leg very slowly, as I maintained the sense of connection I had with Ali. Within a couple minutes, the muscles of this leg also let go completely. Now she had both knees turned outward. For the first time in her life her brain stopped contracting her leg muscles. I wondered if she could actually cross her legs; I decided to explore this possibility, remembering to keep all of my movements slow and gentle. As I slowly lifted her legs they felt very light and they easily moved into a crossed position, knees pointed outward; she was now sitting in a semi-lotus position in her father's lap. The room was silent. You could have heard a pin drop. Nobody said a word as we watched Ali in wonderment. The father, who had barely spoken the whole time, said, "This is unbelievable. It's like a miracle."

The Time to Feel

Our ability to move fast, think fast, and have fast and efficient machines to serve us is closely related to our ability to survive and thrive. Yet it is important to understand that *fast, we can do only what we already know.* When doing anything fast the brain defaults to already existing and deeply grooved patterns. We don't start with fast when we set out to learn a new skill, discover new ideas, form a new understanding, or figure out a new behavior. And it is important to hold off on fast until the brain has formed the necessary connections and patterns for performing that skill. Only then can we gradually move into fast; having these new patterns grooved into the brain more deeply allows for fast and skillful action. Before our brains have figured out how to throw a ball, type on a keyboard, or add and subtract numbers, that ability is not there. This may seem obvious on the surface, yet our expectations of ourselves, as well as our expectations of others, particularly children, demonstrate that it is not always so apparent.

It is important to understand that *fast, we can do only what we already know.* When doing anything fast the brain defaults to already existing and deeply grooved patterns.

I'll never forget the day that Max's mom brought in a sheet of paper with 100 short addition problems for me to work on with him. It was a copy of a test Max had been given in school, and he had failed it. She told me that first-graders' skill levels were being measured not only by how many problems they could solve correctly but by how fast they were able to do it. To pass, the test had to be completed in twenty minutes or less. I was surprised. Here was Max, a six-year-old boy who had no idea what was being asked of him; he barely had any understanding of numbers. So he was certainly not yet ready to do it fast. What he had learned was to guess the answers instead.

As we worked with Max we used Slow and other Essentials to give his brain the time and information it needed to differentiate and to create the patterns he needed to understand and solve the math problems. Max no longer needed to revert to guessing the answers.

When we are good at doing something, we can usually do it fast and reliably. But the reverse does not work. Doing something fast to begin with is not going to make us good at it. Slow is a necessary part of learning and creating new possibilities. In his biographical writings, Albert Einstein describes how he came up with his theory of relativity by imagining himself riding a ray of light, feeling the sensations of movement and of the relationships of his body to the space around him. He did this hour after hour, slowly developing his theory of relativity, later converting what he was experiencing to the language of numbers. Imagine the remarkably rich and complex process taking place in his brain, with billions of nerve cells lighting up, moving in different directions, resulting in his incredible creation and discovery. But what would have happened if someone had been timing him, telling him he had only twenty minutes to come up with a correct answer and then suddenly telling him to stop?

Slow is a necessary part of learning and creating new possibilities.

When a skill is not there yet, it is *really* not there. Before it can be there, millions upon millions of new neural connections, and greater and greater differentiations, need to be created and integrated in the brain. To give the brain maximum opportunity for doing this, we need to slow the process way down. Slow gets the brain's attention, giving your child the time to feel. *The feeling of what happens* is at the core of everything we do; it is at the heart of our ability to think and move. When we go fast, the brain has no option but to revert to already existing patterns, patterns that are grooved in and that we can perform as if on automatic pilot.

Slow gets the brain's attention, giving your child the time to feel. *The feeling of what happens* is at the core of everything we do; it is at the heart of our ability to think and move.

Remember the story of Elizabeth's learning to catch the ball that I described in the first chapter? When the ball was moving too fast for her, no matter how hard she tried or wanted to catch it, her intent to catch the ball translated in her brain to the pattern already grooved, which was to rigidly hold her hands out in front of her and freeze her gaze on me. Similarly, with Ali, whenever another person tried to move her legs she had no option but to respond with greater spasticity. When the movement was slowed way down, however, Ali had time to begin feeling the movement. Her brain then discovered and began differentiating new possibilities. Her muscles let go and her brain stopped sending them messages to contract. And when Max tried solving math problems fast he reverted to guessing.

Slow is an essential part of learning, regardless of whether we're an Einstein or a seriously challenged child with special needs. Slow provides the time for us to feel and to notice. It calls on us to be *present*. Slow amplifies what we feel, making it easier for the brain to perceive differences so there is an opening for us to do something new.

> **Slow is an essential part of learning, regardless of whether we're an Einstein or a seriously challenged child with special needs.**

You may say: "My child is no Einstein. If anything, she is behind the curve." Yes, that may very well be true. However, when you touch and move your child slowly or guide her to go Slow, you help intensify her ability to feel and therefore for her brain to differentiate and create the new. The brain of a child who for the first time figures out how to roll over to her belly—or how to hold an object between her thumb and index finger, or how to make the sounds *mama* or *bottle*, or how to determine that $12 \div 4 = 3$—is a brilliant brain at that moment. It is important to not confuse current limitations that your child has with the remarkable capacities of her brain. The fact that your child cannot stand or talk or solve math problems at this time does not mean that her brain cannot be helped to function at the highest of levels. And Slow is a great tool for getting there.

> **The brain of a child who for the first time figures out how to roll over to her belly . . . is a brilliant brain at that moment.**

Please Help Me Slow Down

Josh, a slight, sweet-looking, three-year-old, bounced into my office with his mom close behind him. He was jabbering nonstop, making a constant flow of sounds that mostly didn't make any sense. Every once in a while in the torrential flow of vowels, consonants and syllables, there was a word that I recognized. He ran to one corner of the room, toward where there was a box of toys, but then, without even pausing there, or seeming to recognize or take any interest in the toys, he changed direction and ran to another part of the room. He kept bouncing off the walls in this way, jabbering away as he poured out his incoherent sounds, frequently tripping and losing his balance.

Any parent with a child suffering from attention deficit disorder (ADD) or attention deficit hyperactivity disorder (ADHD), whose child has been diagnosed as being on the autism spectrum or with fragile X chromosome disorder, or whose child has any other condition resulting in ADD and ADHD-like symptoms, knows how debilitating it is when the child is always moving too fast. The world these children experience is chaotic, and because they can't slow themselves down they have great difficulty learning. Their attention bounces from one thing to another so quickly their brain never has the opportunity to feel and notice enough to be able to make sense of themselves or the world around them in a way that works well enough for them. When faced with new demands, such as learning the complex balance of riding a bike, developing the eye-hand coordination required to catch a ball, learning to read and write, or developing more precise and lucid language skills, their brain cannot differentiate sufficiently to organize and perform these complex actions. What we tend to observe in such instances is an increase in hyperactive behavior.

Less Stimulation for More Information

Some might think these children need more stimulation to try to get through to them, such as having them repeat a desired action, giving more hours to math or reading tutoring, stimulating the tongue with a toothbrush, stretching their legs repeatedly with the hope that it'll help them pedal a bike better, and so on. Yet, it is not stimulation that they lack. Every bit of sensory input stimulates them; the problem is that their brains can't organize the stimulation in a meaningful, coherent way.

If anything, these children need less stimulation; they need us to reduce both the speed and the intensity of the stimulation coming their way. Their brains need the opportunity to experience Slow, to feel and sense what is going on, to perceive differences so their brains have the opportunity to turn the stimulation, coming from both the inside and the outside, into information that they can differentiate, organize, and integrate. Otherwise, any stimulation coming their way, or coming from within them, agitates them and only speeds them up more. Current brain science confirms this, demonstrating the critical importance of Slow and the idea that increased stimulation can be detrimental, exaggerating the very symptoms such children need to change.

> **Their brains need the opportunity to experience Slow, to feel and sense what is going on.... Otherwise, any stimulation coming their way, or coming from within them, agitates them and only speeds them up more.**

Dashing to Slow

During that first session with Josh, I quietly observed him for a few minutes as he ran around the room. Then each time he ran in a certain direction, I gently, without saying anything, stepped in front of him to block his view. At first he seemed oblivious to my presence. He simply bounced off in another direction. After about six times of putting myself in his path, he stopped and looked up at me. It was as if he had noticed me for the first time and wondered what I was doing. In that instant, his flow of sounds also stopped. He was attentioning for a few seconds. Then he dashed off again. Again I stepped in front of him. He looked up. At that point I said to him, slowly, "Hi, Josh, I'm Anat. I'm going to pick you up and put you on my table." I slowly proceeded to reach out to him, picked him up, and placed him on my high table.

> **It was as if he had noticed me for the first time and wondered what I was doing. In that instant, his flow of sounds also stopped. He was attentioning for a few seconds.**

I have discovered over the years that once a child has experienced slowing down, even for a few seconds, and thus has had the opportunity to attention more effectively, she will be able to slow down better and get to Slow more readily on her own. Though we call it an "attention deficit," I sometimes think it would be more helpful to think of it as a "slowing down deficit."

Once on the table that first time, Josh began squirming somewhat. He lay down, sat up, then lay down again, moving his legs in one direction, then another. I sat down, positioning myself very close to him, with my arms on both sides of his body and hovering close to him so that he wouldn't fall off the table. I began moving him very slowly and gently, and with only a tiny amount of change at a time. In the beginning, just as before, it was as if he hadn't even noticed that I was moving him or that I was even there. The flood of sounds continued to pour out of his mouth. I didn't try to stop him from doing whatever he was doing; I just kept slowly and deliberately attentioning to him, moving his legs, his pelvis, and his chest, gently and in the simple basic ways I have described throughout this book. Each slow, attentioning movement was "talking" to his brain through the movements of his body, giving his brain opportunities to feel the different parts of himself, to experience the movements and sensations slowly enough to begin noticing and making sense of them.

Throughout this session with Josh, I served as a coherent, Slow "container" for the noise of his usually fast and disorganized actions and movements. A few minutes into doing this, Josh began slowing down on his own, lying still more and more. And then he became quiet. Very quiet. The incoherent jabbering stopped. The squirming stopped. His brain was calming down! *He was now free to attention and learn.* Josh had come home to himself in a way he had never done before. At the end of the session, his mother said to me, "I have never seen Josh this way."

When Josh came in the next day, he was speaking sentences of two or more words. From time to time he reverted to his speedy flow of unstructured sounds and agitated movements, but then would go back to speaking in a well-organized and understandable way.

Josh improved in leaps and bounds not only with his speech but also with his posture, strength, balance, eating, sleeping, and thinking. This happens frequently with the children we work with. They improve not only in one area but in different areas, and often in ways that nobody had anticipated. Their improvements are generalized because the underlying brain processes have improved.

Time Is Love

Time is love. It's what the child experiences when we take our time with her, being with her where she really is. Unbeknownst to us, when we rush the child, when we ask her to do quickly what she can't do, or we try to get her to do something faster than she can, we often ensure failure. Though we may have the best intentions, the child is left feeling she is not okay or she is somehow not meeting our expectations.

I recall Charlie, a child suffering from a genetic disorder called fragile X syndrome with whom I'd been working for several years. His mother, Sheila, had given him a laptop computer that had a reading program on it. While they were waiting for me in my office, Charlie's mom was trying to help him read. I could hear their interaction as I was walking toward my office. Sheila's efforts clearly weren't helpful. Charlie was getting agitated, angry, resistant, and finally completely stuck. I thought, "They've got to slow down."

Once in my office I asked Sheila if the reading program had an adjustment that allowed them to change the speed at which the words appeared on the screen. She said yes. While she was figuring it out, I sat Charlie on my table. He looked at me and said, "Anat, I'm stupid. I can't read." I told him, "No, Charlie, you are not stupid. The words on the computer are moving too fast, that's all." He looked at me with a puzzled expression for a moment and then smiled just a little.

Sheila then announced that she'd figured out how to make the reading program on the computer slow down. We showed this to Charlie and, sure enough, now that the words on the screen were moving slowly enough for him, he was able to read them. After a few moments he was feeling empowered and delighted with himself. He then declared to me, "I'm not stupid!"

Slowing down the computer not only helped Charlie learn and experience himself being successful with the reading program but also slowed his mom down. Her slowing down that day calmed Charlie and the two of them connected in a way that he felt safe, loved, and accepted, giving his brain the opportunity to figure it out.

Every time you take the time to slow down with your child, it gives you the opportunity to be present with her, letting her true reactions and capabilities inform you. It's as if you were dancing with your child, the way two people can dance together leading and being led, moving as one on the dance floor.

Another Kind of Slow
Babies, Monkeys, and Developmental Stages

In recent years parents have been made increasingly aware of developmental milestones or stages that chart expected timetables of childhood development; the ages their children are expected to hold their heads up, the age they follow moving objects with their eyes, roll over to lie on their bellies, stand, talk, walk, and so on.

In the past few years an increasingly greater premium has been placed on babies achieving these milestones at earlier ages. Parents are often encouraged, by professionals and paraprofessionals, to try to speed up their child's achievement of these milestones; the idea being that somehow the acceleration of such development will provide superior end results physically, emotionally, and mentally. Parents are told to place infants as young as two weeks old on their bellies—what is called "tummy time." That is a few months before babies will do it by themselves. Then there are devices such as jumpers and walkers and a host of other ways to try to accelerate a child's development.

Yet one of the most significant ways humans are different from all other mammals is in *how slowly we develop*. W. M. Krogman, a leading expert on childhood growth and development, writes: "Man has absolutely the most protracted period of infancy, childhood and juvenility of all forms of life."

When we compare the speed at which humans reach developmental milestones with that of chimpanzees (one of the closest animals to us on the evolutionary scale and genetically), we see that at two months of age the latter can already stand upright holding onto its mother; at the same age the human infant is completely helpless and dependent on caregivers to do everything for her.

At five months of age the chimpanzee has taken its first independent steps; it can climb up a sapling or branch and begins to initiate breaking the mother-infant contact for short periods of time. At the same age—five months—the human baby is just beginning to roll to her side.

By the time the chimpanzee is two years old, it has pretty much developed its mature motor faculties. At two years, the human baby is walking but her balance is still very precarious; she is toddling and cannot yet jump up or balance on one leg. Many of her future movement skills and social and cognitive skills are yet to be developed.

Compared to the chimpanzee, the human baby is extremely slow in terms of achieving similar motor and social milestones. However, something very important is happening behind the scenes. While at two years of age the human may still stumble as she walks, she is already talking, with a vocabulary between twenty and thirty words and can string together at least two words to make meaningful sentences. At five years of age the human is likely to have a vocabulary of twenty-five hundred words. The chimpanzee, meanwhile, is making sounds to communicate basic variants of anger, fear, and pleasure and will never develop language as we know it. Nor will the chimpanzee ever develop the conceptual and abstract thinking that the average human will have at nine years of age.

At nine years of age, the human child may be able to play a Chopin sonata, play video games, or solve a math problem. At that same age, the chimpanzee is fully mature, perhaps with its own family, yet its brain will never be capable of the artistic, athletic, or intellectual accomplishments of the human. While we don't yet know if the human baby will become a fast runner, a skilled tennis player, a ballerina, a concert pianist, or a mathematician, we do know that the chimpanzee will never be able to do those things.

Comparison of Some of the Typical Developmental Stages of Humans and Chimpanzees

At Three Months Old

Standing, holding on to mother—
way ahead of the human baby

Helpless, fully dependent on others—
seemingly little is happening

At Nine Months Old

Has full independent movement and already
practices mounting and thrusting females

Crawls on all fours, can't even walk
yet—appears developmentally
way behind the baby chimp

At Eight Years Old

Sexually mature—reached the
greater part of her lifelong potential

Still a child, yet plays the piano—surpassing
what the chimp will ever do—with
enormous potential for future growth

Larger Brain and More Time to Grow

The fact that humans have larger brains only partially explains this enormous disparity in potential compared to the great apes; just as important is the slower speed at which humans reach their developmental milestones. Stephen Jay Gould writes: "Human babies are born as embryos" with brains only 23 percent of the size of the adult brain—the least of all mammals. We are born incredibly unfinished and in comparison to other mammals take a long time to mature. Is there an advantage to our slow development? Gould claims that the marked slowing down of our development, and the growth of our brains, has provided us with opportunities to evolve way beyond any other creature and to achieve what no others have.

The slowing down of the human development allows for an extended and extensive process of differentiation and increased complexity in the structures of the brain from which the unique human skills can arise. This slowing down of the human development takes advantage of the bigger brain that will develop over a period of many years, even decades.

Don't Close the Deal Too Soon

Research shows that efforts to accelerate early development in the healthy baby do not make a meaningful difference in the overall speed of development. There is no evidence that such efforts ensure better performance later in life—and there is a very real possibility that early efforts at acceleration of development can be detrimental. When a child has special needs, she is often behind on the developmental charts in one or more ways. It is understandable that there is a desire to get the child to perform the missing parts, to speed her up so that she can catch up. However, it is not the developmental milestone itself that matters. What does matter is the underlying process that leads the child to accomplish that milestone.

During all the months the human infant is lying there, moving randomly, then very gradually acquiring movement and other skills, behind the scenes there is an incredibly rich activity going on in the brain. Billions upon billions of connections are being formed in the brain; the body is being mapped; the billions of bits and pieces (remember *differentiation*) are going to be integrated over time into what we recognize as the finished product of our developmental milestones and further accomplishments later in life.

We humans, whether with special needs or not, are built so we do not close the deal too soon or too fast, do not commit to a final set of patterns in our movements—thoughts, feelings, actions—that could get grooved in too quickly. That is how we reach the highest levels of development and performance. By slowing down and not closing the deal too soon, we leave the time needed for incredibly complex sets of skills to develop and to be able to continue developing more and more, with new and greater skills throughout our lifetimes. When looking to help the child with special needs, we need to take our time and keep the process open ended, giving the child and her brain exponentially more options for growth. Despite how skilled and intelligent chimpanzees (and other nonhuman primates) are, their brains and general growth close the deal fairly quickly, meaning they can attain a whole lot less than can humans within their life spans.

> **We humans, whether with special needs or not, are built so we do not close the deal too soon or too fast, do not commit to a final set of patterns in our movements—thoughts, feelings, actions—that could get grooved in too quickly.**

Transmission of Signals in Nerve Cells

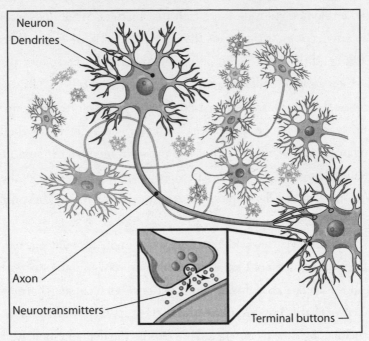

What Science Tells Us About Slow

As your child slows down and begins to feel, notice, and is able to perceive differences better, as she moves and experiences her own body and environment, actual physical changes and growth immediately begin happening in her brain at an incredible rate. The axon, a long slender extension of a nerve cell, called a neuron, gets insulated with fatty material; this is known as myelination, which allows for the electrical impulses to travel faster through the cell and communicate with other nerve cells. The nerve cells connect with and talk to each other through dendrites, which look like the manifold branches of a tree and are at the ends of the axons. During the differentiation process, there is a massive amount of new connections created between nerve cells; in fact, an excess of new connections is formed. A portion of the connections will be selected by the brain to create the new pattern. Any connections that are not selected will disappear over time, through a process called pruning. In the early stages of your child's acquiring a new skill—that is, a new set of patterns—the new connections in her brain are quite fragile until the growth associated with the new skill is complete. They continue to be fragile until the selection of connections and myelination of the involved nerve cells have been completed. Slow and gentle is still necessary during this phase of change.

As your child figures out and more fully masters a new skill, it means the associated structures in the brain have formed enough for her to control and execute what she has learned. Only then can your child perform that skill faster. That is why I say, "Fast we can do only what we already know."

Merzenich, using the principle of slowing down the child and the process, developed a software program called Fast ForWord, which has helped millions of children learn to read and write. Merzenich's team began hearing that the Fast ForWord program, designed to help in the development of language abilities, was having a number of unexpected spillover effects. For example, children with autism were showing improvements in listening, attention, and focus; in handwriting; and in general mental processing, indicating that their brains improved as a whole.

The Tools for Slow

Slow for your child starts with you. You become the model of Slow for her, paving the way for her brain to follow. Slow is a skill you and your child can develop together. Doing something slowly and deliberately with your child in an intentional way requires skill and control. Remember that each of the Nine Essentials improves the functioning of the brain as a whole. As you apply the tools for Slow, look for changes, any changes; they are the bits and pieces from which your child's brain will grow and improve. Watch for the smallest of changes—they are so easy to overlook or dismiss—because they are not the final outcome we are seeking. However, it is these tiny shifts and changes in the brain that are the beginning and are at the heart of all major transformations. Here are some tools to help you introduce Slow into your child's life:

Be with Your Child: Find ten minutes each day to just *be* with your child. Turn off your cell phone. Move away from the computer. Put down the book you are reading. Shut off the TV. You are not going to cook, clean up, or even wash your child's face. Driving with your child in the car does not count, since your attention will be divided. Your only agenda is to *be there* with your child on the rug, or on the bed, or on the sofa, or outside in the yard, or in the play area. Have no agenda for you or your child for these ten minutes; just let feelings of Slow pervade your and your child's experience. At the same time, while making sure that your child is safe, you are going to let her just *be* with you, however that may be at that time. Let her be the leader; follow her cues. If she simply wants to wander around, seemingly doing nothing, just let her wander around and be there with her. If she wants to snuggle or play with your hair, just be there with her while she is doing that. If she wants to play with a ball or a toy car, be there with her while doing that. Just follow any cues she gives. Be there with your child, just the two of you. Even if you find this exercise a bit challenging in the beginning, you will soon discover how pleasurable and easy it is to do. Slow is part of what we are built to do.

Observe Without Judgment: As you slow down when interacting with your child, you will have the opportunity to notice things about her responses to you that you may have never noticed before. When you observe your child without comparing her to anyone else and without trying to change her or control her, you'll be better able to gauge her reactions to what you are doing with her. You can do this when feeding your child, helping her with her homework, helping her get dressed, giving her a bath, or doing any other activity you do with your child. You'll notice more about her responses to the world around her. This flow of rich information will light up *your* brain and will help you be better attuned with your child. The more you are attuned with her, the more her brain can benefit from her interactions with you. You become like the mommy dolphin that swims as one with her baby, carrying the baby in the flow of current that the mother creates as she swims; in time, the baby dolphin is competent enough to separate and start swimming on her own.

Oops, Time to Slow Down: Anytime your child fails at anything, be it a movement she has not yet mastered, trying to play a musical instrument, attempting to read or write, or trying to bring a spoon to her mouth, you will see that your first inclination is to speed up and try to force the failed action. That's a common reaction. But remember, we are going for the extraordinary, not the common. At such moments of failure, just slow down yourself and your child, slow way down. Slow down your own movements, the speed at which you talk to your child, and the speed at which you move your child. If your child has just failed at doing something new and is perhaps trying to do it very fast, slow her way down and ask her to do it again. You may even want to back off from that activity for a while, then come back to it later, but this time use the Essential Slow. Remember when you slow the child down you are giving her brain opportunities to create new solutions. You and she will experience immediate changes and transformations, even if not full success, right away; each of these changes moves the child toward future success.

The Slow Game: The basic rule of the Slow game is that you and your child do whatever you are doing ASAP—that is, as *slow* as possible. If one of you begins to speed up, the job of the other person is to bring it to the attention of the speeder. You could play this game with your child when putting pieces into a puzzle—for example, tell her: "Let's see if I can put this piece in *really slowly*," then proceed to do it. Then say: "Let's see how slowly you can do it." If she moves fast, you can call her attention to it and even help her move slower by guiding her hand gently. Next time you move, do it fast on purpose so that your child has a chance to correct you and tell you to do it slowly. It may take a few repetitions for your child to master the game. Moving slowly, doing anything slowly and intentionally takes much greater control and dexterity than rushing through it. You can bring the Slow game to buckling and unbuckling shoes, riding a tricycle, or any other activity.

The Slow game is especially useful when your child is stuck or unable to perform.. If she is too young to understand or is unable to slow down at first, try to slow down some of the elements of the action your child is doing or trying to do. Keep yourself slow so she can mirror you. As your child slows down, look for fine changes or more obvious changes. You might notice reduced or increased tonus of her muscles, an increase in her alertness and interest, or actual improvement in her coordination or thinking.

Slow Touch: As a parent, you touch and move your child a lot. This touch, this contact, is incredibly important for your child's growing brain. You can help her brain evolve in remarkable ways through what I call *Slow touch*. When caressing your child's hair, move your hand very slowly. Your Slow movement and touch gives her brain the opportunity to feel herself and notice more clearly what is happening. Look for ways that you can do this in everyday interactions that you already do with her. For example, slow down your movements and touch, and use touch when helping her put on her coat or when you are helping to move her from sitting in her wheelchair to lying down or perhaps when you are clapping hands or playing other games with her that involve touch. Slow will *amplify* your child's experience, as well as your own, helping her brain notice what is going on and become more engaged with whatever is going on.

Slow Listening: One of the most important human needs is *to be seen and to feel that we are heard and validated.* So many children with special needs have an especially difficult time communicating with the adults around them. They have difficulty making themselves and their experiences understood, especially when they themselves have a hard time making sense of their world. Your child needs for you to be an especially capable listener. You can become such a listener through *Slow listening*—that is, listening not just to her words but also to her communication through her sounds, movements, inflections, facial expressions, body language, and all other forms of expression. To do so, you need to first slow yourself down internally, quiet down any internal chatter that might be going on in your mind. Take a few slow deep breaths and then shift your attention to your child. Let yourself wonder what your child is communicating through her words or body language or perhaps through the way she moves or interacts with you. You may respond by speaking to your child, describing what you understand her communication to be. Or you may join in with your child, mimicking her communication in a loving and playful way. Or you may simply ask her if that is what she was trying to communicate. You will know if you are on target by your child's response. When you are on target, she will immediately relax and become more responsive and communicative, maybe even playful. When you are not on target, she will tend to withdraw or maybe get upset or even angry. At such times, just continue doing Slow listening until you feel you and your child are connecting.

Be a Master of Kindness: Your child knows when she is failing. Children feel the difficulty and confusion internally, and they certainly are aware of when they are unable to perform as the adults around them are trying to get them to perform. Be generous, be kind. Be your own "League of Slow Parents." Tell your child, "Take your time, no rush, not to worry." Be reassuring. I don't mean that you should tell your child she is succeeding when she is not. Don't try to cheer her along with so-called positive reinforcement when she knows she is not doing well; when you do that, it's distracting and confusing to her brain. Be authentic and kind with your child. Help her with Slow, even hold her close to you and gently guide her with your own body to slow down. When you do this, you communicate to your child: "You are okay as you are. You are doing fine. You are safe." When your child feels loved, accepted, and safe, her brain has the opportunity to turn into a powerful learning machine.

6 Essential Three
Variation

Nature is an endless combination and repetition
of a very few laws. She hums the old well-known air
through innumerable variations.

—RALPH WALDO EMERSON

There are two kinds of variation: The first has to do with *what* we do, the second with *how* we do what we do. An example of the first kind of variation would be when, instead of following your usual schedule of taking your child to the speech therapist on Monday, you drive across town to take him to a play date. An example of varying the *how* of what you are doing with your child would be when, instead of feeding him with a spoon, you let him eat by using his hands. That being said, how do these concepts apply to helping the child with special needs?

Variation Helps the Brain Grow

The brain of the child has a huge job to do. In the first three years of life, the brain grows fourfold, reaching 80 percent of its adult weight. This increase in size is due primarily to an increase in the number of connections between nerve cells. From these connections the brain organizes itself, creating maps of the child's body and its movements, creating cognitive structures, and organizing its emotions.

This remarkable process of growth and development happens through the perception of something new, something different, something that stands out from the background and the habitual in our bodies, our minds, and our lives. That's where the Essential I call Variation comes in. When you bring Variation into the child's life by doing everyday activities in a new or different way, these experiences stand out for him. The perceived differences (leading to differentiation) provide the brain with the new information it needs to create new possibilities. What more obvious way is there to have the brain perceive differences than to intentionally create and introduce differences—Variation—when interacting with our child? That is what this chapter is about: Variation, the intentional creation of differences for the child's brain to perceive and use in its journey to becoming a stronger and better brain, one that figures out ways to move from the impossible to the possible, to find unique solutions in the face of challenges.

....

This remarkable process of growth and development happens through the perception of something new, something different, something that stands out from the background and the habitual in our bodies, our minds, and our lives.

....

Variation Is Everywhere

Variation is all around us, in everything we see, hear, smell, taste, and feel. It also comes from within ourselves: the different thoughts we have, the different emotions we experience, and in our different movements. Even in the movements we have learned to do well, such as walking, no two steps are done exactly the same way even though it may seem they are. Our brains keep taking in new information as we walk, organizing each step, integrating our movements into one constantly changing whole. The brain itself creates Variation all the time.

If we eliminated all variation in our environment we would actually be unable to function. If you are in a space where everything is the same, as can happen to a skier in a heavy snowstorm, you lose depth perception; the light flattens out the landscape, making it impossible to differentiate between what is uphill and what is down or how far away you are from an object.

It is impossible to imagine life without variation. And it is impossible for the brain to function well without sufficient variation. Children's brains require a rich flow of variation to develop successfully. The healthy child spontaneously generates enormous amounts of variation in movement, thoughts, feelings, and emotions.

The child with special needs, because of the nature of his condition, is often limited in his ability to generate variation. For example, the compulsive perseveration of a child on the autism spectrum, by its own nature, denies his brain the variation and information it needs to grow and develop successfully. While the perseveration is the *symptom* we want to help the child get rid of, it is actually the lack of variation that is the most devastating to him. It is our job to help provide the child with at least some of the missing variation it can't get on his own. The good news is that variation is easy to generate and introduce to the child.

....

The child with special needs, because of the nature of his condition, is often limited in his ability to generate variation.

....

The following story illustrates the importance of Variation: how the deprivation of variation early in Michael's life greatly limited him, and how the Essential I call Variation provided opportunities his brain needed to map abilities it could not have otherwise developed.

The Boy in the Cast

Michael was born with what his pediatrician described as dislocatable hip joints, also known as developmental dysplasia of the hip (DDH). His hip sockets had not fully formed. The doctor prescribed a full body cast that would hold the femoral heads in the hip sockets so that the hip would, it was hoped, develop normally. Michael remained in this cast from the age of three weeks to ten months.

When Michael's cast came off, his hips appeared to be fine, but he was unable to move. The first time I saw him at thirteen months of age, he could not roll from his back to his belly or his belly to his back, was unable to bring himself up to a sitting position, and was unable to crawl. Because Michael was having trouble, his parents were referred to a physical therapist, who worked with him for several weeks, running him through a series of repetitious exercises that were intended to teach him to roll over, sit up, and ultimately to crawl. The parents told me that the treatments didn't help.

In spite of being an otherwise healthy and intelligent baby, Michael had no clue about how to move. When he was placed in a sitting position, he could hold his head up and he could move his head from side to side. Often when he moved his arms, it was with an excited, rapid, flapping movement similar to movements sometimes associated with children with autism. His legs, back, and pelvis, meanwhile, were leaden and lifeless. The parents' considerable worry was intensified by the fact that doctors could not suggest further help for their son. They were now on their own in their search for solutions. Like so many parents of children with special needs, they felt deserted and anxious. There seemed to be no explanations for why Michael was not learning to crawl. Everyone they spoke to had suggestions, lots and lots of suggestions, but how did one begin to sort them all out?

....
In spite of being an otherwise healthy and intelligent baby, Michael had no clue about how to move.
....

Michael's parents found their way to me through a mutual acquaintance. In our first session, I observed the beautiful face of this obviously healthy baby and wondered why he didn't know how to move. Then I got a hunch. During the time he was in the cast, all the usual movements of infancy, random as well as the evolving voluntary movements of his back, abdomen, chest, and legs were restricted by the cast and were impossible for him to carry out. He also missed the multitude of possible variations in the dynamic relationships between the different parts of his body that he would have experienced had he been free to move as well as the variations in sensation from being held and touched in the areas covered by the cast. Missing myriad sensations—Variation—that should have come from movement and touch, his brain was unable to map his body and its movements. Because the cast prevented early random and exploratory movements and sensations, Michael's brain very possibly only barely knew his legs, back, and pelvis were there.

I imagined what it must have been like for him and his brain to be stopped in such a manner so early and for so long. His brain was starved of the normal movement variations and the opportunities to feel and discover his body and what it could do; he lacked the information with which to begin the process of making sense of himself and the world around him. Instead he must have repeatedly experienced the restrictions and limitations imposed by the cast. Michael's brain mapped his actual experiences of limitation while living and growing in a cast, creating a phantom cast in his brain. Later, when the cast was taken off, his brain didn't get the news. Michael continued to act as if he were still in the cast, because his brain was missing the information to be able to do anything different.

> **Michael's brain mapped his actual experiences of limitation while living and growing in a cast, creating a phantom cast in his brain.**

He would need to experience some of the movement variations he had missed during the period he was in the cast. I decided to re-create some of them, rather than trying to get Michael to crawl or do other movements that a child his age should be able to do. I wondered if his brain would wake up and begin recognizing and organizing his body more fully. Would it begin forming the maps to move his body better?

I began to very *gently* move Michael's legs, pelvis, ribs, lower back, mid-back, and shoulders in many *tiny movements* and ways I knew he hadn't been able to move while in the cast. I was looking to communicate with his brain, introducing to it the existence of his body and the fact that it could move in all these different ways. Initially, his body was rigid and unresponsive. This told me I wasn't reaching his brain yet. He was unable to follow the guidance of my hands. I was very aware of his phantom cast; for Michael, even though the cast was no longer there, it was real. I made sure that the movements I did with him were tiny, as if the cast were still there. I always pay close attention to make sure I never move a child beyond where it is easy and comfortable for him. To help Michael's brain wake up, I continued to introduce more and more tiny movement variations, and soon enough, as if his brain had reached a tipping point, his face lit up. He was noticing, paying close attention to this rich repertoire of tiny, gentle movements. Very quickly it was as if his phantom cast were melting away. His body was becoming supple and mobile.

> I always pay close attention to make sure I never move a child beyond where it is easy and comfortable for him.

The Big Surprise

Twenty minutes into that first session, Michael's lower back felt alive and vibrant. His brain and lower back were connecting and both were making new connections with all other parts of his body: with his head, shoulders, arms, pelvis, legs, and feet. I decided to see if Michael was ready to take these changes—these lively new connections between his brain and his body—and put them all together into what would become a recognizable and intentional action on his part. I carefully rolled him to his side and lifted his pelvis so that his knees were tucked under him in a semi-kneeling position, making sure he was comfortable and attentive to this dance we were doing together.

A few seconds later he lifted his head and shoulders and straightened his arms. Michael was now supporting himself on all fours! I did not know what he would do next or how far he was going to go with these changes. I waited and watched attentively.

Michael stayed on all fours for a while. It became obvious to me that he had no idea that he could move in this position; it was all very new to him. Noticing how sturdy he was, I trusted that he would be able to manage some movement in this position, so I began, very gently, rocking him forward and back, just a tiny bit. In this way Michael got to experience his weight shifting back and forth between his knees and his hands. That was all he needed. Within a few seconds, and very tentatively at first, he lifted one hand and moved it forward, then lifted the opposite knee and brought it forward, then moved his other hand forward, and brought the opposite knee forward. Michael was crawling for the first time in his life. And he was doing it on his own. He was moving out of his phantom cast.

As Michael's brain took in what he was experiencing, through the rich range of variation, and the differences he perceived with the tiny movements I was providing, billions of neurons in his brain, invisible to the naked eye, were processing these sensations and creating new connections and highly organized patterns, mapping further movements and capabilities. Long before changes are obvious to the outside observer they are nevertheless happening at a furious rate within the brain. *Change always comes from within the child.* The child's special need itself limits the Variation he is able to experience, creating a virtual cast for his brain. That limitation of variation makes it difficult, or even impossible, for the brain to successfully develop in the way it ordinarily would if the child did not have that limitation. Whatever the cast the child has, be it muscular spasticity, as with cerebral palsy, or the kinds of compulsiveness we see with autism, we can always introduce Variation and reduce or eliminate the limiting impact on the child's development. Variation helps make it possible for the brain to do its job.

What Science Tells Us About Variation

Two different scientific studies, one on rats and one on humans, demonstrate the power of Variation to help increase the synapses in the brain and help improve skill acquisition.

In 1990, a group of brain scientists set up a very interesting research project with four separate groups of adult rats. Each group of animals was engaged in a different kind of activity. Here is how the groups were structured:

- **Mandatory Exercisers:** These animals were put on a treadmill for a total of sixty minutes per day. Exercising in this way was mandatory.
- **Voluntary Exercisers:** These animals had a treadmill in their cage, which they used frequently but did so on a totally voluntary basis.
- **Acrobats:** These animals were in an environment that was equipped with a complex obstacle course. While not physically challenging, the course was rich in a variety of activities.
- **Cage Potatoes:** This group had no opportunities for exercise.

The researchers in this study were looking at two key variables occurring in the four groups: (1) the volume of blood vessels in the brains of the animals and (2) the number of synapses—that is, connections—per neuron in the brain.

The results were surprising. The Mandatory Exercisers had the highest density of blood vessels. However, it was the Acrobats—those who were raised in an environment with the greatest opportunity for variation—that had the highest scores in increased synapses per nerve cell—the greatest number of *new connections*.

There is much to be learned from such studies about human possibilities and what we can do to help the brain of the child with special needs.

When we look at the way children are often taught in school, how adults are trained in the workplace, or how various therapy methods are done, we can see that there is an assumption, explicit or implicit, that the best way to acquire a skill is to home in as much as possible and focus attention on that which the person doesn't know, can't presently do well, or perhaps can't do at all. The teacher, trainer, or therapist focuses as narrowly as possible on that which is to be learned and excludes or minimizes Variation from that focal point.

Researcher Melissa A. Schilling and colleagues state that there is an implicit assumption in many organizational learning studies that the learning rate is maximized through specialization. The belief is that the more we narrowly focus on a particular task, the faster our performance will improve. Schilling and coworkers compared three approaches to learning: learning through specialization, without variation; learning with related variation; and learning with unrelated variation. They asked how each of these approaches would affect the learning process.

The research was based on having people learn a strategic board game called Go. They monitored the rate of learning for three groups of participants: The first group practiced only the game Go, with no variation. The second group practiced the game Go as well as a similar strategic game called Reversi, which constituted learning with related variation (which I earlier called "doing the same thing in a different way"). The third group practiced the game Go plus an unrelated strategic card game called Cribbage, which constituted learning with unrelated variation (which I earlier called "doing completely different things").

Schilling's group found that subjects from the groups with no variation and with unrelated variation learned at the same rate. They found that the group presented with related variation—doing the same thing in different ways—learned at the fastest rate, in fact, they learned significantly faster than the other two groups.

One way to interpret these results is that related variation provides the brain with a richness of experience and information that helped the research participants learn the game Go. This is what I call "differentiation around the edges" through Variation—creating new tiny pieces around the edges of what we already know. Specialization, on the other hand, narrowed the focus on the area of the desired learning, which limited the brain's ability to create new information and diminished the ability of the brain to learn.

For our discussion here, *specialization* is trying to get a child to learn something he can't presently do by focusing only on the thing to be learned, by having him repeat only that thing many, many times. This would be like the first group in the study, the individuals who studied only the game Go. For a child with special needs this approach will work only if he is already close to being able to do the thing to be learned, but it tends to produce an inferior quality of performance. For example, he might learn to crawl but not do it very well. With *related variation*—that is, differentiation around the edges—you provide the child with special challenges, variation around the skills he is presently able to do at least somewhat. This Variation, *combined* with the skill he is already somewhat able to do, provides a bridge to a higher level of performance or even to an entirely new skill that he couldn't do before. The third approach, *unrelated variation*, is like trying to make a child do something he is completely incapable of doing at that moment as a result of his special needs. Take the example of making a child crawl when, because of his underlying condition, his brain has been unable to develop the required underlying and fundamental elements necessary for crawling. He might not even be able to roll over to his belly and back yet! This approach very often proves to be ineffective and even counterproductive due to the disorganized patterns that are being grooved in the child's brain as the adult takes him through the crawling motions.

To use the related variations approach with your child, you bring in related elements that are necessary for learning the desired skill, elements that the child's brain is missing and can't acquire by mere repetition. With enough variations that are *close enough* to what your child can do at present, as limited or advanced as it might be, his brain will spontaneously make use of the elements it needs—the missing pieces—that are in the flow of new information coming from these variations. With these new elements the brain can bridge from where the child is right now to *his own unique next level of skill*.

The following tools provide you with ways of applying these concepts in everyday interactions with your child.

The Tools for Variation

Bringing Variation to your child's life can be fun while it is helping usher in desired changes. Even tiny changes in the way the child performs a certain movement increase the synapses in his brain. As synapses increase, so too does the number of connections between nerve cells, expanding the brain's potential for learning new things and adapting to new situations.

Tugging Gently at the Edges of Movement: *Tugging at the edges* means introducing Variation to an area that your child is already able to do on his own or introducing Variation to something he can easily do with a little help from you. Every time you do something in even a slightly different way with your child, it provides opportunities for his brain to grow new connections and create new patterns. Tugging at the edges takes advantage of the fact that learning is made possible and is accelerated when we start where the child already has some skill and can feel what is going on. This will always be with something he experiences as easy. It is where he will be able to be most engaged, participating in whatever you are doing with him rather than being uninvolved and passive or experiencing so much difficulty he begins to resist. You can introduce Variation (tug at the edges) in the movement of the body, in cognition, in emotion, and in social interaction. Always begin Variation in very small, gentle ways, watching for signs in his facial expressions or vocalizations or changes in the quality of his movements that indicate he is engaged and participating.

> **Tugging at the edges takes advantage of the fact that learning is made possible and is accelerated when we start where the child already has some skill and can feel what is going on.**

To illustrate how this works, let's take the example of a child whose hand coordination is wanting. Remember to begin with something that is easy for the child. Let's say it is easy for him to pick up medium-size toy cars, ones that are a bit smaller than the palm of his hand. However, he picks them up in a rough and forceful way. Start by playfully asking him to pick up a toy car with his right hand, making certain it is of the size that is easy for him. After he has picked it up, ask him to drop it. Then ask him to pick it up with even more force than before. Squeeze lightly on his hand as he is picking up the car, saying, "Tighter . . . harder." Have your child go back and forth between lighter and harder a few times.

For the next Variation, ask him to pick up the toy car with both hands, but with his palms and fingers flat and straight. The next Variation is to take off his shoes and have him try to pick up the toy car with both his feet, then with one foot and one hand. Then see if he can pick it up with only three fingers of each hand.

Have him pick up the little car while he is standing up, while he is sitting down, lying down on his back, on his belly, and so on. Then just have him lift the car with his right hand and observe if the movement is already more refined and better controlled. Say nothing to him, let him discover and feel it on his own.

You can do a very similar version of Variation with behavioral issues. For example, if your child tends to have tantrums and yell, you can, when he is not in the middle of a tantrum, play a game with him making different sounds (Variation) and making the sounds louder on purpose, then even louder, and then really loud. Then ask him to make the sounds softer. You and he can make sounds with your mouths closed, with your mouths open, while lying down and rolling from side to side, while sitting, or while standing or running and jumping. Then if and when he has a tantrum, you can ask him to vary the ways he yells—louder, softer, with his mouth open, with it closed, and so on. Most likely the tantrum will evaporate.

Keep focused at all times on your own stated purpose here, of tugging gently at the edges as a way of providing opportunities for your child's brain to experience more Variation, new information to form new patterns and more fully map his body.

Any movement that your child can do or that you can do with your child can be varied. You do not need to create a new regimen or set aside special time for what I'm describing here. Variation is easily introduced to nearly every daily activity that you already do with your child or that your child does on his own: getting dressed, drawing pictures, changing diapers, eating, bathing, and so on. Variation with any activity increases differentiation and complexity in your child's brain, which leads to greater motor control, better intellectual capacities, and a happier child.

Trust Small Changes: Some parents may initially find it challenging to give up on exercise regimens that include repetitive techniques and routines they may presently be following with their child, such as forced exercising or goal setting intended to make their child do what he can't. They may also be reluctant to introduce Variation to what is more or less already working with their child, afraid of messing it up and losing prior gains. If you find yourself feeling this way, take baby steps with tugging at the edges. Try taking only one day during which you stop the exercises you have been doing and take just five or ten minutes, three or four times that day, to experiment with movement variation the way I described it. Notice any positive changes in your child, then try taking a whole week during which you experiment with variation while avoiding more preprogrammed approaches. As you see more changes in your child, including his becoming happier, gradually bring Variation to anything you do with him, wherever he needs help, including with structured therapies and exercises.

Follow Your Child's Lead: As your child gains more freedom in his movement, he will begin to vary what he is doing spontaneously on his own. This might be in the movement of his body, his arm, leg, head, shoulder, back, in his thinking and ideas, in his emotional expressions, or in his interactions with others. At such times, be like a good ballroom dancer. Follow your child's lead and join in. Be flexible and ready to vary. For example, if your child is usually very quiet and timid and all of a sudden he expresses himself with a loud voice and hits the floor with his hand, demanding something, in a playful and nonthreatening way, join in: Mirror what he is doing. Mimic him by raising your own voice a bit and by gently hitting your own hand on the floor. Partner with your child, both of you playing together, with you following his lead. When he sees your participation in something he is doing, it is affirming for him and adds another kind of Variation. Another way to follow your child's lead is to describe what he is doing, such as, "Oh, your arms are up, up in the sky, now they are down, down. . . . Oops, you just landed on your tush!" Take an interest in your child rather than trying to correct him according to a rigid notion of what he should be doing.

Mistakes, Anyone? When your child does something the wrong way, do not correct him. Yes, you read that right: *Do not correct him.* (Of course, if his behavior endangers himself or someone else, make sure that you stop him right away.) As glaring and obvious as his mistake might seem to you, more often than not he doesn't recognize it; he has no idea what he is doing. He does not feel it!

Be assured that when I say don't correct the mistake, I am not advising you to ignore mistakes but rather to use the opportunity to introduce greater Variation. You will be helping your child become aware of what he is doing and acquire alternatives that work better. Think of your child's mistakes as a wonderfully rich resource of Variation and think of his limitations as opportunities for introducing Variation for him to be able to learn what he needs to learn. How do we make use of these treasures? You can take any mistakes your child makes and begin varying that mistake to help him perceive what he is actually doing. Through such variation you help your child gain greater freedom and mastery in his actions.

....
Think of your child's mistakes as a wonderfully rich resource of Variation.
....

Getting Good at Variation: When your child's brain has an underlying difficulty in creating variations, any variation, it is important to focus on helping his brain become more skillful at generating variation from within and integrating variation that arises from without. Variation to the brain is like light to the eyes: Without light the eyes cannot see, and without Variation the brain cannot learn or organize action very well. Children on the autism spectrum often have difficulty with variations. They often have an adverse reaction to any change or variation, especially if unexpected. It is as if their brain has gotten stuck in a rut of compulsive or repetitive patterns and has difficulty changing what it is doing. But this kind of rigidity of the brain can be seen, to a greater or lesser extent, with most children who have special needs. When a child has this kind of difficulty with compulsive behavior—be it emotional, cognitive, or physical—it is important to first introduce Variation in an area where he is already doing well. This is where he is most likely to be able to allow for Variation and make use of it.

....
Without light the eyes cannot see, and without Variation the brain cannot learn or organize action very well.
....

To try to help the brain improve its Variation capabilities, it is often easiest to begin in the area of physical movement. It is important to select a movement that your child can already do and, it is hoped, one that he likes and that is the easiest and most comfortable for him.

For example, if your child likes to clap his hands, even if he does it somewhat compulsively, that might be a good place to start. You could start with imitating his movements, clapping when he claps, then varying the tempo a bit. Or perhaps you clap with him on every other clap. Then you might gently take hold of his right hand and clap it to your own right hand; then, if he is barefoot, gently lift his leg and clap his foot to his hand. All of these are variations for the brain. You are not doing this with your child to get him to be more skillful at clapping his hands; you are introducing Variation where there is a chance that his brain will be able to perceive differences and get more comfortable with changes. If he resists and doesn't like any of these moves, do not insist; instead, look for other opportunities in which you can introduce gentle Variation that might appeal to him.

You are helping your child's brain get better and more skillful at doing Variation. You are helping your child's brain become a stronger and better brain, a brain that can create new information and overcome limitations.

Discovering the Difference: Some children have difficulty with academic or cognitive skills not because they lack intelligence but because for some reason their brains are not perceiving certain differences that are essential for mastering those skills. Variation can help these children's brains perceive differences that they are not presently seeing, hearing, or feeling, though these differences may seem obvious to everyone else.

One of the ways this manifests is when a child has difficulty learning to read and is unable to recognize the different shapes that make letters. He does not perceive the difference between a *p* and a *q*, or a *W* and an *M*. Or he may not yet recognize the difference between drawing a line from the right to the left of a page and drawing a line from the left to the right.

One of the ways I use Variation to help a child with this kind of challenge is that instead of having him try to recognize and write the letters, I select three simple shapes: a dot, a straight line, and a wiggly line. I have the child watch me as I slowly draw each of these shapes on a piece of paper and I name each of the shapes as I'm drawing them. I say, "Dot. Straight line. Wiggly line." Then I use my finger to draw these same three

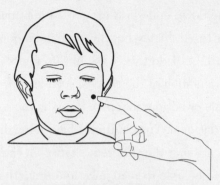

Touch your child's face lightly with the tip of
your finger and retract it to draw a dot

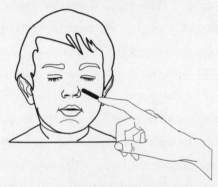

Lightly and slowly draw a straight line with your finger
on your child's face and ask: "Is it a dot or a straight line?"

Lightly and slowly draw a wiggly line with your finger on your child's
face and ask: "Is it a dot, a straight line, or a wiggly line?"

shapes on the back of the child's hand, naming them as I did before. I then have the child lie down and close his eyes. I continue to draw with my finger these same three shapes, but this time in random order, on his arm, face, belly, or back. As I do this, I ask him to guess each of the shapes. I also vary the orientation of the shapes, such as drawing the wiggly line from top to bottom or bottom to top, or drawing the straight line horizontal or vertical or diagonal. The children I have done this with have gotten very adept at identifying the different shapes on their own bodies, and that leads them to be able to recognize and draw these same shapes on paper.

With combinations of these three shapes we can begin constructing all the letters of the English alphabet. For example, a straight line becomes an *l*, a wiggly line becomes a *u*, and so on. Four diagonal lines become a *W* and two vertical lines with two diagonal lines become an *M*. I also have the child make these different shapes with his body, for example by standing up tall like the straight line or lying down on the floor curved like a wiggly line; I might ask him to walk in a straight line or jump up and down for a dot. These variations provide the brain with important distinctions it needs to be able to organize reading and writing.

Whenever you introduce Variation to your child, his brain begins perceiving differences and creating something new with this information. That is what needs to happen if anything is going to change. And once children feel the freedom and the playfulness associated with Variation, they become happier, more engaged and alert, and better learners.

7

Essential Four

Subtlety

Nothing is so strong as gentleness, nothing so gentle
as real strength.

—ST. FRANCIS DE SALES

The dictionary definition of *subtlety* is the "ability to
recognize and make very fine distinctions." As we've
observed in the previous chapters and in the stories of the
children I've shared with you, the brain's ability to perceive
fine differences is at the heart of its ability to generate new
information for organizing new, more refined and more ex-
acting action and for overcoming limitations. This is true
whether this change involves your child learning to move her
body, being able to improve her intellectual capacities, or
changing and improving something in her emotional life. To
be most helpful to your child, whatever you do with her
needs to foster and empower her own spontaneous ability to
perceive differences. And that's where Subtlety comes in.

Without it, her brain will have little or no new information to work with. The more Subtlety and gentleness that you bring to any action you do with your child, or that your child does herself, the more her brain will perceive differences and the more brilliant she will be at creating new solutions for overcoming her challenges. Let's look closer at subtlety and gentleness, and how they help your child perceive differences.

....

To be most helpful to your child, whatever you do with her needs to foster and empower her own spontaneous ability to perceive differences. And that's where Subtlety comes in.

....

Greater Intensity Lessens Sensitivity

You have probably had the experience of standing in a crowded room, perhaps at a party or during a theater intermission, trying to carry on a conversation with a friend. After a few frustrating minutes of struggling to hear each other above the din of the crowd, you suggest that the two of you go outside so that you can talk. Once outside, you at first find you are still yelling to be heard. But you quickly lower your voice, as does your friend. You both speak more softly, in your normal tone of voice, which includes thousands of different tonal inflections, changes of volume, and subtle innuendoes. Here in this quiet atmosphere you enjoy a pleasant exchange.

During moments like this, you are experiencing what Ernst Heinrich Weber, a psychophysiologist, discovered more than a century ago: Our sensitivity to a stimulus (in this case, the sound of our friend's voice) diminishes as the intensity (the roar of the crowd) of the background stimulus increases. (This is known as the Weber-Fechner law, which I'll discuss later in this chapter.) Due to the roar of the crowd, you have difficulty hearing your friend's words; you cannot communicate finer nuances and inflections in your own thoughts and feelings since you are straining, using your voice forcefully, to be heard above the crowd.

This same principle holds true for all of our senses. When you are standing outside in the glaring light of a sunny day—an intense stimulus—you won't notice the light of a flashlight turned on beside you. Our sensitivity to the light created by the flashlight—our ability to perceive the difference—is diminished by the greater intensity of the sunshine. But the same flashlight turned on in the dark immediately gets your attention. In total darkness, even the flash of a match igniting will do it. If you put five teaspoons of sugar in your tea, you will not notice the change of sweetness if someone added an extra quarter teaspoonful of sugar. If you are carrying a ten-pound box up the stairs, you won't feel any difference in weight if someone adds a single piece of paper to the box.

You might imagine yourself doing this little experiment: Pick up and hold a two-pound book. Now place a pen on top of this book. Will you feel the very subtle difference in weight that the pen adds? You won't. The sensations coming from your muscles and joints as you hold the book are too strong for you to notice the very slight increase of weight of the pen, a principle I first learned from Dr. Feldenkrais. Your brain cannot perceive the subtle difference. Now put down the book and hold a one ounce letter in your hand. Place the same pen on the letter. Your brain will now notice the additional weight of the pen.

So Simple Yet So Powerful—Subtlety in Action

In our efforts to help a child improve and go beyond her current limitations, be it with the movement of her body or with cognitive, emotional, or social skills, it's important to recognize that any excessive force that we apply with her or that she exerts on her own, will make it more difficult for her to feel nuances she must be able to feel if she's going to improve. Any force greater than the minimum needed to perform the intended action will interfere with your child's progress. The more you can help create the conditions for your child to perceive *subtle differences*, to feel more of what there is to feel by ensuring ease and comfort—that is, by reducing force and excessive effort—the more her brain can change and she will improve. Any forcing or excessive efforts exerted by you or by your child herself will degrade her brain's ability to perceive subtle shifts and differences in her own movement, thinking, or emotions, which will make it much harder, and at times even impossible, for her to improve. Subtlety—increasing gentleness by reducing the force and effort in your and your child's actions—is one of the most potent and immediate ways to increase creativity and intelligent action exponentially in both you and your child.

> **The more you can help create the conditions for your child to perceive *subtle differences*...the more her brain can change and she will improve.**

Welcome to Lazy Land

Lily was three years old when I first saw her. She was so tiny that she could easily have passed as a one-year-old. As I observed how she interacted with her mom and her baby-sitter, who were very loving and protective of her, Lily's behavior was developmentally like an infant. This was later confirmed by her mother, who told me that Lily had just gone through a battery of tests that had determined she was at the developmental level of a five-month-old. Lily had been born very premature and now suffered from severe cerebral palsy. Her muscles were very tight, mostly her flexor muscles, which kept her elbows always tightly bent, and her hands in a fisted position; her legs were crossed with knees always somewhat bent; her belly muscles were constantly contracted and tight so that her back was rounded, making it impossible for her to support her own weight. Lily had no voluntary movement. She couldn't roll over to her belly or even lie on her belly when placed in that position; she would stay curled up and very uncomfortable. When placed in a sitting position, she could, with great effort, hold herself in that position, with her back extremely rounded, for only a few seconds and then she would topple over. She couldn't use her arms and hands. She could talk, but her diction was poor and she spoke very faintly. Often it was impossible to understand what she was trying to say.

In spite of these limitations, I could see that she was very awake and alert. She followed what was happening around her with interest, her big brown eyes taking everything in.

I gently placed Lily on her back on the worktable. Even in that position, her muscles remained contracted: her legs bent and she held them somewhat elevated off the surface of the table. Her arms were bent, clutched close to her body, and her belly muscles were tight. It was as if her brain didn't know that she was lying down. It didn't know how to let go.

When I gently held her left leg and began moving it ever so slightly, immediately her already contracted muscles contracted even more, and with great intensity. She curled in on herself like a little ball. I stopped moving her and waited until she calmed down. I then tried moving her pelvis, again just a tiny bit, and very slowly, yet still she responded with the same intense muscular contractions as before. I tried many different ways to see if Lily could be moved without these reactions. I slowed way down, doing the tiniest movements possible, working at subtler and subtler levels. I talked with her while moving her, engaging her and seeking ways to help her feel safe. But still she contracted her muscles with every movement. It was as if each time I tried to move her, her brain was hijacked by this incredibly forceful and undifferentiated early pattern of movement—rounding herself into a ball.

After ten minutes, it dawned on me that this pattern of contracting into a ball was not just the cerebral palsy at work; it was also a learned pattern for Lily. It was clear to me that she really wanted to move. She wanted to help, and from her point of view she was actively participating.

I learned that she had gone through close to two years of therapy during which, from early on, she was rolled over to her belly and was placed in a sitting position. People working with her tried to get her to open her hands and use them. Attempts were even made to get her to stand up. Due to her condition, each time these movements were done with her, the only thing her brain could do was to contract in powerful and undifferentiated ways that put her into this constricted ball position. She had learned to associate any intent to move herself, or to be moved by others, with that pattern of constriction.

The intensity—the great force with which her muscles contracted anytime she was moved or tried to move herself—created a vicious circle. The great intensity made it impossible for Lily's brain to perceive any differences, thus denying her brain any new information with which to differentiate and learn how to move.

I realized that in order for Lily to learn to move, I had to somehow help her decrease the excessive efforts she was making when she was trying to move. Then it dawned on me. I needed to find a way to help Lily learn how to *not try* to move. She needed to learn to feel the difference between contracting and not contracting her muscles, between doing more, doing less, and doing nothing.

Thus I decided to teach Lily how to be *lazy*. She needed to learn how to not do anything so that she would have an opportunity to feel herself and her own movements.

So I made up a story for Lily. I told her that my office was a very special and different kind of place called Lazy Land. This was a kingdom where everyone was *lazy*. We all spoke V-E-R-Y S-L-O-W-L-Y and we B-A-R-E-L-Y moved. We slouched and lay around, doing nothing at all.

I leaned over and brought my head down to the table, resting there lazily next to her. Lily found this hilarious. I used my voice, my own movements, and my words to convey to her what I meant by *lazy*, modeling for how to reduce her excessive efforts.

After a while, I told Lily that I was going to begin moving her, but that we were both going to be very, very lazy. I proceeded to lift her leg, and sure enough she immediately got all tight as before. I stopped the movement and pointed out to her, in a playful way: "Hey, you forgot to be lazy!" I continued with this process, with many variations, always as gentle as I could be, over the next two sessions with Lily, always lazily telling her to be lazy. Then, for the first time, after Lily involuntarily tightened her whole body, she realized that she had done this, and then was able to voluntarily let go. It was the most exciting moment, like a miracle! We continued for the remainder of the week to practice being lazy, for her to do nothing while I was moving her. More and more, Lily was able to allow me to move her very gently without her forcefully contracting her muscles. She was able, for the first time in her life, to *feel* the different movements of her body. Her brain was now perceiving and differentiating in ways that it had been unable to do before.

Lily soon began opening her hands and was able to grasp and play with small toys. By the end of her first week of sessions, she began to roll spontaneously onto her belly and to her back all by herself, and she was doing it with grace and refinement. Her brain was integrating the flood of new information resulting from Subtlety into these new skills.

Lily's family continued to bring her in for clusters of lessons, one or two weeks at a time, over the next three years. In each visit she continued to transform. She learned to crawl and to sit up by herself. She was able to use her arms and hands freely and with great dexterity. Her alert and bright mind and personality showed itself through her intense interest in playing and learning. Her speech improved, getting clearer and clearer, and her voice gained strength and expressiveness. All of these changes and new skills demonstrated that her brain was perceiving subtler differences, giving her ever increasing control of her body and her intellectual capacities and enriching her emotional expression. Lily began feeling good about herself.

The last time I saw her she was able to pull herself up to standing but still struggled with being able to fully use her legs. By this time she was in school and was a very bright student. Her parents elected to get Lily a power wheelchair, which she used mostly in school and which she loved because it allowed her to move in the classroom and between classrooms faster and more easily. At home she hardly ever used the wheelchair. Her parents wanted her to maintain as much of her own mobility and independence as possible.

The Powerful World of Lazy Land

Lily's story illustrates how, like the sunlight drowning out the subtler light of the flashlight, her intense, involuntary muscular contractions made it impossible for her to benefit from the various therapies and attempts to help her. I discovered that all the children I work with, whether they have been diagnosed with autism, attention deficit hyperactivity disorder (ADHD), or any other condition, need Subtlety in order to improve and thrive. After identifying the source of the intense stimulus limiting Lily that was drowning out her ability to feel subtle differences in her movements (her contracting into a ball), it was essential to find a way to reduce the intensity of that stimulus. We helped her do it through the imaginary world of Lazy Land, where she transformed her idea of what it meant to move from the incredible efforts that led her nowhere to the experience of ease, comfort, pleasure, fun and *not trying hard*—it led her to learning and change.

You have a remarkable opportunity to use the power of Subtlety—the reduction of the intensity of a stimulus your child is experiencing—to immediately wake up her brain and help it differentiate and integrate new patterns and skills. All you need to do is find out where your child is experiencing or exerting excessive efforts and force that are drowning out her brain's ability to perceive differences and that stunt her development. Excessive intensities of stimulation can occur in many different ways. Some may be characteristics of the child's condition, while others may be unique to your child. A child with attention deficit disorder (ADD) might try to draw a picture but use so much force that she breaks the crayon. A child on the autism spectrum might be trying hard to make sense of something being asked of her, but the intensity in the voice she is hearing overwhelms her and she begins to scream or revert to perseveration. A child with cerebral palsy might be trying to learn how to use a walker but tightens her whole body so that she is too rigid to move her legs. These are all moments of opportunity for you to introduce Subtlety, to look for ways to help your child reduce excessive efforts and intense stimuli and open up to new learning.

You, the Subtle One

If we are to be effective in helping the child we need to turn our attention to ourselves.

When a child has special needs it is clearly a call for action. Everyone caring for that child will quite naturally focus their attention on the child. What is sometimes less obvious, yet of equal importance, is that if we are to be effective in helping the child we need to turn our attention to ourselves. That means bringing Subtlety to yourself—to your own actions, your own thinking, your own emotions, and your own movements. Anyone I've ever known or worked with, and this includes myself, always has a lot of room to reduce unnecessary efforts and intensities, which leads to increasing our own sensitivity and our ability to perceive differences. We need to be a Stradivarius rather than a $50 fiddle. When you bring greater Subtlety to yourself, you will increase *your* sensitivity and ability to feel. You will also increase your ability to *feel your child*, to perceive finer and finer changes in her body, in her movements, in her thinking, and in her emotions as well as in her relationship to you, other people, and the world around her. All of this provides information that will guide you to what your child needs and is ready for in the here and now. You will be able to interact with your child in a way that is relevant to her, to what she is feeling and experiencing, rather than following an idea of what you "should" be doing with your child or simply acting in an automatic fashion. You will have so much more information to work with, coming from your child and from within you. You will be more creative and effective in your efforts to help your child.

> **When you bring greater Subtlety to yourself, you will increase your sensitivity and *ability to feel*.**

As you become more refined and sensitive within yourself, you will spontaneously find yourself more attuned with your child. The quality of your own movements, thinking, feeling, and expressions will serve as a model for her. You will provide a model of greater Subtlety to help her brain reduce unnecessary intensities within herself that otherwise would block her from improving.

What Are Numbers For? Subtlety for the Mind

Very often my clients say to me: "Anat, I see how what you do works for the physical body, for movement, but I don't understand how it works with the mind." I'm asked this question even when the parents are able to recognize clear and even dramatic changes in their child's cognitive abilities, be it in her starting to read, starting to write, understanding math, or improved understanding of what is asked of her.

One parent, once he did get it, said to me, "I think I know why it has been so hard for me to grasp this. It's because I can't see or touch thinking. But I can see my child moving and touch and feel her body." The intellectual, emotional, and physical are not separate; they all are an integrated whole and require a brain that can perceive differences and organize that information into effective action. In the words of Michael Merzenich, "Thinking is the same fundamental process in the brain as organizing movement."

Examples of the need for Subtlety in areas of cognition to help the child's ability to perceive differences and improve her thinking skills come up in almost every session I have with a child. John, one of the children I worked with some years ago, had been diagnosed on the autism spectrum. He had been coming to me since he was a baby and then now in second grade. He was doing very well in many respects but was having great trouble with math. I asked his mother to bring John's math homework to the session. Then I watched him as he attempted to solve a couple of the math problems. Very quickly it became clear to me that he had no idea what numbers meant or what they were for. He could read the symbols and name them correctly, but that was about it. I asked him, "What do you think numbers are for?" He looked at me surprised, then said, "I don't know." I asked again, cajoling him a bit. This time he thought and thought. Then he brightened and happily told me, "It's for the teacher to ask questions."

"True," I said. "And are they for anything else?"

He thought a moment, and then replied with great self-assurance, "Nope."

I had an idea. I knew he had a birthday coming up, so I suggested that we might pretend to plan his party. He liked this idea. "Let's start with a small birthday party," I said. "Let's say you are going to invite only one friend. Is that okay?"

He replied, "Yes," mildly enthusiastic.

"Who would that be?" I asked.

"Sam, my best friend," he said.

I took a piece of paper and drew the image of John and next to him the image of another boy, Sam. Then I asked: "Would you like to have some party favors at your party?"

"Yes," he said, clearly more enthusiastic. "A puzzle and a little box of crayons."

"How many puzzles will you get for the party? How will you know if you have enough when you go shopping with your mom?"

"That's easy," John replied. "I'll get one for me and one for Sam."

Great! He understood "one." I proceeded to draw a puzzle and a crayon box next to John and next to Sam on the paper.

Then I asked John, "Is this what you will get?" He studied the pictures for a second, then answered yes.

"Would you like to invite more kids for your party?" I asked John. He was all for that. He began naming kids he would like to invite, naming each one. I stopped him at eight. "I think that's probably enough kids," I said, and then drew his image and the image of the additional eight boys with their names on a separate piece of paper. I then took the first page with the drawing of John and Sam with the two party favors drawn next to them. I asked him: "Are these enough party favors for all the kids in your bigger birthday party?"

John looked at that drawing, then at the drawing of the nine kids, then back to the first drawing and said, "Oh no, it's not enough for everybody."

He was now perceiving the difference in the quantity. So I decided to ask him: "You need to go with your mom and get party favors for all of these kids. How are you going to do that?" Then immediately added a question: "What are numbers for?"

He took a few seconds and all of a sudden he looked at me, as if surprised, and said, "To know how many party favors to get at the store with my mom!"

"Yes," I said. "Numbers are for knowing how much or how many we have of something, like how many kids in a birthday party or how many car toys you have and how many your brother has."

John was delighted with his discovery. It was like a wide door into the workings of his mind had been opened. In the next few sessions he insisted that we do some math problems. He declared to me: "I love math!" This was a 180-degree change from his dread and sense of failure regarding math that he had expressed up to that point.

To help John I needed first to find where he was: His understanding was that *numbers are for the teacher to ask questions about.* I then looked for a way for him to begin feeling the meaning of numbers, rather than giving him more math problems, which we already knew he couldn't solve. His efforts to do so were undifferentiated and very stressful for him; this great intensity didn't allow his brain to figure it out. Once I reduced the intensity of his experience of math and at the same time created the opportunity for his brain to perceive differences associated with quantities that were meaningful for him, he was very quickly able to associate those quantities with the idea of numbers. His brain was now differentiating patterns of quantities, or groups, and their relationships to the words that represented these numbers. His brain was putting order into disorder through the help of Subtlety.

Intuitive—Counterintuitive

So much about the Essential Subtlety is counterintuitive. The natural inclination is often to bring in more force when something isn't working as we would like it to. Not until you have some experience with Subtlety and have experienced its power to transform you and your child, does it become more natural for you. As you reduce the force and intensity with which you yourself move and with which you interact with your child, you'll begin to *feel* much more and to notice finer and finer nuances that were nonexistent for you before.

> **You'll begin to *feel* much more and to notice finer and finer nuances that were nonexistent for you before.**

One of the gifts that arise from this process is that you will become more intuitive. I am not talking about intuition in the *woo-woo* sense. What I mean by intuition is your brain's ability to generate and integrate greater amounts of information at any given moment, guiding you to know more clearly when your child is ready for something new and when she is not. Intuition is knowing when she has had enough, when she is feeling empowered by what she is being asked to do, and when it is diminishing her sense of self. As contradictory as it might seem, the increasing richness and refinement of your own feelings will serve as an important additional resource for your logical mind in the service of your child. Observe yourself and notice if and when you begin to experience your intuition. You don't have to trust it at first, but as things unfold, notice how often your intuition is on target. Over time you will learn to bring everything to the table: your logical thinking, the information you get from others, especially other professionals, and your own feelings and intuition. Intuition becomes yet another tool that you can rely on and that helps you decide what is best for your child at any given moment.

What Science Tells Us About Subtlety

As I mentioned earlier in this chapter, the Weber-Fechner law is an established neurophysiological phenomenon. It helps us understand why it is that reducing the intensity of the background stimulus increases the ability of the child to perceive differences. And those perceived differences are information for the brain to work with, for creating new connections and for moving the child from the impossible to the possible.

Researchers have found that babies' ability to recognize differences followed the same Weber-Fechner law that applies for simple sensory perception: Infants as young as six months of age were able to notice the difference in the number of elements, both visual and auditory, when those differences were large enough in relation to the initial amount introduced.

What the Weber-Fechner law and continuing research around it tells us is that to help your child develop intellectual or any other skill, parents, teachers, and those in other helping professions need to find ways to reduce the background intensity. Once they do, many differences become big enough for the child to perceive, and the brain gets the information it needs and the child becomes more intelligent and skillful.

The Tools for Subtlety

The following tools offer you ways to employ Subtlety to help your child's brain perceive differences better. As discussed earlier, the more the brain is able to perceive differences the more information it has to work with and the more your child can move beyond her current limitations.

There Is a Difference to Be Made: Whenever your child is stuck, unable to progress despite all your and your child's efforts, it is almost certain that she is not perceiving *enough* differences or *any* differences whatsoever in the areas of her limitation. She might not see, hear, feel, or understand what is obvious to you and others. This tool calls on you to discover where your child might be making excessive efforts or where you, or others are using excessive effort or force on her. It can be excessive physical efforts, great emotional intensities coming from you or your child, or forceful cognitive efforts that make it difficult or impossible for your child's brain to perceive differences. Remember, until she is able to perceive a difference that difference simply doesn't exist for her; until she has the opportunity to perceive that difference, she cannot learn and improve. The first step is for you to look for ways to reduce these excessive intensities.

Become a Stradivarius: Think of your ability to feel more and to be able to perceive finer and finer differences as a lifeline to your child's brain and its ability to overcome challenges. Subtlety calls on you to grow and evolve in the service of your child. Any investment you put into learning how to reduce unnecessary efforts in your own actions will immediately reflect in your child's ability to learn and change.

Subtlety in Movement: It is easiest for most people to learn to reduce excessive efforts in body movements. Next time you drive your car, for example, experiment with reducing the force you apply in your arms, hands, and fingers to move the steering wheel. See how much less muscular effort you can exert and still control the car perfectly well. Experiment in the same way with washing dishes, getting dressed in the morning. If you follow an exercise regimen, be it yoga, running, tennis, or whatever, experiment with reducing force and effort there. You will discover that as you reduce force, you will feel more and actually get better at what you are doing.

Subtlety in Movement with Your Child: Immediately begin using your emerging Subtlety skills with your child. With every movement you do with her—changing diapers, getting dressed, picking her up or putting her down, or any other way that you move your child or help your child move—use less and less force. Notice your child's immediate response to your greater Subtlety. Combine it with slowing down—remember the Essential Slow, and you will witness your child's brain waking up even more and beginning to change.

Subtlety and Emotional Expression: Next you can apply Subtlety in your emotional expressions. Look for opportunities to reduce the emotional intensity that you bring to any interaction you have with your child. You can do this through the gentle tone of your voice, the feelings of ease with which you approach your child, or by reducing the intensity of your expectations of your child at any given moment. That is not to say that you give up or become disinterested in her progress: on the contrary, you reduce the intensity of your emotional expression with your child so that you become more attuned and in synch with her, and your child becomes more attuned with herself.

Any time you provide your child with a model of Subtlety, through your own thoughts, feelings, and actions, she will experience that Subtlety firsthand. Through you, your child will learn Subtlety, mirroring and integrating what you bring to her.

Working Smarter

Now that you are using Subtlety in your own actions, you will be able to detect much better when your child is using excessive force and efforts and when she is making a change and lessening her use of force and effort. Whenever you do detect her excessive efforting, use this as an opportunity to guide her into her own Subtlety.

Comfort in Movement: If your child has difficulty doing a certain movement and is trying to do it with excessive force, find ways to *gently* guide her to use less force. That might require taking her out of the position she is presently in and having her be in a different position where she is able to reduce the force of the movement she is trying to do.

For example, when a child tends to trip and fall a lot and places her feet far apart as she walks, you can be sure that she is using excessive muscular effort when standing and walking. At such times she is unable to feel the difference between her feet being right under her, being farther apart, or being close together. Think of her excessive efforts as being like a very loud noise that drowns out her ability to perceive the gentler and more refined communications coming from her joints and muscles to her brain, which she will require if she is to articulate her movements better. You could play a game with her to turn down the volume of her excessive force, to help her feel finer differences. For example, instead of starting from a standing position, from which she is using so much force trying to avoid falling, have her sit down in a chair. In this position excessive effort will be reduced and she will be able to feel more. Make sure she is comfortable and that her feet reach the floor. Have her look at her feet and show you with her hands how far apart her feet are. Don't worry if she is accurate or not. Then move her hands farther apart and say, "Now your hands are farther apart." Then move them closer and say, "Now they are closer." Have her put her hands down.

Ask her to close her eyes and then you gently move her feet farther apart but not farther than is easy and comfortable for her to do. Remember that you are after helping her reduce intensity and force anywhere that is possible for her to feel what she is doing. Ask her, "What do you think? Are your feet closer together or more away from each other?" Don't worry if her answer is correct, and *do not correct her.* Just let her feel what she is feeling and guess at where her feet are. Then have her look at her feet.

Ask her to close her eyes again. Then move her right leg closer to the left and ask her, "Did you feel that I moved your leg?" Most likely she will say yes. Then ask her, "Did I move it closer to the other leg or did I move it more away?" (If your child is too young or unable to speak, simply name what you are doing rather than asking her questions.) Then repeat this whole process with the other leg, each time reducing the force in your own hand and arm as you move her leg. After that, ask her to move one leg (either right or left)—with more force and then with less force.

Do this game for five minutes or so, then have her stand up. Give her a moment to feel any changes in the way she is standing. Most likely her brain has recalibrated ways of using her legs more efficiently. Now repeat the same steps as above while she is standing. If she has any difficulty doing any of these variations standing, have her do it again in the sitting position. After about ten minutes total of playing this game, stop altogether and simply have her move around. Do not point out to her that her feet are now closer or not, whatever the case may be (see Chapter 8 for more).

There are many variations of this game, for different movements or conditions, for reducing effort so your child can feel and notice finer differences in what she is doing, giving her brain opportunities to organize her movements better. You will be amazed how quickly the brain figures out what had seemed out of reach for years.

Lazy Land: To help your child reduce excessive force and effort while trying to move, you can encourage her with your words to try less hard. Reassure her that it's okay to do less. You can play the Lazy Land game with her if you like or invent any other game that will help her reduce her efforts as she moves. For example, have a contest to be the last one to cross the room.

Emotional Ease: If your child has a tendency to use excessive force emotionally—such as having tantrums, banging her head, or getting into compulsive repetitive behaviors—know first of all that this is an involuntary and automatic behavior. At that moment, the intensity the child is generating is so high she is not able to perceive any differences or change her behavior. Later, when your child is calm, sit down with her, even hold her if she lets you, and tell her a story about what happened earlier when she was having a tantrum. Use a gentle tone and be nonjudgmental. You might say, for example: "Remember how earlier you got upset? You wanted to watch TV and Mommy said no, it's time to have dinner. Remember how you were really loud?"

As you speak very gently and softly, you might say: "Let's try to be a bit louder for just a moment. Okay?" Then, if your child doesn't indicate resistance to this idea, go ahead and speak in a voice that's a bit louder. Then ask your child to do the same. Once she has, "Okay, good!" you might say. "Now let's do a gentle voice." Then go ahead and do that. Go back and forth, creating smaller and greater differences in loudness. Through Subtlety you are helping your child shift from automatic, undifferentiated behavior to having more differentiated feelings, leading her to have greater emotional freedom and choice. Later, if and when you see that your child is about to have a tantrum, remind her about the louder and softer game. Ask her in a gentle and loving way: "Can you be a bit louder? And now softer?" Make sure that there is no trace of teasing, sarcasm, or anger in your voice. Doing it this way will help her brain shift from her automatic, undifferentiated, involuntary, and forceful emotional expression to her newer more differentiated feelings and her easier expression.

As you and your child get better at Subtlety, you will both feel more and your child's brain will get better and better at perceiving differences. These perceived and felt differences are the information your child's brain will use to move beyond her present limitations. You will observe your child becoming more intelligent, more astute, and a better and faster learner. Past struggles and suffering will be replaced with delight and discovery.

8 Essential Five
Enthusiasm

Enthusiasm is contagious; be a carrier.

—SUSAN RABIN

We often think of enthusiasm as a feeling we have for something that pleases us. The origin of the word is the Greek *enthousiasmos*, meaning "inspired by the gods." Merriam-Webster's dictionary defines enthusiasm as "strong excitement of feeling." When referring to a person who has an ardent interest in a sport or other activity, we may say: "She's a golf enthusiast" or "He's a football enthusiast." While such definitions are useful in everyday life, the way I am using it here is somewhat different.

Think of Enthusiasm as a skill that you can develop within yourself, one that you will apply in the service of helping your child overcome his limitations. Enthusiasm as a skill is your ability and your willingness to acknowledge as important the smallest of changes in your child, and for you to experience joy, internally celebrating those events or actions. In that respect, Enthusiasm is not about paying compliments, such as saying "Good boy!" or "Good girl!" Nor is it about clapping your hands to applaud something your child has accomplished—what is generally labeled *positive reinforcement*. What I'm talking about here is developing your ability to create and amplify your own internal experience of deep delight and appreciation for your child's tiniest changes and improvements.

When you amplify the Enthusiasm you feel within yourself, *your child feels it*, even if you say nothing. While I have witnessed this silent interchange between caregiver and child thousands of times in my work, it has been heartening, in recent years, to discover scientific research verifying this phenomenon. In 1996 Giacomo Rizzolatti, a neuroscientist at the University of Parma, discovered the activity of mirror neurons in the brain, which "allow us to grasp the minds of others not only through conceptual reasoning but through direct simulation. By feeling, not by thinking." In an article in the *New York Times*, science writer Sandra Blakeslee observed: "The human brain has multiple mirror neuron systems that specialize in carrying out and understanding not just the actions of others but their intentions, the social meaning of their behavior and their emotions."

All this clearly indicates that your own Enthusiasm powerfully affects your child's brain. Your skillful Enthusiasm helps your child notice and feel changes—the differences—within himself, and the positive emotions your child feels coming from you tells his brain that these changes are important to notice and groove in. In other words, your Enthusiasm— your feelings of delight, appreciation and hopefulness—will be felt by your child. Your child's brain, we must remember, will also mirror and adopt feelings of discouragement, hopelessness, disappointment, disapproval, or indifference from the people around him. Aside from wanting your child to feel good about himself, which is a very worthy goal, why is Enthusiasm important?

> **Your skillful Enthusiasm helps your child notice and feel changes—the differences—within himself, and the positive emotions your child feels coming from you tells his brain that these changes are important to notice and groove in.**

Look at Me!

When you notice the smallest of changes in your child and generate Enthusiasm at that instant, your Enthusiasm pulls into the foreground of your child's attention a thought, a feeling, or movement that distinguishes it as important. This makes it possible for his brain to perceive the change, to differentiate it from the background noise—activity—that is going on in his brain. We don't know which small change will end up being important for your child's future improvements. We do know, however, that your child's brain needs billions of these small differentiations to gain new skills. Enthusiasm is another way to help your child's brain perceive differences that become a source of information for the brain to work with. Your Enthusiasm amplifies for the child small changes, making it easier for him to notice those differences. Without your enthusiasm, these small and seemingly insignificant changes may never be noticed by your child's brain and can become missed opportunities.

> **Enthusiasm is another way to help your child's brain perceive differences that become a source of information for the brain to work with.**

We can see this Essential in action with healthy children all the time. Children get very excited—the child's version of Enthusiasm—whenever they do something new, calling their brain's attention to it. The excitement generated from within them helps them amplify changes the same way that your Enthusiasm does for them. And frequently they look for a witness with whom to share their excitement. Often it is nothing that we would think is a big deal. For example, when a three-year-old draws something on a piece of paper, he will run to his mother, pull on her hand and say, "Mommy, Mommy, look, look what I did!" What mom sees on the paper is a scribble. Nothing to be excited about. Or is it? For the child it is a huge thing, something very new. It is one small, yet very important piece in his future ability to draw, to write, and much later, perhaps become an architect. His own Enthusiasm helps his brain distinguish this new piece and groove it in his brain. Without his Enthusiasm it is likely to leave no permanent impression and change in his brain. Recently, while taking a walk, I happened to pass a playground and noticed a little girl hanging upside down on a climbing structure. As she did this she called out to her father, "Look, Daddy! Look at me, look at me. Look what I'm doing!"

The little girl was so excited about hanging upside down that she wanted her experience to be noted and amplified for her by feeling her dad's Enthusiasm. This is something that happens probably millions of times every day, on playgrounds around the world. What is important to note here is that the child's Enthusiasm, her spontaneous excitement about what she is doing, gets her brain to pay attention and to select the relevant connections that are being created at that moment. Her performance of the action, combined with her Enthusiasm, wakes up her brain, alerting it that these are successful connections that get selected over other connections; as a result, these patterns get grooved in more clearly and powerfully, becoming available for future use. The adult's participation in that excitement aids this process in the child's brain.

Is It Real?

Jacob suffered brain damage at birth that led to developmental delay, both physical and cognitive. When he was first brought to me, at age two, he was unable to roll over to his belly; couldn't tolerate lying on his belly; his eyes were crossed; and he was unable to sit, speak, or do much of anything. I was happy to note that he seemed to enjoy his lessons with me; he was very attentive and quick to respond. After a few lessons he gained some mobility in his back, was able to hold his head up better, and was more aware of his environment. At the same time, the changes were small compared to the achievements of other kids his age. If he were more like them, he would be running around, talking, playing, learning to say no, asserting himself, and much more.

As I usually do, I always had at least one of Jacob's parents in the room during each of our sessions. Tom, the boy's father, was very attuned to his son and took great delight with the smallest of changes he saw in Jacob. For Tom, any change, even a seemingly insignificant one, was proof that his son was intelligent and that there was hope for him. Tom was a quiet man, so he never said much during the sessions. However, he watched very closely, and his interest and love for his son was palpable. After each session he expressed his enthusiasm about the changes he had observed in his son during the lesson.

Jacob's mother, Jackie, was fierce in her commitment to her son and dearly loved him. But her style was very different from Tom's. She seemed constantly aware of her son's challenges. Changes Jacob made appeared to bring her no joy, hope, or relief. She certainly was not enthusiastic. At first I thought she simply wasn't aware of Jacob's changes, so I began to gently point them out to her. She readily acknowledged the changes. But these small changes only reminded her of how far Jacob was from where he "should" be, and this perspective increased her feelings of discouragement. I clearly understood how she could feel this way as long as she was seeing only Jacob's limitations, not seeing value in the small changes and not knowing what kind of future he could have.

After a few sessions, I noticed that whenever Tom was present, Jacob progressed a lot faster. It was as if Tom's internal experience of delight with the changes Jacob was going through uplifted the boy and amplified his ability to respond to my work with him. When Jackie was in the room, it was just the opposite. Working with Jacob felt like trying to drag his brain through wet concrete. Jacob became timid, sluggish, and shut down.

Coming from a scientific background, I questioned my perceptions. But after a while, I could no longer deny that the absence or presence of Enthusiasm can be the make-or-break ingredient for a child. Jacob's wonderful parents taught me that Enthusiasm is real and it needs to be recognized and to be fully acknowledged. I discussed my realization with Tom and Jackie. At first, as Jackie became aware of how her own lack of Enthusiasm affected Jacob's progress, she felt embarrassed and worried. Then she asked, "Is this something that can be learned?" I reassured her; absolutely yes it can be learned. She quickly declared her intention to do just that. Together they agreed that Tom would bring Jacob to his sessions as often as he could while Jackie would hone her Enthusiasm skills to be more attuned to the small changes in her son. As she changed, not only did Jacob immediately respond positively to her newfound abilities, but Jackie herself became happier, finding genuine delight in Jacob's progress.

Please, No Applause!

It's important to not confuse Enthusiasm with what is often called *positive reinforcement*. Positive reinforcement is praising or rewarding your child for something you have been trying to teach him or perhaps for ceasing to do something you've wanted him to stop. We often clap our hands enthusiastically at such times. Or we reward our child with a treat or a gift.

Nearly every parent uses positive reinforcement, intentionally or instinctively, to encourage a child to learn and improve. And often this is an empowering and positive experience for the child.

Enthusiasm, as I am speaking of it here, is not about your child earning external rewards or praise. In fact, it is the opposite. One of the first things we teach parents is to not clap their hands or make loud and excited exclamations when their child has just done something for the first time, such as taking his first steps, saying his first word, or interacting socially with another child. Instead, we ask parents to act as if whatever their child is doing were perfectly normal, as if he had been doing it forever. We do, however, encourage the parent to quietly and fully feel their own delight and excitement, relief and joy—to internally experience their emotions. Why is that? Because we want the child's change or achievement—small or big—to be *felt* by the child. We want it to be the child's own experience. Applause and external rewards will distract the child and shift his attention, taking the brain away from the process it's engaged in. We don't want the child's attention to be shifted to *our* feelings and reactions. Nor do we want to try to reinforce his new accomplishments at such times. It is extremely important that your child stays attuned to what he himself is feeling and experiencing as he figures something out for the first time. His experience itself is the reinforcement. This is especially important when a child has special needs; the child needs the time and space to feel himself and stay immersed in his own process of self-discovery. That doesn't mean you should be stoic. Understand that your internal Enthusiasm, while allowing your child to have his own experience without interruption or distraction, is your best way of supporting your child at such moments. When all is said and done, it is up to your child's brain to figure out how to move, think, and act. We want the child to feel, to perceive differences, to notice and focus on his own experience as it unfolds. It is all new for her. Neither your child nor you, the parent, can know what will happen in the next second. Enthusiasm felt and experienced in the way I've described supports this internal process, this unfolding in the child, and allows your child her own process of discovery.

> We want the child to feel, to perceive differences, to notice and focus on his own experience as it unfolds.

Please, No Encores

Another common way that the child's attention is hijacked is when we ask him to do it again—that is, to repeat what he has just done for the very first time. This demand will often short-circuit the process in the brain of forming the new skill.

It's thrilling to see a child do something for the first time. No doubt about it. And we want to see him do it again, perhaps to confirm for ourselves that what we have just seen is real. What most people don't realize is that when a child does *anything* for the first time, be it to say *Mama*, or to make eye contact, or to roll over onto his belly, or to sit up, or to stand up, he did not *intend* to do it. The child very often doesn't even know what he has just done. That first time of doing anything is often a mistake. Unintentionally, his brain somehow put together many of the bits and pieces that quite unexpectedly resulted in this new outcome. Doing something for the first time, the child is having an internal experience of what he's just done but he does not have an external idea of what that is or what to label it or how to do it again. What the child needs at that moment is some time to continue focusing inward and integrate his experience. When asked to do it again, the child most likely will not know how to do it and, as a result, will fail. That well-meaning call for an encore may very well forestall the child's brain's integration of this new ability.

> What most people don't realize is that when a child does *anything* for the first time . . . he did not *intend* to do it.

I have learned over the years that when a child does something for the first time, for example, pull himself up to standing, he will do it again in one minute, one hour, one day, or perhaps one week later. After a while, as the new skill matures, it becomes available to the child all the time. I have also observed that when pressure was placed on a child to repeat his performance of a newly acquired skill, this new skill often seems to disappear. When we overwhelm the child this way, there is an active inhibition of the fragile new connections that takes place, making it much harder, and at times impossible, for the child to do it again.

Enjoy the Inner Celebration

A few years ago I walked out to the waiting room to invite in my next client. There I saw Jeffrey's parents sitting side by side, their backs as straight as if they had each swallowed a stick, hands in their laps, and with stoic, inexpressive faces. I knew that their son Jeffrey had just had a lesson with one of my colleagues. I said a jolly hello but they barely responded. I was confused. When I asked if everything was okay, Jeffrey's dad silently pointed in the direction of the long hallway outside the waiting room—in the direction of little Jeffrey, who was about four years old at the time. He was walking without a walker, all by himself, up and down the hallway that was just outside the waiting room. When I asked his parents why they were being so quiet, the mother answered, "We're not supposed to be excited or tell him anything. We're just sitting here making sure we are doing nothing to spoil the moment." I assured them that what they were doing was fine, and it was what I had coached them about in the past. But I also assured them that it was okay to relax and to enjoy this wonderful moment.

The next day, before Jeffrey's next session, I asked his parents how he had been for the rest of the previous day. They told me that when they got back to the hotel, Jeffrey wanted to stay downstairs in the large lobby and continue walking. They agreed, leaving it up to him to guide them. Jeffrey had been so excited about his newfound ability that he wanted to keep doing it. But that wasn't all. He felt the need to share it and to be witnessed by others, similar to the little girl I'd seen in the playground.

The parents told me how they sat in the lobby watching Jeffrey experiencing their own Enthusiasm as they watched him. Jeffrey, who had been so painfully shy and subdued when I first started working with him, was walking up to complete strangers, standing right in front of them and saying, "Hi, my name is Jeffrey. I'm walking all by myself for the first time in my life." His proud parents smiled as they related this story to me. "You can imagine the looks on the faces of the unsuspecting strangers who he'd invited to rejoice with him," they said. Jeffrey continued doing this for several hours, until he was completely exhausted and it was time for dinner and bed.

No one had needed to cajole Jeffrey into walking, nor had he required his parents' applauding him or telling him how proud of him they were feeling. His parents gave him the space to experience his newfound skill and express his pride and delight in this very unexpected way. Note here how Jeffrey is the one who initiated the experience, amplifying his own delight in his newfound ability by walking and by approaching strangers with his news. Meanwhile, his parents sat close by, filled with their own Enthusiasm. The positive reinforcement Jeffrey got was spontaneous, coming from his own actions. His newfound ability was all the reward he required. It was his. His loving and patient parents had five hours to watch their son and digest the enormous transformation we had been building toward for more than a year and a half.

What Science Says

Our own enthusiasm can have a powerful impact on the moods, behavior, and even the physical abilities of both our children and ourselves. It can help amplify our child's ability to learn. Others' emotions as well as our own can affect us, even when we are not consciously aware of it. And these emotions can initiate synaptic changes, activating new neural connections. Negative emotions generally have a more powerful effect on the brain than do positive ones. For instance, if a child experiences repeated failures because he is being asked to do something he cannot do, it is easy for him to acquire feelings of learned helplessness, and it is difficult to undo those feelings. If the emotions he experiences are positive, they turn on the Learning Switch and help consolidate, or groove in, the new patterns of learning.

There is a good deal of research demonstrating how our facial expressions communicate our emotions and affect other people. A fearful face is fast-tracked to the amygdala, the primitive brain, alerting us to danger and causing us to be vigilant and anxious. Studies have shown that even when researchers made fearful faces that were invisible to conscious awareness, states of vigilance and anxiety were communicated, causing the subject's amygdala to light up and trigger a state of vigilance and anxiety. Knowing what we know about the communication of our emotions, it becomes clear why our own Enthusiasm is so important for our child.

Emotions such as enthusiasm and the spontaneous excitement that we experience when, for example, we do something successfully get the brain to pay attention and to select the relevant neural connections that are being formed at that moment, strengthening those connections in the process. An emotionally arousing stimulus, which we can help provide our child through our own Enthusiasm, places the child's brain in a "motive

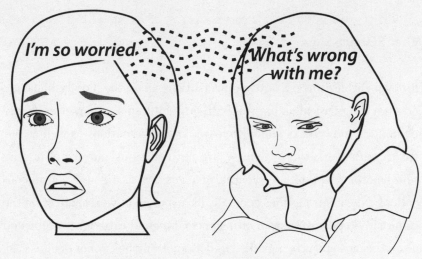

Our facial expressions communicate our emotions
and impact other people

state," coordinating information processing in the brain. Chemicals produced in our brains, such as dopamine, a neuromodulator, facilitate synaptic transmissions, amplifying circuits that are involved in the control of movement in various regions of our bodies.

Some emotions, such as the anxiety and stress we feel when we repeatedly experience failure, has a detrimental effect that impairs our ability to learn and to perform even the most basic activities. These emotions generally manifest as stress, raising cortisol levels that, if prolonged, can destroy hippocampal neurons associated with learning and memory. And even short-term elevation of cortisol in the hippocampus can hinder our ability to distinguish between important and unimportant elements of a memorable event. Prolonged stress in infancy leads to excessive cortisol activity, resulting in synaptic reduction and even cell death in the hippocampus. This results in losses in self-regulation, memory, positive mood, and other functions. When these negative changes happen they can be at least partly ameliorated by nurturing in subsequent development.

It is of great importance that we all remember and accept as real the fact that children pick up on the emotions of their parents and of other adults caring for them. They feel these emotions, which affects their brain, their Learning Switch, and their ability to change and improve.

The Tools for Enthusiasm

It is easy to get enthusiastic when your child has an obvious breakthrough such as saying his first word and taking his first step. Look for opportunities to experience Enthusiasm with small changes, rather than only when your child achieves a known developmental milestone. Every child goes through a multitude of these tiny, seemingly unimportant changes on his way to achieving the more obvious developmental stages.

When your child has special challenges he needs you to be a very special parent, and part of this is noticing and experiencing Enthusiasm for the tiny changes along the way to the bigger more obvious accomplishments. He needs you to develop your ability to notice and recognize the smallest of changes and differences in him, and for you to know and feel their significance as he tries to master new skills. Your special challenge is to become an astute observer of the *small* so that you can be enthusiastic about those changes.

Ask yourself, "How much evidence do I need before I recognize—before I know—that my child has just done something new and different?"

Ask yourself, "How much evidence do I need before I recognize—before I know—that my child has just done something new and different?" The less evidence you require, the more you will empower your child.

Start with observing your child during your typical daily activities and interactions. You might notice changes in the color of his cheeks—redder or paler; you may notice his eyes get brighter and that he is more alert during certain activities than during others. You may notice that while applying some of the other Essentials his movements become smoother. Take note when his movements become faster, slower, or choppier than a moment earlier or at some time in the past. You might notice that for the first time he is showing interest in other children because today he stopped what he was doing and intensely watched another child playing. Recognize that at such times changes are occurring within your child's brain, tiny changes that can become very large ones. And, yes, each small change is an occasion for your Enthusiasm.

At this point, you are not trying *to do* anything with your perceptions of these changes other than to recognize them and to know that they are real and potentially important for your child's development. You are becoming better at perceiving whatever there is to perceive in your child.

Taking Mental Notes: As you become more accustomed to doing this, you may find it helpful to make a mental note or you may want to write your observations down: "Hey, he just turned his head and looked at his sister squarely for the first time." Or "When I support his pelvis while he is sitting, his usually stiff right arm gets freer." Or "He is tantrumming less intensely and recovering faster when I transition him from one activity to another." By naming and describing what you have noticed in this way you create greater clarity for yourself of how your child is changing—including the very small and fine changes. You will be amazed by how much more you will see, feel, hear, and otherwise notice in a very short period of time and how much Enthusiasm you can bring to your own experience of these changes. Keep practicing this tool whenever an opportunity lends itself, perhaps while doing home therapy programs with him, or during a regular play time, or during any other daily activity. You will know you are successful with this tool when you require less and less evidence to recognize your child is changing and learning. After a day or two of noticing that you are getting better at this, move on to the next tool.

Changing Emotions, Generating Enthusiasm: Now that you are recognizing small changes in your child as real and you are perceiving each of them as one of many thousands of tiny milestones, you can choose to be enthusiastic about them. At times this can seem quite difficult. You can, however, change what you are feeling in the moment. The four steps that follow can help you hone your Enthusiasm skills. Each step is designed to work with activities you are already doing in your life and with your child.

1. *Ask what is stopping you from generating Enthusiasm.* It may be the disparity between the dreams and expectations you have for your child and what is going on with him right now. Or perhaps what is making it difficult for you to generate Enthusiasm is the knowledge of the diagnosis and prognosis he has received. There's no denying that your child's challenges are real and serious, but it's also essential for you to be present for his progress, every small step of the way.

2. *Remember a time when you were feeling enthusiastic.* Without trying to deny or block out your more negative thoughts and feelings, remember a time when you were feeling content, empowered, and thrilled with what was going on. This can be a large or small event from the past. It can even be the little stuff of daily life, the smell of an orange, your sight of the first blossoms of spring, or a minor success at your work. Re-create the sensations—warmth or cold, visual images, sound, touch, smell, taste—that you experienced at the time. Amplify those feelings and sensations and savor the experience for a moment, staying with it for five to twenty seconds without letting your mind skitter away from it. Focusing on these feelings increases the release of dopamine (the so-called feel good hormone) in your

brain and wires together neurons to strengthen that memory, making it easier to access those feelings in the future. The more you do this consciously and with intent, the more that memory and other positive memories will become a resource you can use for building your Enthusiasm "muscle" and bringing it to other situations.

3. *Transform your experience.* Think of a daily chore that you dislike, perhaps washing the dishes, folding the laundry, or grocery shopping. Just before you are about to do one of these chores—let's say it is washing dishes—call up your Enthusiasm memory and feel it as fully as you can. Feel satisfaction, delight, safety, hopefulness, curiosity, gratitude, appreciation, or any other positive feelings associated with the memory. Once you are steeped in those feelings and can hold them for a few seconds, begin doing that chore as you usually do but this time see how the experience of doing it changes when you can maintain the feelings of Enthusiasm that you have created. If you lose your Enthusiasm, simply stop doing the chore for a brief moment and take the time to re-create the feeling, then go back to doing the chore.

   Keep doing this exercise three times (or more if you like) every day for two to three minutes at a time. Do it along with any chore that you don't ordinarily enjoy doing as well as with activities you already like. You will be surprised at how good you can get at generating Enthusiasm, even under challenging conditions.

4. *Bring your Enthusiasm to your child.* Once you know that you can generate and keep generating Enthusiasm intentionally, begin applying it as you perceive the smallest of changes in

your child. Remember that your Enthusiasm is experienced internally. Notice how your child responds to this change in you. Many children, at first, simply become happier, more expressive, and exuberant. As you continue applying other Essentials and generating Enthusiasm in response to the smallest of changes in your child, you will see him changing in new and often surprising ways.

Know that from time to time you will lose it, when all of this may just seem like too much to do; reality can sometimes bring you down. But you can always re-create and further strengthen your Enthusiasm skills. This phenomenon of recalling, strengthening, and accessing feelings in this way is not simply make-believe but has been shown to lead to measurable changes in neural structures in our brains.

....
Be the leader. Do not look to your child for reassurance.
....

Become the Leader: When *you* develop your ability to perceive the finest of changes in your child and *you choose* to take delight in these small and seemingly insignificant differences, not just the big and obvious ones, you become the leader in your child's life. So often the people who love the child and want the best for him look to the child for reassurance. Be the leader. Do not look to your child for reassurance. If the child does something well, he feels good and hopeful. If the child struggles or simply can't do something you are expecting him to be able to do, he feels upset, discouraged, and fearful. The child feels the anxiety and disappointment and gets the message that "something is wrong with me." By taking a leadership role, as this tool invites you to do, you turn this process on its head. Rather than being brought up and then down by the daily challenges of your child, like a leaf floating on a wave, you can hold a vision for your child. You become the leader. You generate Enthusiasm within yourself, independent of the child's performance. This is one of the hidden secrets of great teachers and great leaders, the ability to be a vessel or container for an intention, to generate Enthusiasm for others. You will take leadership with your spouse, grandparents, friends, and strangers. You will find yourself taking greater leadership with your child's teachers, therapists, and doctors. That does not mean that you ignore their advice. They all have very important and, at times, vital knowledge that can ensure your child's well-being and future development. But you will be able to see your child as the growing and improving human being he really is, even when not fulfilling specific expectations. You will remember that the only way to get there is by moving in that direction while empowering your child's brain and spirit to grow and evolve.

> **You will be able to see your child as the growing and improving human being he really is, even when not fulfilling specific expectations.**

Enthusiasm, Generosity, and Spirituality: The root of the word *enthusiasm* can be traced to the Greek word *enthousia*: "inspired by the gods," or "having the god within." As clever, knowledgeable, or skillful as we may be, the process of growth and personal evolution is miraculous; what we know and can do is just a small speck of what there is yet to be known. When a child figures out how to do anything, no matter how small or large, the actual doing of it by that child is mind-boggling, miraculous. Your Enthusiasm calls on these miraculous powers to inspire you and your child. Enthusiasm requires your generosity: generosity of heart, mind, and spirit. Your willingness to notice, delight in, and give importance to those smallest of changes in your child is generosity in action. You celebrate your child and his changes long before the full evidence that he is doing fine is fully there. Your willingness to empower your child through your Enthusiasm is a profound act of bringing godlike inspiration to the process. Your Enthusiasm helps your child gain access to his own genius. It helps usher in the miraculous in very real ways.

Michael Merzenich, one of the world's leading neuroscientists, has observed:

> **Moment by moment we choose and sculpt how our ever-changing minds will work. We choose who we will be in the next moment in a very real sense, and these choices are left embossed in physical form on our material selves.**

These words are both inspiring and encouraging for any of us who have children with special needs in our lives, confirming that where Enthusiasm is concerned you not only are sculpting yourself but are also helping your child sculpt himself.

9 Essential Six
Flexible Goals

It is not the mountain we conquer, but ourselves.

—EDMUND HILLARY

Even before our children are born, we consciously or unconsciously have goals for them. We want them to be brilliant and successful. And most certainly we want them to be healthy and happy. Our goals for them may be far-reaching, extending into the future. Some of us enroll our children in preschools before they are even born. Others have academic goals for our children, to earn good grades and go to the best high schools so that they can graduate from a prestigious college. Perhaps we want our children to make lots of money, marry well, settle down, and raise their families nearby.

These goals are based on assumptions that our child will be healthy and fully capable, that her constitution and makeup will be much like our own. The moment we learn otherwise, the moment we find out that our child has special needs, our world is turned upside down. We start asking very different questions: What will this diagnosis mean for my child's future? What goals should I set for her? Should I aim for her to achieve the usual developmental stages at the expected ages? What should I do if she is not progressing in our pursuit of a certain goal for her? Is this happening because I have not done enough as a parent? Should I continue trying to get her to do it, pushing her even harder? And if the answer is yes, which interventions are best for her? If the answer is that I shouldn't continue pursuing my present goals for her, does this mean I am giving up on my child? What is it that I can expect for my child, and what can I do to help her achieve those expectations?

Every child is unique, even when she shares the same diagnosis with thousands of others. In this chapter I offer ways to go about answering questions that are empowering for you and your child and that fit your unique situation. It is about what is the best way for you to go about setting goals for your child and then trying to help her achieve those goals. Everyone has had the experience of pursuing personal goals, and we all know the importance of setting goals. The most commonly recommended way to approach goals is to narrow the focus on that goal while trying as hard as possible to achieve it. This approach is manifested in phrases such as "Go for it," "Keep your eyes on the prize," "No pain, no gain," and "Never give up and never give in." But when it comes to trying to help your child with special needs, this approach can often prove to be counterproductive. Rigid goals approached in a forceful and inflexible way can limit the child even further rather than advancing her.

Luckily there is another way to go about goal setting for your child, one that is much more in harmony with how the brain, body, and spirit work and with how the child learns and changes. Our child can accomplish more, with less suffering, while we stay open to possibilities otherwise not available, by *holding our goals loosely*. Holding our goals loosely means that we approach goals for our child with clear intent yet with a light touch, and with lots of flexibility.

Holding goals loosely may seem like an indirect, laissez faire, out-of-control, or even scary way to go about trying to achieve desired outcomes. We are much more accustomed to try to help our child reach a goal—whatever that goal might be—*right now*, by the fastest, shortest route possible. We often believe this is the only way to get there. When our child fails, we think we should focus on that goal even more, that for our child to attain this goal we should be even more tenacious, more disciplined, and more single-minded. Try harder. And if our child still has not reached the goal set for her, we often revert to thinking that it's the child's special needs that prevent success or even that there's something wrong with us.

> **Our child can accomplish more, with less suffering, while we stay open to possibilities otherwise not available, by *holding our goals loosely*.**

Yet paradoxically, as you will discover, it's by holding goals loosely for your child—having a flexible attitude toward those goals—that you and she will begin having breakthroughs that would otherwise be impossible. As you learn to hold goals loosely, many of the regularly accepted limitations dictated by specific conditions and the customary prognoses will be proven wrong. You will begin to have a more joyful and collaborative effort with your child, seeing her less as a project and more as a full human being with her own feelings, desires, and life path.

Baboons, Humans, and Reversible Goals

When introducing the concept of Flexible Goals to my students, I often share the following story. Baboons in the Kalahari Desert have excellent caches of water and are intelligent enough to hide the locations of these caches from humans and other animals. Quite an achievement. When native hunters want to find these water caches, they first look for a giant anthill, which the baboons like to frequent. Being curious creatures, the baboons often watch from a distance as the hunters make a hole in the rocklike clay of the anthill, big enough for a baboon to reach into. They drop a few seeds, of the sort that baboons like to eat, down into the hole. When the hunter moves off, a baboon moves in, sticks his hand in the hole to get the seeds, closes his hand in a fist and then tries to bring the seeds out. Because he is clutching the seeds in a fist, and won't let go, he can't get his hand out of the hole. The baboon is stuck. He tries to yank his hand out more forcefully, but to no avail. As the hunter approaches, the baboon panics, screaming in fear, even somersaulting as it tries to escape. But because he won't open his hand and let go of the seeds, the baboon remains trapped. Long story short, the hunter keeps the animal on a leash for the night and feeds him salt, which baboons can't resist. When the animal is released the next morning the baboon races off to quench his thirst, unwittingly leading the hunter to the precious cache of water.

For the baboon to reverse this course of events, all he would have to do is open his hand and let go of the seeds. But his brain lacks the evolutionary complexity and freedom to override his drive to have the seeds. He clings to that goal even at the expense of his freedom and thus his survival.

Most of us have been taught to pursue a goal by sharply narrowing our focus, trying to get our child to do what she *should* be able to do. When we too rigidly focus on attaining specific goals for the child, we and the child are less able to respond to feelings, experiences, information, and new opportunities. We end up limiting our child and ourselves. At such times we often overlook the potentially undesirable consequences of following goals too rigidly and may even ignore the child's well-being and our own.

> When we too rigidly focus on attaining such goals for the child, we and the child are less able to respond to feelings, experiences, information, and new opportunities.

Having goals for your child is important. Without them she most likely will not be able to thrive. Your child's challenges are real. For your child to be able to find solutions to overcome her limitations, she needs her brain to work on the highest, most potent level that it can. However, when you go about trying to achieve goals too rigidly, like the baboon trapped by his own fist, rather than helping your child's brain upgrade to its highest potential, you are most likely driving it to its more primitive levels where little choice, discovery, or invention can occur.

When Will She Talk Already?

We began working with Alexa when she was two and a half years old. Her condition: undiagnosed developmental delay. She was a very unhappy little girl with little voluntary movement. She was cross-eyed, her jaw hung open, her tongue stuck out of her mouth most of the time, and she drooled. The parents' immediate goals were to get her to roll over to her belly, to sit, to crawl, and to begin responding to verbal communication.

Before our visit, Alexa had been working intensely with a number of therapists who were trying to reach these goals directly. They attempted to have her do these movements and positions, such as crawling or sitting, but with little or no success. For the first year and a half, her parents had been hopeful that these efforts would help Alexa. But as time went on, and they realized their daughter was hardly progressing, they started looking for another approach. They were ready to move their eyes away from the prize, the obvious goals, and try our approach.

Our goal was to wake up Alexa's brain by starting with whatever she could presently do. This would open up the opportunity to help her brain differentiate and create the small changes that could lead to the bigger milestones. I explained to Alexa's parents that this is what I call *differentiating*, or working around edges.

....

Our goal was to wake up Alexa's brain by starting with whatever she could presently do.

....

It took Alexa's parents a while to surrender to this way of working. It felt scary to them to stop trying to have Alexa achieve the obvious goals. But soon they were seeing small changes they had never seen before. For the first time, they realized that Alexa could learn, that she was intelligent despite her tremendous limitations. We worked with her in this way over the next two and a half years. We intentionally looked away from the obvious goals and kept to Flexible Goals. This allowed the freedom for Alexa's brain to wake up to new possibilities and to herself, over and over again. Through the many different, small changes in her brain, Alexa learned to roll over to her belly, crawl, and finally stand and walk. She changed in many other ways as her abilities grew, becoming a happy, clearly intelligent and loving child, a very different kid from the one I'd seen that first day. She far exceeded all expectations for children with her prognosis.

Coming Around to the Loosely Held Goal

With these goals accomplished, Alexa still was not talking except for saying "ahh" for yes. As she started kindergarten, her parents felt a great pressure to get Alexa to talk. This became their focused goal for her. The school strongly recommended speech therapy. When her parents discussed this with me, I reminded them of how Alexa learned to roll, sit, crawl, and walk. It wasn't until we looked away from these goals and worked with her where she was—*working around the edges to produce small changes*—that Alexa's brain had been able to figure it out. I told them that speech therapy would be fine, provided the therapist would keep the goal of speech very loose. The therapist would need to completely avoid drilling Alexa and trying to get her to talk in a direct and inflexible manner, thereby avoiding the risk that Alexa's brain would get more stuck in its current patterns and perhaps make it even more difficult for her to talk. They agreed.

For a number of months I didn't see Alexa. Then I received an email. Alexa's mother had found a new speech therapist whom she was very happy with. "While they are making wonderful progress," the mother wrote, "Alexa still isn't speaking. The therapist told me that her facial muscles are weak." Alexa's mom wanted to know if I could give Alexa a few lessons to "help strengthen those muscles." In addition, the mom wrote me that her extremely sweet child was, for the first time in her life, having serious behavior problems. She was having tantrums, was very difficult to calm down, and wouldn't follow her parents' or teachers' instructions. The parents felt at a complete loss. I emailed back, telling Alexa's mom, "I have no way to fix or control Alexa's face muscles. I work with the brain, not the muscles." And I asked, "If the therapy she was getting was working, how come she wasn't progressing?" I agreed to see Alexa for two sessions to evaluate whether I could help her brain begin organizing the highly complex skill of talking. I truly didn't know if I could be helpful.

When Alexa came in for her lesson, she was at first a bit tentative, but once I lifted her onto my work table, she leaned into me, and we hugged. I knew one thing: I was *not* going to try to make Alexa talk. I would do my best to have her feel confident that I wasn't expecting her to talk. Instead of asking her to talk, I talked and talked. I told her how happy I was to see her. I asked her, as part of the stream of words coming out of my mouth, if she was now in kindergarten. I didn't wait for or expect an answer. I kept right on talking. Yet, she nodded her head, affirming that she was. I said, "Wow, that's amazing." Then I told her some about my own child's kindergarten. At some point I asked her if her kindergarten was like that. Again, I didn't expect or wait for an answer. To my surprise, she very quietly said yes. The word was not perfectly formed but it was clearly a yes. I acted as if nothing unusual had happened but realized that the word yes had come out when she was *not* being asked to speak and when she was *not* trying to talk. She and I were connecting. She was deeply engrossed, and we were both looking away from the talk-now goal.

I then began uttering nonsensical syllables and vowels, using no real words but with the intonation and rhythm of conversational language, in this way taking our lesson away from the final goal of having Alexa speak. Now Alexa was lying on her belly, and I was working on her back, ribs, and spine to try to get more movement in her back and to free her diaphragm to move and let the girl breathe more fully. Alexa had always loved her lessons. She lay very quietly, attentive to the sensations in her body, but she also seemed fascinated with my nonsense talking. After a few minutes I paused, and to my amazement and delight I heard Alexa say a few nonsense sounds. When she stopped I responded with my own nonsense sounds. Then the two of us had this ongoing conversation with full intonation as if we were really saying something but with no real words.

Alexa was obviously enjoying herself. At one point I "asked" Alexa a nonsense question—using the inflections of my voice but no words—and she responded by saying yes very clearly. Then she spoke a nonsense-language question and I answered no. After thirty minutes into the session, I felt it was enough. I didn't want to exhaust Alexa and have her brain inhibit this newfound skill.

I sat Alexa up and told her that the session was over and it was time for her to go home. She looked at me, pointed her right index finger at me and in a very loud voice said: "No!" Saying no was new for her. I laughed, pointed my index finger at her and said in an equally loud voice: "Yes!"

Before leaving I impressed on her mom how important it was to make sure that everyone in Alexa's life, including her teachers, intentionally avoid trying to make Alexa talk for at least two months, while we continued working with her. That also meant putting speech therapy on hold for a few weeks. Deeply moved by the changes she had witnessed in her daughter, the mother readily agreed.

They left my office. A few seconds later, to my surprise, Alexa ran back into my office pointing her finger at me and almost yelling, saying, "No, no, no!" I pointed back at her and said, "Yes, yes, yes!" Her mother and I looked at each other in astonishment at Alexa's new sense of empowerment. She was like a bird released from a cage, celebrating her new freedom and absolutely delighted with herself. I finally walked her out the front door, reassuring her that I'd be seeing her again the next day.

From No to Yes, to So Much More

The next day Alexa came in and resumed nonsense communicating with me right away, just as we'd done before. She had obviously been looking forward to this. She had planned on doing it! After a while, when the nonsense conversation was flowing I very gradually began inserting into the mix a real word and a while later another. My concern at first was that the real words might stop Alexa. Instead, she began doing the same thing, inserting a real word here and there.

The teachers at Alexa's school reported that, after only two of these lessons, Alexa was unexpectedly, and without prompting, saying two- to three-word sentences once in a while. Her rage attacks and tantrums had disappeared completely. After three months of working with us, Alexa was clearly saying longer sentences and was speaking more frequently, *when not prompted or cajoled* by another person to speak. Alexa had learned and improved when all those caring for her looked away from the final desired goal and instead had Flexible Goals that provided the freedom to work around the edges, seeking ways for her brain to differentiate and produce small changes at the edges of what she was already able to do.

The Importance of Success

Your child's experience of success plays a critical role in her ability to change and grow. But what exactly do I mean by this? When a child takes any action—small or large, intentional or unintentional—and gets an outcome that she finds pleasurable and interesting, that's the experience of success. For example, when a baby grabs Mom's hair and pulls on it unintentionally, the mom says, "Ouch!" The child is surprised and delighted with the sounds she produced. When she experiences such a success, her brain is more inclined to reinforce whatever patterns led to that success. Her brain lights up. The child *wakes up*, becomes more alive, and learns better and faster.

> **When a child takes any action—small or large, intentional or unintentional—and gets an outcome that she finds pleasurable and interesting, that's the experience of success.**

Success feels good. It empowers the child. It is another *amplifier*, a marker for the child's brain to notice that, "What you just did is valuable. Groove this in for future use." Success breeds success. Most of a child's experiences of success are not what we adults normally consider as success because these successes are often not obvious, full-blown accomplishments such as walking, talking, and other obvious milestones. However, this multitude of the child's small experiences of success is what leads her to the big achievements. These kinds of experiences of success can occur only at the edges of the child's present abilities. A child cannot move from crawling to jumping rope. But she can progress from crawling over flat surfaces to crawling over obstacles. Your understanding of this principle, of success starting at the edge of what your child can presently do, is of utmost importance in your efforts to help your child.

The child with special needs requires lots and lots of small successes for her brain to wake up and figure out unique solutions to her condition. If asked to do what is way beyond her present capabilities, her brain can't figure it out; she will actually be stopped from learning that skill. Having Flexible Goals means always moving around those edges of present ability where the experience of success—and change—are most accessible to the child.

> **Having Flexible Goals means always moving around those edges of present ability where the experience of success—and change—are most accessible to the child.**

If there is a solution to be found for a child who is unable to relate to others or is unable to stand or walk, it will be found by beginning where she is right now. This is the essence of having Flexible Goals, of knowing how to create opportunities for your child to experience success at the edges.

The Universal Application of Flexible Goals

The same Flexible Goals principle of tugging at the edges of what the child can currently do and where she can presently experience success is true for the evolution of any function. Often, when parents bring their child to me for the first time, they ask, "When will she be able to walk?" Or "Is she ever going to talk?" Every time I'm asked such questions, I search inside for an answer, and I always come up with the same realization: "I don't know. If I had to know right now, and had to somehow directly *make* your child walk, or talk, or stop being hyperactive, as a mechanic might tune up a car's engine and get it running again, I would have no idea what to do. And I'm sure both your child and I would fail." At the same time I know for certain that if I can *connect* with the child and help her begin differentiating and doing new things that she can follow and that she experiences as success, *starting where she is right now*, she will progress. And if that process continues, she will eventually reach more and more milestones.

When parents hear my answer they initially tend to feel somewhat confused because the only way they know to gauge their child's progress is by the standard milestones. Often they feel that the only way they can help their child is by trying to have her achieve such common goals. I explain that what I look for at all times are *changes at the edges of where the child is at the present time*—that is, changes that expand the child's vocabulary of movement, thought, and feelings. Change of this kind indicates that the brain is in the process of doing what it must do to reach that child's next developmental stage. I tell parents that to be useful to their child I need to have Flexible Goals and look away from the milestones. What I'm looking for is the child's responsiveness to what I do; I'm looking for her participation, even if that response is tiny. I am looking to see that the child is having experiences of success and am watching for the delight in the child's various expressions that come with it.

A friend who is a golfer told me about a basic rule of the game: Play it as it lays, which means that you always play the ball from wherever it lands. This saying was also popularized in a literary novel by Joan Didion. As applied to Flexible Goals, it means connect with your child wherever she is right now: Discover what your child is able to do *at this moment*, and seek ways to tug at the edges, thus helping your child's brain find its own unique path of development. Place bigger goals and developmental milestones in the background of your mind. Know the milestone you would like your child eventually to attain, be it walking, talking, socializing, reading, or writing, but hold that goal very loosely. Do not let the projected milestone drive what you do with your child. Have the here and now of your child guide what you do.

I know that these many tiny changes will lead children who have special challenges further along in their individual, and often unique, development. When you stop letting the normally predictable milestones tyrannize you or dictate what you do with your child, you will start to see greater progress.

What Science Tells Us About Flexible Goals

One example of imposing a rigid goal is the practice called tummy time, which involves placing infants on their bellies before they are able to roll over onto their bellies by themselves. The claim for doing this is that it strengthens the infant's body and accelerates her ability to achieve certain milestones—namely, turning onto her belly, crawling, and coming up to standing. Some of the early literature on this practice proposed that tummy time would help the child also achieve other milestones more quickly, ensuring that she would be more successful in life.

One of the things that happens, however, is that by putting the infant on her belly, she is denied the aimless activity that a child would normally be able to do on her back. You'll remember from my earlier chapters how important this aimless activity, with all its random movements, is for the process of differentiation and the development of the child's brain.

A number of follow-up studies have looked into the long-term effects of children raised with tummy time. Such studies found that these children learned to roll *from their bellies to their backs*, crawl on their abdomens, crawl on all fours, and tripod-sit as much as three months sooner than babies who were not raised with tummy time. It is interesting, however, that this early accelerated development did not carry over into the achievement of later milestones. There was no difference between tummy time children and non–tummy time children in their accomplishing milestones such as walking and in gross and fine motor development.

One might conclude from this that accelerating the time it takes the child to achieve these early milestones wasn't very useful in the long run, but at least it might reassure parents to see their child achieve those goals sooner rather than later. But when we look at this practice more closely we need to ask what impact imposing these goals might have on the *quality* of how the child moves, thinks, and feels. Is she missing anything as a result of tummy time?

One of the studies of tummy time focused on infants with low birth weight and found that placing such babies on their bellies before they were able to roll onto their bellies by themselves led to postural problems—both short- and long-term—and to other developmental problems.

Emmi Pikler, a pediatrician, founded and operated a large orphanage in Europe, just after World War II. She was a big advocate of providing safe and loving conditions for children to grow and develop at their own pace—without adults imposing rigid goals in their efforts to accelerate children's different milestones before they could do it on their own. She trained the nurses and all the caregivers in her institute to apply Flexible Goals at all times. She observed how "parents and other persons engaged in child care attempt repeatedly to promote developmental phases (milestones) by active manipulation and verbal stimulation." She also found that the children raised at her orphanage who were provided the time and space to develop at their own rate and in their own way—following her Flexible Goals approach—without any attempts to accelerate their progress, were slower to reach the initial milestones by as much as three to four months, just as later research of tummy time would show. More important, however, she observed that: "Not only did the children learn to sit, stand, and walk by themselves, but they were apparently more independent, more sure in their movements, and, in general, *more content and quiet in their behavior than were other children of the same age.*" She wrote: "We regard the secure and well balanced movements of the children reared in our institute as significant. They not only move well, but if they fall—which is unavoidable—they fall well." They fell so well that among the fourteen hundred children who were raised in her institute from infancy none of them had any fractures.

These findings show us that healthy babies will grow and reach their milestones whether or not they are helped by caregivers applying rigid goals regarding those milestones. The children ultimately work around it either way. However, for children with challenges, denying them Flexible Goals can have very detrimental effects. When we move our own eyes away from the prize of having our child achieve a specific goal through rigid means, it becomes possible for the *quality* of that child's movements to improve.

These findings and the importance of Flexible Goals can be better understood when we remember, as discussed in Chapter 5 on the Essential Slow: We humans are blessed with a slow, protracted period of development that keeps the learning process open-ended for longer than any other species. When we take our time and keep the process of helping the child with special needs reach her goals open-ended, reversible, and flexible, we give that child and her brain exponentially more options for growth. Don't try to close the deal too soon! Do not let trying to make your child cross the finish line be your primary goal. Your child's brain is built to take its time, moving from one stage to another just like all children do. When you follow the practice of Flexible Goals, you give your child's brain the opportunities for becoming most ingenious in discovering solutions to challenges. That is when your child becomes most alive.

The Tools for Flexible Goals

What follows are nine methods for applying Flexible Goals, opening new paths for your child to find solutions to her challenges, paths that might otherwise be unattainable. The skills I describe here will also help reduce stress, and increase happiness, for both you and your child. You may wish to keep a journal of your work with these nine tools.

Identify: If your child has been given a diagnosis, identify what this means to you. What do you understand to be your child's specific challenges? And what goals do you currently have for your child? For instance, a goal might be to have her respond to her name, develop the ability to pay attention, learn to stand up, or improve her fine motor coordination. What, in the best of all worlds, would you like your child to accomplish? If your child does not have a specific diagnosis, identify what behaviors or limitations she has that you would like her to change or overcome.

Focus on the Process, not the Goal: Remember that no one, not even the healthiest child, reaches any new milestone by simply jumping to that point or solely by practicing that activity. Rather, we achieve new goals *through a process*. Whenever you find yourself pushing your child to achieve the desired goal directly, either by manipulating her body to do it or by asking her to do it, you deny your child's brain of opportunities for having the information it needs; you are limiting yourself and your child at that moment. Instead, look away from the goal, reminding yourself that you play a very active part in this process. Simply stop what you are doing, take a deep breath, and look away from the goal to allow the child's needed process to take place.

Wonder: Whenever you are applying any of the Nine Essentials, *wonder* what your child will do next. Wonder leads to discovering previously unknown possibilities. Wonder how your child is going to react. Is she going to like or get interested in what you are doing with her? Wonder what small or large changes may occur. Wonder about the ideas and feelings you and your child are coming up with and experiencing, moment to moment. We never know in advance the way we will attain a goal or the exact path the child will take to attain a goal. When you allow yourself to wonder, you create space for that which you couldn't have known to be part of the solution. You keep the field of possibilities wide open for your child.

Back Off: Always put process ahead of outcome. You will find yourself in countless situations where you will be expected to go for narrow and predefined goals around something your child is presently unable to do. That might involve a goal that a doctor, therapist, or perhaps a teacher suggested through an individualized education program (IEP) conference. If another person accuses you of being neglectful of your child or risking your child's future because you have chosen to work with Flexible Goals, you will need to be the leader. Explain to others who work with your child how to employ Flexible Goals. Ask them to work with your child by tugging around the edges of her current ability, always looking for that edge where the child can experience success. Know when to back off with a goal that is too far ahead of what your child is presently able to do; back off on any goal that is too hard, is too fast, or is introducing too much too soon. If trying to attain the goal creates discomfort, pain, or distress for your child, back off. Anytime you put outcome ahead of process you risk having your child learn the limitation she is experiencing. This can eventually lead you or your child to give up on the possibility of ever achieving that goal. By not knowing when to back off, you risk falling into the belief that your child's failure is due to her condition rather than seeing that the failure results from the path taken to help her.

Play: Let your path with your child be playful. Learn to *meander* with your child, spontaneously taking different directions in what might seem to you to be a waste of time. Keep the importance of aimless activity and randomness in mind, being always attuned with your child and guided by her responses. Know that every time you take on a goal for your child, you are both stepping into the unknown. Your child's brain will thrive with all the new information it gets, all the while discovering new possibilities. In this way your child might very well surprise you by improving and growing in ways you didn't even know to expect.

Embrace Reversibility: There might be times when unexpected opportunities will arise and you will want to adjust one or more goals for your child. At such times, be open to changing course on the spot, to change the intended goal—what I call *reversibility*. There may even be times, as your child's path unfolds, that you will want to totally change some of the goals, again requiring you to reverse your intended goals and any corresponding actions you are taking with her. So many great breakthroughs were discovered on the way to seeking something else. Your reversibility allows you to be responsive to your child, making it a priority over holding to a rigid goal or path.

Let Go: *Do not try to control the outcomes with your child.* You can have enormous influence and contribute in profound ways to the quality of your child's process, greatly increasing her chances of doing better and better. However, what your child does or is able to do at any given moment is beyond your direct control. When we try to control the outcome, things begin to go awry. The child's brain needs freedom to create and integrate billions of bits of information; this is how we form the new. When we are too willful and rigid about trying to control the outcome, we are presuming to know what we cannot know; at best, our efforts to control limit the child and diminish the opportunities for new possibilities.

Cherish the Connection: Have what is happening in the here and now with your child guide you to what you do next. This will give your child's heart and mind what it needs from you to be able to better overcome her limitations—to be *seen* by you, to *feel the connection* between the two of you. You will both feel empowered through this focus.

Embrace Mistakes: Allow your child—and yourself—the room to make lots of mistakes. Do not worry about doing the Essentials *right*. Don't worry about your child doing things right. Don't even worry about doing Flexible Goals right. Mistakes create a treasure trove of information from which your child's brain (and yours) can discover ways to achieve different goals and figure out how to attain the goals you have for your child. The brain is a self-organizing system that arrives at goals spontaneously through lots of experimentation and approximation. The greater and more challenging the goal, the more room your child needs for mistakes, self-correction, and self-discovery.

Having a child with special needs puts enormous demands on the parent. It creates extraordinary challenges that none of us are ever prepared to take on. There is great uncertainty that can lead to fear, worry, and confusion. These feelings tend to push us toward adopting rigid goals in the hope of finding solutions and a sense of safety. As difficult as it may be, and despite your uncertainty and fear, come back again and again to Flexible Goals whenever you can. Don't let fear and uncertainty dictate either the goals you set for your child or the path you take in trying to help her attain those goals.

10 Essential Seven
The Learning Switch

Always walk through life as if you have something
new to learn and you will.

—VERNON HOWARD

The *Learning Switch* is, of course, a metaphor, not a bio-mechanical device in our brains. It is a way to describe the fact that at any given moment, your child's brain can either be poised to learn—being the learning machine it is designed to be—or not. When the switch is turned on, it can be on a higher setting, for your child to be a more powerful learner, or on a lower setting, for a less effective learner.

Most of us have a pretty good idea of what it means to have the Learning Switch turned on or off. It is an actual change in the way your brain is working. You become more alert and you find yourself interested, suddenly grasping what you couldn't understand before or being able to do something you couldn't do before.

Using an electroencephalogram to measure brain waves, we can detect a significant difference between the activity of the brain when the Learning Switch is turned on and when it is turned off. But we don't need electronic devices to be able to recognize it in our children. We can sense when children are taking in what we are saying or doing. We recognize when they are aware of what's going on around them or within themselves. We notice that they are responsive. We might see that responsiveness in their eyes, in their movements, in their facial expressions, or in a word or sound they make.

It is important for you to recognize whether your child's Learning Switch is on or off. When it is off it doesn't matter what you do with your child he is not going to learn or change. When it is turned on, the brain is receptive not only to the sights, sounds, smells, tastes, and sensations of touch from the world around him but also is receptive to the feelings and sensations within himself. The child begins doing something new with all of that stimulation. He begins to learn. Changes begin occurring in the brain.

Scotty's Breakthrough

Scotty had been diagnosed with developmental delays and had been slow with every developmental stage. He began walking after he was two, and then only with lots of therapy and assistance. He had all the symptoms of attention deficit hyperactivity disorder (ADHD) and had been unable to learn to read and write, even with the help of a private tutor. Scotty was a bit overweight, walked rather clumsily, and had poor space perception. He was very sociable and highly verbal. He was emotionally attuned to the people around him, showing that he had emotional intelligence and was a very loving and lovable child.

Before I met with Scotty, who was ten years old and in the fourth grade at the time, I talked to his parents over the phone. Judging from what they told me, it was clear that the boy wasn't learning what others were trying to teach him, despite their considerable efforts. According to his parents, Scotty could more or less recognize the alphabet but with little consistency.

I realized from the parents' descriptions of Scotty that what he had learned was his *experience of failing at reading.* The patterns his brain had created as he tried to figure out reading and writing had led to his repeated failure; these patterns of failure were getting more and more deeply grooved in his brain. His brain had narrowed down to repeating what he already knew, generating no new information around this challenge; his brain re-created the experience of failure again and again. All of this told me, loud and clear, that his Learning Switch, at least when it came to reading and writing, was turned off.

I wasn't surprised when his parents told me that he was resistant and uncooperative during his tutoring sessions in reading and writing. I would expect him to demonstrate at least some aversion and resistance to such efforts to teach him. Who, after all, would want to fail at the same things over and over again?

....
Who, after all, would want to fail at the same things over and over again?
....

I suggested to the parents that before I could work with Scotty I would need him to stop getting any tutoring or making any attempts to read or write, for at least two months. I wanted Scotty to have a period of time away from the repeated patterns of failure he was presently experiencing. The parents met with the school psychologist and others who were working with their son. Everyone was horrified by the idea of stopping their teaching efforts for two months. They said they were afraid he would lose all the progress he had made so far. But what progress had he made?

The only thing he had to lose was his deeply ingrained and limiting patterns of failure—and losing that would be good.

After considerable discussion, I suggested that we wait until Scotty's summer break, when it would be easier for his parents to bring him to me for two or three intensive series of lessons. They agreed. The first time I saw Scotty, he seemed a bit shy but was very sweet and polite. I asked him if he would write his name for me, something that most children like to do. He complained and resisted a little but said yes and began tentatively moving his pencil around on the paper in a slow, small, circular, jagged motion. Then he stopped for a second, as if he had finished writing the first letter, though the scrawl he made did not resemble the letter S or any other letter. He began again, as if to write a second letter, writing this second letter on top of the first, drawing the same kind of small, jagged, circular line. He continued in this way five or six times, layering one letter on top of the other, then stopped as if he had completed the task of writing his name. He looked at me as if hoping that I'd approve whatever he did, obviously not knowing whether he succeeded or failed. I thanked him, said nothing more about it, and proceeded with the session.

It was abundantly clear to me that Scotty had no idea how to read or write. It was clear from his rigidly held shoulders and arms and the tense and grim expression on his face that his Learning Switch was turned off. Further evidence of this was in the fact that he was repeating the same grooved-in ritualized actions that he had learned over the past four years. He wasn't expecting or looking to create something different or to change. His Learning Switch was turned off.

Throughout that first session and the next, I observed that Scotty never moved his eyes to the right, nor did he voluntarily turn his head that way, though his head turned in that direction when I moved it. He seemed to lack awareness of the right side of his universe. The clumsiness of his walk as well as my observation about his efforts to write indicated to me that his brain was missing some of the underlying differentiation and mapping needed for coordinating his movements well. The first thing we needed to do was to turn Scotty's Learning Switch on. Otherwise any attempts at trying to have him learn to read and write would be a waste of time.

I began employing a tool that I described in Chapter 6, drawing a dot, a straight line, or a wiggly line on his face, arms, hands, back, and chest with my finger to wake up his brain to begin to perceive differences. At first he was unable to tell what the shape was, and couldn't distinguish between the shapes. But very quickly he became good at doing it. I also helped him become more and more aware of his whole body by gradually having him do more complex and refined movements, which he greatly enjoyed. Within a couple of sessions Scotty stopped complaining alto- gether. He came into each session enthusiastically, and with his Learning Switch turned on. He began offering his own ideas and suggestions about what we should do. He laughed more often. He was noticing a lot more in his environment and commenting about it. Each day he was sharper in his thinking and visibly becoming more powerful and skillful in his move- ments. And he was funny. The world was beginning to make a lot more sense to him and he was clearly empowered by his new knowledge.

At this point I asked Scotty if he wanted to write his name again. With great excitement he said yes. He took the pencil in his hand and slowly and deliberately wrote S-C-O-T-T-Y. This time, each of the letters had its own separate space and each letter was easily recognizable.

The following week Scotty and his parents went home, where he saw his tutor. She had stated that her intent was just to play with him, as prom- ised, not to have any reading or writing lessons. However, she called me later to tell me that Scotty had walked into her office, and had gone straight to the basket where she kept a collection of wooden letters. He brought the basket of letters to the desk that they used for reading and writing. She told him that they were only going to play today. Nevertheless, he insisted on forming words with the letters. The tutor told me how stunned she had been by his initiative and progress. "He is a completely different boy," she exclaimed. "Not only does he know the letters but he wants to experiment with writing and reading." Even more impressive to her was how happy he was, that there were no complaints or distractions. He kept his focus the whole time. His attention and concentration were remarkable. He wanted to learn. I told her, "His Learning Switch is now turned on and I am sure you're going to see him developing in ways that will surprise all of us."

One Whole Child

Focusing narrowly on the specific area of the child's problems or limitations is a normal and natural response. But there is one big problem with that. When we do so, *we stop seeing the whole child*. The full scope of the child, with his rich internal experiences and complexity, tends to elude us—and we ourselves tend to get grooved in in limited ways. Unbeknownst to us, our own Learning Switch gets turned off. When we open up and widen our focus so that we are seeing our child beyond his limitations and beyond our concerns, we turn our own Learning Switch back on. We begin to see our child more fully, more holistically. We discover things about our child we didn't notice before. We discover new possibilities for interacting and helping our child. Suddenly new opportunities useful to our child present themselves to us. We become more creative in helping his brain differentiate and evolve in areas that are not directly or obviously connected to the known problems. Yet often, in ways we couldn't have predicted, the child improves in the areas of his greatest challenge. This process turns on our own Learning Switch and turns on our child's in the process. It upgrades the brain's organizational capacities as a whole.

....

When we open up and widen our focus so that we are seeing our child beyond his limitations and beyond our concerns, we turn our own Learning Switch back on.

....

Seeing the Whole Child

While I didn't ignore the limitation that Scotty's parents were concerned about, I knew from past experience how important it was to put that awareness in the back of my mind and keep my Learning Switch turned on to see a child holistically. By doing so I quickly learned a number of things about Scotty: that he was sweet, that he had an emotional intelligence and an awareness of other people, that he didn't have the vaguest idea of how to write, that he did not move his head to the right, that his eye movements were limited, and that he appeared to have a very undifferentiated sense of spatial organization. I also noted that while he was able to walk, he did not walk well; the message to me was that because his brain had been able to organize this highly complex activity despite insufficient differentiation and awareness of his body meant that he actually had a very good brain.

I knew that turning on Scotty's Learning Switch—and with it his brain's ability to better differentiate and organize his movements and sensory perceptions—would improve his life. But I did not know in advance the specific ways he would improve. Thinking, feeling, walking, running, and, yes, reading and writing, all depend on the brain's ability to differentiate and organize all aspects of the child's self. So I let my holistic view of Scotty continue to guide me. I started by leading him through gentle movements that helped increase his awareness of his body, which obviously he was lacking. Then I drew the different lines on the surface of his skin, starting on his face, which is where he was able to first successfully differentiate between the dot I drew, the straight line I drew, and the wiggly line I drew with my finger. Note that all of this provided his brain with the opportunity not only to differentiate between the diverse sensations he was feeling and to link them to their corresponding shapes but to get better in differentiating in general. Learning to move his eyes and head to the right opened up for him the space on his right. His world began making more sense to him; he felt safer to move and was able to take more risks.

> **Thinking, feeling, walking, running, and yes, reading and writing, all depend on the brain's ability to differentiate and organize all aspects of the child's self.**

I always try to keep my own Learning Switch turned on and kept on high during my sessions with the children I work with, not only to maintain my own holistic awareness of the child but to observe changes that tell me that his brain is awake—that his own learning switch is on. In this way the child can experience himself as a whole, not as his limitations.

Throughout the lessons my attention was on Scotty's whole being, not on his limitations. I stayed open to *any opportunity* for him to learn and grow. I was using the different Essentials to provide his brain with opportunities to experience greater and greater differentiation, to upgrade its own organizational capabilities and to develop. Scotty was experiencing himself as successful and with it came a sense of joy and excitement about learning.

When you have your own Learning Switch on and see your whole child, you will find that you'll be helping your child turn his Learning Switch on, too.

What Science Tells Us About the Learning Switch

While the term *Learning Switch* does not describe a mechanical device in the brain that one can turn on or off like a light switch, it does describe an observable reality. I have seen this thousands of times in my work with children; a child's brain can be in a learning mode or not. When the child's brain is in a learning mode, almost anything we do with him will move him forward in his development. When the Learning Switch is off, no matter what you do there will be little or no change; in most cases, the child's limitations will just get more grooved in.

> **When the Learning Switch is off, no matter what you do there will be little or no change; in most cases, the child's limitations will just get more grooved in.**

Much about the brain's ability to learn remains a mystery to science though new discoveries are being made in laboratories every day throughout the world. Perhaps one of the more important observations of science is that there are certain conditions, measurable in the laboratory, that must be present before learning can occur. For example, for the learning mode to turn on, there must be a sufficient level of arousal. This arousal state is physiological, biochemical, and psychological.

Our emotions play a key part in this process of arousal, affecting communication between nerve cells and either increasing or decreasing both synaptic sensitivity and the transmission of information between nerve cells, which is the basis of all learning and development. Science tells us that there are chemicals produced in the brain, called neuromodulators, that are triggered by our emotions. These neuromodulators alter the influence of neurons on one another, either increasing or decreasing the level of arousal in the brain, depending on what the emotions are. In this way, emotions greatly affect information processing throughout the brain. They have the potential for putting the brain into an attentive, learning state or shutting it down so that little or no new learning occurs—turning the Learning Switch on or off.

Emotions, most brain researchers agree, also guide our attention, which is necessary for any new learning to occur. Sad emotions will affect what we pay attention to and the way we pay attention—very different from the way we pay attention when we are happy. Our emotions influence not only how our brains process information but how our thinking is organized. Interest, one of the most ubiquitous of emotions, appears to be necessary if learning is to take place at all. Animal research shows that motivation and engagement synchronize the whole brain, helping the animal organize itself better.

Knowing what we know of emotions and the brain, it is especially important for parents of children with special needs to understand the effect anxiety and fear have on the child's learning process. Anxiety and fear narrow down the child's attention; these emotions focus the child's attention on trying to feel safe, and nothing else. As Alan Fogel, researcher and author of books on emotional and sensorimotor development in children, writes: "The ability to respond to threat and to seek safety is the most important job of our nervous system." Anxiety and fear turn off the child's Learning Switch.

A prolonged stress response to threat (perceived or real) is particularly damaging. It can damage receptors in the brain that result in a negative effect on mood and memory and create hyperactivity in the child. Anxiety, fear, pain, and fatigue all tend to turn the child's Learning Switch off. Safety, connection with the parent, playfulness, joy, comfort, acceptance, and love all help turn the Learning Switch on.

....

Safety, connection with the parent, playfulness, joy, comfort, acceptance, and love all help turn the Learning Switch on.

....

Tools for Turning on Your Child's Learning Switch

The tools given here will help you flip your child's Learning Switch and dial it up to a higher setting. Your child will become a better learner. He will learn how to learn, he will grow and develop faster and further.

Is the Switch On? Learn to recognize when your child's Learning Switch is turned on. Some parents describe this as the impression that "a veil has lifted." Your child's eyes get brighter, and he moves them as he follows what you are doing. He becomes more animated, more vocal, and begins to move more. He participates in whatever you are doing with him, even if in the most minimal ways. He smiles, laughs or in other ways indicates that he is happy. Maybe you notice that he is curious and interested, more aware of what is going on within him and around him.

Turn on Your Own Learning Switch: To be able to help your child turn on his Learning Switch you first need to have your own Learning Switch turned on. When you bring yourself into the here and now you have turned your Learning Switch on. Once you have done this, pay attention. Get interested in and notice what is going on with your child. Attune yourself with him so that you can provide him the conditions and the ever-changing input he needs to thrive. This begins with just knowing that turning on your Learning Switch is possible, then proceeding with your intent to do that. Next, imagine a room or other space in which you have the image of a luminous switch you can turn on anytime you wish. Give this switch a color and shape that pleases you. Then imagine reaching into this space and turning the switch on. In your mind's eye, see your brain lighting up, humming along, ready to create new ideas and possibilities for you in your interactions with your child. The more you do this, the easier it gets until it will be second nature to you.

Avoid Turnoffs

Even when you have the best of intentions, there might be things you do with your child that turn his or her Learning Switch off; it is very important for you to watch out for these turnoffs and avoid them. Here are some common Learning Switch turnoffs to watch out for.

Pain: No doubt you've heard the saying, No pain, no gain. When it comes to turning on your child's Learning Switch, just the opposite is true; pain and discomfort definitely turn off the Learning Switch. There are situations when there is no choice but for your child to experience pain, such as having to go through a certain medical procedure or experiencing the pain that is symptomatic of his particular condition. At such times we do our best to comfort our child and help him to feel safe and loved. However, there are times when, fortunately, pain can be avoided—and needs to be avoided—if the child and the all-important capacities of his brain are to thrive.

If your child cries and resists a particular therapy, most likely he is experiencing physical or emotional pain and with it mental anguish. His brain's job is first and foremost to ensure his safety, to make certain that he feels protected and secure. Pain signifies danger. Anxiety is his response to danger. Despair and even depression are his responses to pain, danger, and fear that won't go away or that keep recurring. Whenever he feels this way, one thing is quite certain: His Learning Switch is turned off. Whatever you do with your child, be it the daily routines or any kind of home exercises and therapies, always look for ways to do it that are comfortable for your child. Be sure that what he is doing is pleasurable and that he feels safe. Avoid painful routines.

Excessive Repetition: Whether it's drilling the child in language, or having one or more adults *crawling* the child, or repeatedly doing range of motion and stretching exercises on a spastic arm, know that when it is done mechanically and with excessive repetitions, such activities will very quickly shut off the child's Learning Switch. When this happens, the exercises or routines will tend to groove in the existing patterns of limitation, discomfort, fear, anxiety, and a desire to escape from the unpleasant experience.

Repetition is good only after your child has figured out how to do something well that he couldn't do before. When that happens he will repeat his actions spontaneously, over and over again, enjoying himself and, in the process, grooving in the successful new patterns with feelings of pleasure and success. That's what all children do. Until such time, instead of repeating the same thing over and over again, hoping to get a different outcome for your child, stop! Then begin applying the Essentials. Start with Variation, Flexible Goals, and Enthusiasm, which are excellent antidotes to excessive repetition. You will be turning your child's Learning Switch on.

If learning isn't taking place . . . stop what you are doing; it's not working.

Fatigue: One of the more elusive ways your child's Learning Switch gets turned off is fatigue. When the Learning Switch is on, your child's brain creates new connections in the millions per minute, changing at an incredibly rapid rate. This is hard work for your child. Brain work consumes huge amounts of energy. Researchers have discovered that the ideal span of time for learning is *no more than twenty minutes*. That's assuming that learning is taking place. If learning isn't taking place—that is, if you suspect that your child's Learning Switch has turned off—stop what you are doing; it's not working anyway. Any longer than twenty minutes will often get the brain to lose or inhibit the new, still-fragile connections and the child loses access to what he has just learned.

I often tell parents that when your child does something new, stop immediately. Don't listen to your own inner drive to try to have your child repeat that new learning so that you can be sure it's really learned. Either shift the activity that you are doing with your child to a very different one or, if you see that your child is tired or has become internally focused or otherwise preoccupied with his thoughts, feelings, and sensations, give your child time to integrate. Let him eat if he is hungry, sleep, play, recover; you can resume interacting with your child later.

Powerlessness: When a child is experiencing pain, discomfort, boredom, or confusion or is not connecting with what you are trying to have him do, if you stay the course and insist on continuing, your child feels powerless, which turns off his Learning Switch. When your child is engaged and interested, and when you are responsive to your child's experiences, he will feel empowered, and his Learning Switch turns on. He becomes emotionally involved in the process. You can feel his excitement and his increased vitality. That doesn't mean doing just anything your child wants to do, but make sure that you are being authentically responsive to your child's experience at all times.

Provide Turn-Ons

The following are tools that you can use intentionally to help turn on your child's Learning Switch. Use them as often as you can.

Your Child's Interest: Find out what interests your child. It could be certain sounds, colors, shapes, games, activities, or certain foods.

Use the Other Essentials: Movement with Attention, Slow, Subtlety, Variation, Enthusiasm, Flexible Goals, Imagination, and Awareness. Combining any of the Essentials with something your child likes is almost certain to turn on his Learning Switch. One parent discovered that her child, who was on the autism spectrum, loved to touch and feel colorful fabric ribbons. The mother collected a wide variety of little strips of colorful fabric and used Variation to help the girl's brain differentiate, using colors and tactile sensations of the fabric in creative ways.

Get Curious About Your Child: Always observe how your child is being affected emotionally, physically, and spiritually. Know that everything your child is thinking, feeling, sensing, seeing, and hearing when his Learning Switch is turned on is in the service of his growth and development. Whenever the Learning Switch is on, he will be making new discoveries that will be meaningful to him.

Regardless of the intent we have for our child or the issue that we are focusing on, our child discovers the new not by us *trying* to make him learn but by our helping and allowing his brain to do its work, with the Learning Switch turned on and without limiting how he will use the new information. Einstein spoke of something he called "recombinant play," which simply means that one allows information to mix all together like in a wonderful stew in which flavors mingle, find their own connections, and produce something one could never have predicted or systematically formulated. This is where exponential change is born.

11 Essential Eight

Imagination and Dreams

The Possible's slow fuse is lit by imagination.

—EMILY DICKINSON

I like nonsense, it wakes up the brain cells.

—DR. SEUSS

The human brain provides us with the capacity to imagine, to dream, and to create something new from within ourselves, as if out of nothing. The ability of the child to imagine, daydream, and envision is an important part of her successful growth and development. The degree to which the child is able to do this will determine, to a great extent, the life path that she will follow. It will help mold the personal power she will experience around everything she does, from the most fundamental skills to the goals she may choose later on in life.

Imagination turns the lights on throughout the brain, creating billions of new connections. This ability to form new connections through imagination and dreaming into the future is our ultimate human gift, allowing us to move beyond our limitations, creating new possibilities and realities that would not otherwise be possible. As Einstein has said: Imagination is everything. It is the preview of life's coming attractions.

We can think of imagination as a treasure trove for the child's future. The creative powers associated with imagination are intensely alive and active in healthy children. They are essential as the child reaches out into the world, developing new skills and abilities and discovering seemingly endless new possibilities.

We can think of imagination as a treasure trove for the child's future.

When a child has special needs, her spontaneous inclination to imagine and dream may be fully or partially stopped. This can happen due to the challenges and, sometimes, the pain that take up all of her attention as she simply tries to cope and survive. Or it may happen when the brain itself is limited in its capacity to imagine as a result of her condition. No matter the reason, it is of utmost importance that we try and wake up the child's capacity for imagination, to give her access to this treasure trove that all healthy children rely on for their learning and development. Through Imagination and Dreams the child's brain upgrades itself to its highest level of functioning where it is more able and likely to find solutions for overcoming her limitations.

Let's Go Down a Brand-New Track

I met Ari for the first time when he was five years old. His diagnosis: autism. He was a tall boy for his age, lanky and handsome with very large brown eyes. He had many of the typical symptoms of children on the autism spectrum but perhaps the most striking was his severe perseveration and lack of the use of personal pronouns *I* and *me*. His parents brought Ari for his first session and with them they brought along a portable DVD player ready to play Ari's singularly favorite children's video, featuring Thomas the Tank Engine.

Before beginning his first session, his parents suggested that I play the disc while I put Ari on the table, because they believed that would help keep him less anxious. I asked to first try working with Ari without the video to see how he would act and whether I could connect with him. Within a few minutes it became clear that Ari was too anxious to be able to participate in the session, so I said yes to playing the video. Once it was turned on, Ari became transfixed on the little screen and the most remarkable thing happened. He began reciting every word of the story verbatim, just a fraction of a second ahead of the recording itself. He knew the whole thing by heart, all ten minutes of it! In addition to all the obvious problems that this behavior entailed, I realized that Ari was not using any imagination at all while doing this. His recitation was like a machine. There was no variation in his words or tone of voice; he brought nothing of himself into the story. When the video ended he would instantly reach out and push the button to start the video all over again, always reciting it exactly the same way.

After working with him for a while through Movement with Attention and the other Essentials, the tonus of his muscles began changing, and he moved his body in a smoother, more coordinated way. From this it was clear to me that his brain was waking up and responding. At a certain point I paused the DVD player for just a few seconds. Ari seemed alarmed yet kept reciting the movie, and with increased intensity. I quickly turned the video back on. When it started playing again his recitation was out of sync with the soundtrack of the movie. He stopped and for a moment seemed disoriented. I gently encouraged him to resume reciting the video from where it was now playing. After a moment's hesitation, he did. I let the video run for a bit, then told him to be prepared because I was going to pause the recording again. When I did he again kept reciting determinably as if the video were still running. But this time when I turned it back on, and he realized he was out of sync with the sound track, he was able to reverse himself and get himself back in sync quite quickly.

The next day I made sure the DVD player was on when I started working with Ari. This time I tried something new. After pausing the video, I began asking him some questions regarding the story line. By this time I knew it pretty well! For example, I suggested the following: "Maybe Thomas the Tank Engine didn't try to go up that hill right away. Maybe he decided to go to McDonald's to have some french fries first. What do you think of that?" By bringing my own imagination to the story I invited him to take an imaginary ride with me. His first reaction was again to get very anxious and recite the story with greater speed and vigor. I backed off and said: "Oh, okay. Not a problem." I repeated what he had last said from the script, then turned the video back on.

One or two minutes later, as I was helping Ari move in different ways, I was aware of his body getting more limber and his back getting stronger. This told me that his brain was awake and in learning mode. I paused the video again, and again suggested an imaginary alternative to the story line. This time Ari responded with much less anxiety than before. All of a sudden it was as if he had awakened from a deep trance that he had been in for a long, long time. He looked at me and suggested his own change in the imagined next move of Thomas the Tank Engine. Thomas, he said, went off to fight the monster. Ari was imagining!

Very soon this had become our game—making up new adventures for Thomas. Ari was no longer upset when I paused the video. He became imaginative and was helping create new story lines instead of only reciting the script over and over again. He even learned to tell the story backward and let me know when what he was saying was following the script and when it was his own invention.

Another thing Ari really liked to do was to throw a small ball back and forth with his father. Whenever he wanted his dad to throw the ball to him he would say, "Throw *you* the ball," when he meant "Throw *me* the ball." A couple days after Ari began using his imagination, I wondered if his brain would now be able to figure out pronouns. I attempted to help him differentiate *I*, *you*, and *me* by using a multitude of Variation. At first Ari didn't seem to be able to change. But then he stopped for a moment and seemed to go into a very internal, contemplative state. He then turned to his father and said: "Throw *me* the ball!" Having imagination not only allowed Ari to create new worlds, it allowed him to recognize himself and use a pronoun that differentiated himself from others.

The Reality of Imagination

As we see from Ari's story, imagination is real; it is a real function of the brain, something that the brain can do. It is invaluable for creating the new, vitalizing both the inner and outer worlds of your child. Imagination has the power to upgrade the quality of the functioning of your child's brain, creating new pathways and inventing new and refined ways of moving, thinking, and feeling.

Imagination has the power to upgrade the quality of the functioning of your child's brain.

Because imagination is intangible—that is, we can't touch, see, smell, or hear it directly, it can be difficult to think of it as really real or to believe it is important. On the contrary, it is not only real but it is essential for all change and growth. Research shows that adults who practiced playing the piano in their imagination got as good results or better than those who physically practiced playing the piano. Those who used their imagination for practicing gained the advantage for *further skill learning with minimal physical practice*. They became better at using this powerful tool—imagination.

Imagination and creativity go hand in hand. Think of a child playing with a wooden stick. In her imagination she turns the stick into a magic wand and in doing so she creates a whole alternative reality. She then continues playing in that reality, inventing endless ideas and actions emerging from it. All the while her brain is building new connections and patterns that become part of forming the whole child.

With Ari, the introduction of imagination helped reduce his compulsive perseveration—reciting the script of the video endlessly—and the anxiety that came with it. The awakening of his own imagination helped his brain work better. It also put him on the very important path of being able to differentiate the *I* and *thou* and to become more himself.

The Genius in Your Child

We all have a capacity for *divergent thinking*—that is, the ability to envision multiple solutions to a specific problem. A simple example of this would be finding how many uses we can think of for a paper clip. According to the researcher J. P. Guilford, who developed a test for divergent thinking, divergent thinkers were not only facile at generating multiple solutions to a single problem but were also able to simultaneously judge the relative usefulness, originality, and effectiveness of each solution.

Using Guilford's criteria for divergent thinking abilities, researcher George Land tested fifteen hundred children between the ages of three and five; 98 percent of the children scored in the genius category, based on his divergent thinking index. They were incredibly imaginative and creative. When he tested the same group five years later, when the children were between the ages of eight and ten, only 32 percent tested as geniuses. Five years after that, only 10 percent of the children from the same group tested as geniuses. And when he tested two hundred thousand adults, only 2 percent tested as geniuses in divergent thinking.

How is this relevant to your child who has special needs, you might ask. First and foremost it is important to note that very young children are geniuses in *divergent thinking*. This means that their brains are built to be creative, to imagine, and to find divergent ways of reaching one particular outcome. When a child has special needs, she needs her brain to use its highest potential for finding the unique solutions to her unique challenges. There is no one set way for the child to get from crawling to walking or from babbling to talking, for example. There is no one single correct path that the child can somehow find and then follow to get her to the specific destination of walking, talking, or whatever. Imagination feeds into this amazing freedom that the human brain has to invent ingenious and original solutions.

> **When a child has special needs, she needs her brain to use its highest potential for finding the unique solutions to her unique challenges.**

I believe we miss great opportunities for helping children with special needs attain their full potentials when we try to have them take a singular, well-defined path that we believe so-called normal children take to develop a particular ability. By presuming that we can precisely map out and prescribe a particular path to mastery—for example, to walk or talk— we deny the child opportunities for using her own brain's innate capacity for imagination, divergent thinking, and original problem solving so necessary for answering the unique challenges of her condition. When we support the child in the use of her own imagination, we support her brain to find its own solutions.

This Boy Is a Genius

Many years ago, while traveling with Dr. Moshe Feldenkrais, parents brought a four-year-old child with cerebral palsy to work with him. It was the boy's first session, and he had to go up about five steps to get from where he was waiting to where Feldenkrais had his work table. The boy used a walker since his legs were quite spastic and he had a very difficult time moving them. Feldenkrais stood by and waited patiently as the boy laboriously negotiated the stairs, with his metal walker and his spastic legs.

After a few moments, when the boy was between step two and three, intensely focused on his task, Feldenkrais turned to me and said, in Hebrew, "This boy is a genius!"

"Why do you say that?" I asked, finding it difficult to see any genius in this boy's arduous movements.

Feldenkrais answered, "Look at the *way* he is figuring out how to come up those stairs!"

This experience helped define how I think about children with special needs. Over time I have realized that we discover the genius of any child not in the seeming perfection or gracefulness of her specific achievement—such as climbing stairs effortlessly—but in the ability to use imagination and divergent thinking to find unique ways of accomplishing a task in response to tough challenges.

It is this facility of imagination, divergent thinking, and creativity that the child with special needs must draw on to grow and develop successfully.

The Magic of Daydreaming

A close relative of imagination is daydreaming. Children daydream a lot. Daydreaming allows them to explore endless possibilities in the safety of their own minds. Their daydreams create a context in which they can make use of the multitude of sensations, feelings, movements, ideas, and interpersonal experiences that they are having every moment of their lives. Neurophysiological research shows, for example, that all physical activity is organized in the brain by images of the person moving through space, just as it might appear in your mind when you dream or daydream of yourself walking or running, swimming or playing tennis. That three-dimensional movie in your mind, organizing the constantly moving images of that activity, is not only visual but contains information from all of our senses. Children don't learn to walk, for example, by imitation alone. Watching others walk provides the context in which their brains differentiate and use the information to organize itself to eventually stand up and walk. When we watch those around us walk or run or move in other ways, we imagine that experience in ourselves. Our imaginings and daydreams bring that activity alive in our own minds. A child who was raised with wolves learned to walk and run as the wolves walked and ran; he moved incredibly well on all fours and never learned to walk fully upright. Similarly, children can be heroes or princesses, doctors or artists or school-teachers in their daydreams and later in life choose a profession in which they can *make those dreams come true.*

When we find ways to support children in the use of Imagination and Dreams, helping them tap into their dreams, fantasies, or make-believe play—either through action or in their minds, if they have difficulty moving—we help them access the limitless wellspring of energy and passion they have within themselves. Many parents do this spontaneously with their children all the time, especially through play. It can be something as simple and fun as having the child pretend her hand is a kitten walking around and looking for its friend or Mommy's hand becomes the kitten who walks gently up and snuggles next to the child's cheek. If the child happens to have some spasticity in her hand, this might be the way for her to take interest in her hand and be willing to move it.

Daydreaming can often seem like a waste of time. Most of us have been raised to believe that our minds need always to be focused and clear, paying close attention to whatever we are doing. We give ourselves permission to daydream only during idle and unguarded moments. We might even think of daydreaming as unproductive and thus see the child who's daydreaming as lazy. Research shows that just the opposite is the case. Although we have traditionally assumed that we spend most of our time engaged in goal-directed thought that is periodically interrupted by blips of irrelevant thoughts, research shows that most of the time we are engaged in less directed, unintended thought. So, in fact, we are mostly daydreaming and are routinely interrupted by periods of goal-directed thought. While we are daydreaming, a wide variety of regions in the brain light up: those associated with impulse control, judgment, language, memory, motor function, problem solving, socialization, spontaneity, and the processing of sensory information. In other words, the child's brain comes to life—*it lights up*—when she daydreams.

While we are daydreaming, a wide variety of regions in the brain light up.

It is normal and healthy to daydream. And when the child is daydreaming, her brain may very well be integrating information, organizing it, and creating new connections for later application in her life. *Daydreaming is a fertile state that allows the child's brain enormous flexibility to pull together unpredictable solutions and inventions, something that the child with special challenges has a great need for.*

The child who's sitting in class daydreaming and is seemingly not paying attention to what the teacher is saying will most likely be missing the specific information being presented at that moment. That by itself is not great because we want her to be listening and paying attention. However, perhaps at that moment, through her daydreaming, her brain is in a creative process making sense of what she just heard from the teacher. Or perhaps, what the teacher said has triggered an idea in the child's mind, one that takes the original teaching a step further.

It is important to remember that a child is not an empty closet that we just stuff information into. The child's learning process is a creative one, one that constantly draws on the powers of Imagination and Dreams. Everything the child learns is imagined and invented within her own brain, formulated from within herself and from scratch. Nothing we might attempt to teach her becomes fully useful to her until this process takes place within her. And daydreaming is a huge part of her ability to do just that.

What Science Tells Us About Imagination and Dreams

You may find it difficult to shake the belief that intangibles, such as imagination, daydreaming, and fantasizing, are not all that useful. Certainly it is difficult to accept the idea that they could be very practical when you are faced with the grave challenges of trying to help your child with special needs. That is where further research can be helpful. Steven Jay Lynn and Judith Rhue, both psychologists, studied six thousand men and women. They found that those who fantasized—*daydreamed*—were more creative and stronger at problem solving and empathy than those who didn't fantasize. They were also more flexible, spontaneous, and far more interesting. All this was presumably a result of their brains' ability to create new information and new patterns through Imagination and Dreams.

But it's not only in mental or cognitive functions that Imagination and Dreams make a difference. Alia J. Crum and Ellen J. Langer worked with a group of eighty-four female room attendants employed in seven different hotels. The researchers divided their study participants into two groups: The first, called the "informed group" was told that the work they did, cleaning hotel rooms, was good exercise and that it satisfied the surgeon general's recommendations for an active lifestyle. The second group, the "uninformed group," was told nothing. Both groups continued doing their usual work. After four weeks the informed group showed a decrease in body weight, blood pressure, body fat, waist to hip ratio, and body mass index. The uninformed group had no significant changes. This study demonstrates how imagination brought about measurable physical changes. Applying imagination with your child, with its upgraded brain energy, can transform the outcomes of anything you do with her.

The Tools for Imagination and Dreams

Children begin participating in pretend play, or make-believe, by their second year of life. They are able to distinguish between real and not real and play imaginative games. Their ability to recognize the difference between reality and imagination provides opportunities for divergent thinking and the creative powers of their brains to bring forth remarkable new possibilities. The tools I provide will help you bring the powerful Essential of Imagination and Dreams into your child's daily life.

Let's Play: Play is one of the most common ways to activate a child's imagination. So much of what we do with our children, and what we ask them to do, is very serious and structured. It is usually even more so with a child who has special needs, particularly when she is receiving therapy and extra tutoring. Any opportunity to turn these activities into a game filled with imagination makes those activities more fun and effective. It brings levity, joy, and interest to the experience your child is having. By doing so, your child will become more engaged; this will actually upgrade the organizational capabilities of your child's brain and wake up its creative powers.

Co-Imagine with Your Child: Your child might be limited in her ability to imagine at this time, as we saw in the story about Ari. Begin introducing imaginary ideas and suggestions as you are interacting with your child. While doing this, look for any signs that she is trying to join in. If your child can talk, listen to her very carefully and integrate what she suggests into the image, story, or game that you're creating. Remember how Ari added a new element to the train story by saying that Thomas the Tank Engine went off to fight the monster? Do not change or correct what your child brings in! Don't worry if it doesn't make much sense in the beginning or if somehow she presented it in a faulty way. It's her first approximation. It needs to be nourished and appreciated as is. And it's all imaginary anyway. No one can do it wrong.

If your child cannot talk or express herself very well yet, and you see she is trying to participate, ask her yes or no questions, lots of questions. (Yes can be a blink of the eye and no a tiny movement in her index finger, for example). So you might say, "And does the bunny go to sleep now (in the imaginary story) or is she playing with her brother?" Wait for the child's response and integrate her choice into your cocreated imagery.

Discover the Dream: When you notice that your child is spacing out when she is supposed to be paying attention or listening or following instructions, back off for a moment. Let her be in her space, whatever that may be. If your child is very young, just leave her alone for a moment and wait for her to come back. If your child is old enough to understand your request, *very* gently, and in a friendly and loving tone, after giving her some time, tell her: "I'm so interested to know what you are doing now in your mind. Could you tell me?" If she doesn't seem to understand, create a fantasy of your own that you can share with her and then ask her if she has one to share with you. Most kids will pick up on this and cooperate very quickly. With an even older child you can ask her to write down her daydream or she can dictate it to you while you write it down for her. Make sure that you *do not* use the daydreams to try to manipulate your child to do what you want her to do or hope she will be able to do. So if your child is frightened by the noise of a vacuum cleaner, *do not* make up a daydream where you tell her that she is not afraid. Or if your child cannot run, you do not recount to her your daydream where she walks or runs. Make sure it is your child's dream.

Take a Co-Daydream Break: Next time you are with your child and she is a bit stuck or is resistant to what you are trying to have her do, stop and take a co-daydreaming break. You have probably done a similar thing many times where you describe to your child something you are going to be doing later with her, something you know she likes, as a way of calming her down or having her stay focused on what she is doing at the moment. Here you intentionally daydream and imagine with your child. You can say to your child something like: "Okay, let's take a break here [from doing homework] and think of somewhere you would like to be right now." After she tells you where she wants to be, you can embellish it a bit. "You'd like to be outside on the climbing structure? Oh and on the tire swing." Bring in more detail, even imaginary beings and things beyond the real. Then ask your child to describe what she would be doing if she were there right now. You can be there with her or not, depending on what she wants. You can introduce movement and music to the dream. Maybe you sing a song or introduce dancing movements. Notice how your child comes to life. At times you might be able to connect the content of the co-daydreaming with where your child was stuck or simply co-daydream with her in any topic she is interested in and see whether your child can all of a sudden problem solve where she was stuck earlier.

Story Telling: Story telling is one of the ultimate ways to imagine and daydream. Encourage your child to tell you her own stories, her daydreams, even write them down for her and read them back on another day. Perform—play act—the dreams, or portions of the dreams. Wherever your child has limitations, work around them with imagination. You and your child can make believe anything. Have your child plan scenarios and act out those scenarios for a fair amount of time. Act out the stories, using everyday items as props. Write them down, and add to them later. Become animated in your expression; this will wake up your child's brain to create new connections and possibilities.

Honor Your Child's Dreams: Dreams call to us from our future.

They organize our brains and provide the wind under our wings that lift us to our greatest heights of achievement. It is of utmost importance for each of us to have a dream, big or small, something we strive for, something that we feel we are called by and that we are on a path to fulfill. Your child has dreams, too. Always remember that they are *her dreams*, not yours. Your child's dreams are not *your* dreams and hopes for her. Honor your child's dreams, take an interest in them, treat them with respect. Dreams, by their nature, are not rational and cannot be justified; they just are. They often grow and change as the child matures. I recall working with a teenage girl with mild cerebral palsy whose dream was to become a dancer. Even though it was quite clear that she was unlikely to be hired by a professional dance troop, everything we did was in the context of her dancing. And she did indeed dance! She blossomed; she grew to love her body despite its limitation. She was empowered!

Free to Invent: The more you work with Imagination and Dreams, the more you and your child will find yourselves inventing your own ways of bringing this Essential into your lives. You know your child best. Go for it. Have fun on the road to discovering new possibilities.

12 Essential Nine

Awareness

If we could see the miracle of a single flower clearly,
our whole life would change.

—BUDDHA

Early on in my work I realized that if a child were to make profound and often immediate changes for the better, he needed to have present a *certain quality* that had to do with his *presence.* At the time the best way I could describe this quality was that "there's someone home." I observed that the more the child was *present* in this way, the more remarkable would be the outcomes of our work together. This quality was different from the wakefulness, attention, safety, comfort, and involvement of the child, all of which are indispensable. There was an extra ingredient beyond these that was necessary if the child were to make transformational changes. Over time I came to realize what this "secret" ingredient is: It is the child's *Awareness* of himself, his Awareness of his surroundings, his Awareness of what is going on within him and around him. It is his being an *observer*, actively figuring out relationships within different parts of his body, and relationships among what he does, what is done to him, what he feels, and the outcomes that he can anticipate or generate. From his own observations he can even anticipate outcomes, including novel situations he had not previously experienced.

The child's Awareness catapults his brain to a level at which he can figure out his world and the world around him in ways he couldn't otherwise do. Awareness is behind his evolving intelligence, the process that imposes order in the otherwise random and chaotic flood of sensations. All of this amounts to that special quality of what I first called *there's someone home*—of the child *awaring*. (I use the word *awaring* here as a verb—that is, the act of being aware. *Awaring* reminds us that what the child is doing is an action, dynamic and ongoing. We ordinarily use the word *awareness*, which is a noun. It names the action, but it causes us to think of awaring in a static and detached way.)

Before I began working with children, I didn't give much thought to whether infants, babies, and young children possess the capacity for generating Awareness. This concept was brought to my attention during a conversation with Dr. Feldenkrais, when he said to me: "Babies are highly aware. Without awareness they wouldn't be able to develop properly." His statement surprised me. It was difficult for me at the time to link in my mind the idea of Awareness with a baby. Those sweet, babbling, barely-able-to-do-anything little beings certainly didn't seem to have what I had been thinking was an exclusively adult capacity. Over the years my experiences would prove my earlier belief to be wrong. Babies can and do *aware*.

Sneeze After Me

Oliver was brought to me at five weeks of age. He suffered a congenital condition called *arthrogryposis*, in which his elbow joints weren't fully formed, and in place of his biceps, which bend the arms, he had connective tissue. His arms were rotated inward and were lifeless, never moving, not even at the shoulder joints, wrists, hands, or fingers. Before being brought to me, when people tried to exercise his arms, he cried in pain.

Oliver responded well to our work together. He improved quickly. His arms began moving and so did his fingers and hands. Because he was a tiny infant, he was often nursing during his lessons. He seemed to enjoy the work I was doing with him. When Oliver was nine weeks old he felt safe enough for me to work with him lying on my table, when not nursing, instead of being held in his mother's arms. One day, with him on his back and with me moving him gently in a variety of ways, I needed to sneeze. I took my hands off him and waited for the sneeze to materialize. After a few seconds I felt the sneeze forming. I breathed in and out, *Haaa . . . hehh; haaa . . . hehh; haaa . . . hehh!*"

Oliver stared at me intently, his eyes wide open and not blinking. Then I sneezed loudly. *Ahh-choo!* Oliver lay completely still, continuing to stare at me for what seemed to me a very long time. He still wasn't blinking. I looked at him, wondering what was going on for him, then said to him, "Yeah, I just sneezed." Then, to my utter surprise, he began breathing in a way very similar to what I had just done: *"Haaa hehh, haaa hehh, haaa hehh."* I was sure he was going to sneeze, too. Then he made a final louder sound—an imitation sneeze. *Ahh-choo!*

The first thought that went through my mind at that moment was, "Oh, my God, he can think!" I didn't know that nine-week-old infants could actually see, hear, feel—and witness something—then process it internally, and intentionally come out with what they had figured it out to be. Oliver was *at home* within himself, able to observe, take interest in events outside himself; he was aware enough to then organize an action in response, as was evidenced by his imitation of my sneeze. There was no doubt in my mind that little Oliver was "awaring."

Awaring Is an Action

The role of Awareness in our child's life, and in our own, becomes clearer when we think of Awareness as an action. Awareness is not a thing or a state of being or something we possess. Just as we don't possess walking or thinking or talking—they are only there as we do them—these actions don't exist on their own. Awareness, like movement, is something we do. Just as you might say, "I'm walking or cooking or playing with my child," I propose that we learn to say, "I'm *awaring*," or my child is *awaring* at this moment, or not. Once you start thinking of Awareness as an active verb, you can learn to recognize when your child is doing it—awaring or not awaring.

> **Awaring allows your child's brain to make a quantum leap from where he presently is to his next level of abilities.**

When your child is awaring, he is drawing on the transformational capacities of his amazing brain. Awareness catapults your child's brain to higher and more potent capacities of organization and creation. Awaring allows your child's brain to make a quantum leap from where he presently is to his next level of abilities. By awaring he gets better at that which he *awares*: his movements, thoughts, feelings, and actions. He transforms in ways that often seem miraculous.

Your child is awaring whenever he observes himself in action and realizes what he is doing, realizes that he could continue doing what he is doing, do it differently, change what he is doing, or stop altogether. He can begin awaring long before he has language. Awaring, like any other skill, is subject to growth and evolution. Over time, as your child applies his awaring capacities more and more, he will get better at it, and this improved ability to aware can help him greatly in overcoming his challenges.

Getting Better at Awaring: Awakening the Observer Within

We all possess this capacity we call Awareness, by which we are able to observe, know, and change ourselves. As we saw with Oliver, even at nine weeks of age he was clearly awaring. His ability to aware not only got him to fake sneeze but would eventually serve a significant role in his becoming aware of his arms and learning to use them in creative ways that defied all the predictions of his future limitations given to him at birth.

Awaring is an integral part of any child's successful development. The more a child uses the skill of awaring, the more that capacity will expand, becoming stronger and more integral with the inner workings of his brain. One of the central qualities of awaring is that it is the opposite of automatic, compulsive behavior or action. Awareness is a source of freedom. Awareness elevates the brain to a place of discovery and choice rather than being reactive and on automatic pilot. Whatever your child's special needs may be, you may find that the areas of challenge are fraught with compulsivity and automaticity—with seemingly little or no freedom to go beyond those challenges. Awaring opens the door leading out of the prison of present limitations.

To aware requires having a virtual *internal observer*. It is as if your child shone a light revealing something he had not seen or realized before. Awareness is different from attention, which we explored in detail in earlier chapters. Your child could be paying attention, focusing on something he feels, hears, sees, thinks, or is doing but not be aware, at that moment, of himself doing it. In other words, his internal observer of himself and his own actions is not active at that moment. He may be watching a program on TV, paying close attention, getting very absorbed, perhaps clapping his hands with excitement from time to time, even talking to the characters on the screen and yet, at the same time, he is completely oblivious to the fact that he is doing all this.

> **Awareness elevates the brain to a place of discovery and choice rather than being reactive and on automatic pilot.**

As improbable as it might seem to others who are observing him, a child who is tantrumming may very well be completely unaware of what he is doing and how his behavior is affecting him and other people. His inner observer is not present at that moment. His brain is on auto pilot with no choice but to complete the cycle of the behavior. It is operating at a lower level—that is, with little or no awareness and with no choice or freedom. If an outside observer can at that moment help to awaken the child's own observer, to have the child begin awaring, it will often transform the behavior instantaneously and possibly change how that child acts in the future.

It is important to remember that the observer self is *neutral*. It observes; it does not judge, cajole, manipulate, or punish. It is what I like to call a benevolent observer. Once the observer is awakened, awaring immediately begins to take place, and with it comes a transformation that would otherwise not be possible for your child.

Your Awareness Is Key

Have you ever had the good fortune of being in the presence of a person whose awaring powers are highly developed, who is obviously more aware of himself and his surroundings than most mortals? The Dalai Lama comes to mind as such a person, as does Mother Teresa, Mahatma Gandhi, and other highly evolved spiritual teachers. Perhaps there has been someone like this in your own life, such as a teacher you had the good fortune to learn from. For me such a person was my teacher, Dr. Feldenkrais.

You may have noticed that in the presence of such a person you change, at least temporarily. Perhaps you notice that being in the presence of that person brings out the best in you or allows you to recognize things you hadn't recognized before. You think more clearly; you are emotionally calmer and more balanced; and you're more generous, benevolent, and compassionate in that person's presence. The power of one person's expanded Awareness elevates those around him. In the same way, your own elevated Awareness—your increased awaring capacities—can lift your child and help transform his brain. The powers of your awake and benevolent observer are such that they can have a domino effect, changing your whole family, reducing stress, increasing bonding, and getting the best from everyone more often.

....

The power of one person's expanded Awareness elevates those around him.

....

Am I Doing This?

Julia is a medical doctor. Highly successful, married to a very successful professional, she brought her daughter Sheila to me a few years back. Sheila was diagnosed with having a severe case of attention deficit hyperactivity disorder (ADHD) and delayed development in all areas: motor (even though she could walk), language, and cognitive.

At the end of our first session, Julia tried to put Sheila's shoes back on. Sheila seemed completely oblivious to her mother's intent and efforts. She kept running around while the mother implored her to come over to her and sit down, with ever increasing intensity in her voice. The more intense and fast Julia's speaking became, the more Sheila was bouncing off the walls, becoming increasingly hyper in her behavior. Julia, brilliant and very much a type A personality, was speaking very fast and with long elaborate sentences. It was clear to me that Julia's inner observer was asleep at that moment. She was running completely on automatic pilot. As bright as Julia was, she had no idea what she was doing or how her tense voice and long and complex sentences were affecting her daughter. In her own mind she was trying only to get the shoes on Sheila's feet so that they could leave.

I sat down facing Julia and asked permission to coach her. She immediately said yes. At that moment I took the role of being her benevolent observer. I told her that she was very bright; she thanked me for the compliment. I let her know that I wasn't trying to compliment her but I was helping paint a picture of something I wanted her to become aware of. I then told her that she is a very fast thinker and speaks very quickly, with highly elaborate sentences. She seemed surprised. She had no idea. She had never thought of herself in those terms. I continued to tell her that when she spoke to her daughter so fast, with great intensity and with complex sentences, Sheila simply couldn't follow. I assured her that her daughter was quite intelligent but Julia's speech was too fast, too intense, and too complex for her daughter's brain at this time.

During this exchange with Julia, I spoke slowly, and Julia was watching me and listening with great intensity (of course), and I suggested she observe herself so that she could slow down her speaking, simplify her sentences, slow down her movements, and try to generally *do less* whenever she was with her child; I suggested that she become aware of her own anxiety and, when she felt anxious, to stop a moment and take the time to calm herself down.

Right then and there Julia began speaking very slowly, with a softer tone of voice, telling Sheila with short simple sentences to come and sit down so that she could put her shoes on. Then she stopped and waited for Sheila to respond. It took a moment and then it was as if the message had landed. Sheila turned toward her mom, walked to the chair and sat down, calmly letting her mom put her shoes on.

A few weeks later, Julia told me that her increased Awareness of her type A behavior, as she called it, allowed her to make changes, transforming the atmosphere in their home for everyone. Nowadays Sheila understands what is said to her, even when it is fast or complex, but Julia has adopted the aware, more present way as her preferred way of being, particularly when she is with Sheila.

What Science Tells Us About Awareness

Scientists who study Awareness recognize the great challenge not only of researching it but of forming a precise definition of what Awareness is. Many use the terms *consciousness* and *awareness* interchangeably. In this regard, all animals have a certain degree of consciousness. Without it they would not be able to seek the basic necessities of life. Dogs recognize what's to come when they see their master's suitcases by the door or when their master gets out the leash to take them for a walk. As I use the word here, *awareness*, is not the same as, or interchangeable with the word *consciousness*. Rather, I use awareness to signify an extraordinary capacity to observe and be aware of oneself. It is the ability to know that you know. We look in the mirror and recognize that "I am looking at a reflection of me," and we realize that you and I are different. Philosophers have also referred to this capacity as "meta-consciousness" or "meta-awareness"— the awareness of awareness or the awareness of our ability to think about our own thoughts, desires, feelings, and beliefs. We humans are not endowed with instincts such as those that most other animals have.

Instead we depend on our awareness of ourselves and of our relationships with the world around us to guide us. Awaring facilitates learning and the immediate integration of new neural patterns.

Given the role that awaring plays in forming the human brain and upgrading its organizational and learning capabilities, it is not surprising that researchers are finding out that infants as young as seven months old demonstrate at least some capabilities of awaring. Researchers Agnes Kovács and colleagues have shown that seven-month-old babies can take into consideration the perspective of others. This ability requires some form of awareness of self and others, an ability that was once thought to first emerge around the age of four. Kovács found that these infants encode the beliefs of others and that the beliefs of others have similar effects as their own beliefs in performing tasks that they were given. They also discovered that the beliefs of others continued to influence the infants' behavior even after that other person had left the scene.

Scientists at MIT have shown that twelve-month-old babies can use knowledge to form surprisingly sophisticated expectations of how novel situations will unfold. They have shown that babies only a few months old have a solid grasp of basic rules of the physical world and can make rational and accurate predictions of the way events will proceed.

If we stop to think about it, it makes sense that awaring, which is such a fundamental and central function for the successful development of the human being, is present from the beginning of life. And it continues to develop over time, just as do all other skills.

The Tools for Awareness

You cannot overestimate the power of *your child's own awaring* to transform him in quantum leaps. And never underestimate the importance of your own awaring in helping your child's brain do its own awaring. The following tools can help both you and your child awaken this remarkable and necessary human capability.

Awaring Begins with You: It is helpful to remember that the ability we call Awareness is an action rather than a thing—that is, *awaring*. To be able to help your child develop and more fully benefit from his awaring skill, you first have to develop and bring into intentional use your own awaring. You can actually decide to exercise or practice your awaring, just as you might exercise by walking or running. We all aware spontaneously, from time to time, in our daily lives. Maybe we get up in the morning and notice that our back is feeling stiff; then perhaps we link that stiffness with moving a heavy chair the day before. After *awaring* this for a moment, we realize: "I'm always thinking I've got to do everything myself." Then we realize that the next time we have the option to act in a new way—we could ask for help.

With this tool you are invited to go beyond the spontaneous awaring and begin to bring your intentionality to this action. You may choose to aware while you're standing in the line at the supermarket. You may aware that you are feeling rushed and that you are standing too close to the person in front of you in a futile attempt to accelerate the process.

You may also choose ahead of time certain situations in your life where you will be awaring. Intentionally become aware of your thoughts, movements, feelings, and actions. You are exercising your awaring skills by simply noticing what you are experiencing, what you are thinking, feeling, and doing in everyday situations as they occur. Everyday activities and events provide endless opportunities for awaring. This will help you develop your awaring skills to new levels, just like developing a muscle through intentional exercising.

As you become more skillful at awaring, gradually apply it to more complex, more emotionally and cognitively demanding situations, such as when you try to do something new and challenging that you have never done before. As you feel you are getting good at awaring, and have expanded your Awareness of your awaring, you are ready to bring these skills into your interactions with your child.

Awaring with Your Child: Once you have practiced your awaring skill for a while and you are feeling that you can call on it intentionally, begin bringing it into your interactions with your child. In the beginning, choose a situation or activity that is low stress for both of you. For example, this might be watching a video together. From time to time observe him instead of the movie. What can you become aware of in him? Perhaps you become aware of some change in his posture whenever he is absorbed in the movie. Or maybe you become aware of facial expressions that you have not seen him make before. Or you notice expressions that you have seen on his face at other times when he was happy or sad or frightened. Then shift your attention and observe yourself. See if you can become aware of what you feel at that moment, what thoughts you may have, what do you desire at that moment? How is your own body organized? Are you comfortable? Are you sitting close to your child? Do you like the closeness?

After a few days of practicing awaring with your child in low impact situations, begin awaring in situations and interactions with your child that are more challenging for him and possibly for you as well. This may be during a home therapy session or while you are helping your child with schoolwork or handling your child's challenging behavior on the playground. Before you do anything with your child, stop and become aware of what you are feeling. Are you confused? Are you feeling that you are in charge? Are you calm? Frightened? Overwhelmed? Tired? Hopeful? Hopeless? Are you feeling love for your child at that moment? Are you irritated? What are you thinking? What do you need at that moment? Are you content and feel self-sufficient and in control or would you like to have some support yourself? Do not censor yourself. There is no right and wrong here. *You are focusing on awaring; there is only what is.* Become aware of what it is you are driven to do, if anything. All this should take only a moment or so of your time. *Think of your awaring as a quick, internal scan.* Awaring like this will pull you away from your own automatic reactions and actions and give you more freedom to choose what to do and to come up with creative new ideas as to how to be and what to do with your child.

Who Am I Doing It For? Once you aware with your child, shift your awaring to your child. What do you see over there? Decide what it is that you want to do with your child next, including the possibility of leaving him alone and just continuing to observe him. But before you proceed, ask yourself, Who am I going to do this for? Is it for my child, or is it for me? Or is it for both of us? You may find that the answer you come up with will surprise you.

So often parents find that the action they were about to take with their child, with the best of intentions and believing it's for their child, realize, after awaring, that it's not the case. Often we take actions to reduce our own anxiety. Or we may be following the dictates of an authority figure we feel we don't dare question. Maybe we do what we do because we believe that it is in the best interest of our child without confirming that it is so. And sometimes we are simply on automatic pilot. No matter what you decide to do, the sheer fact that you are awaring gives you more freedom and choices about what you do or don't do with your child. Your own awaring, irrespective of the content, will help elevate your child's potentials and move him to aware more himself, helping his brain to be able to more successfully resolve his challenges.

Awaken the Observer and Genius in Your Child: As long as your child is awake, anything you do with him or any activity he is involved in is an opportunity to guide him to use his awaring skill. For the child it will mostly occur as a game. Once it is awakened, awaring becomes a core skill that is applied everywhere. Again, start where it is easiest for your child and for you. Choose an activity or situation that your child likes and feels comfortable with. This might be feeding your child. If your child is still an infant and you are feeding him with a bottle, instead of just bringing the bottle to his lips and placing the nipple in his mouth, thus starting him to suck automatically, pause for a moment. Hold the bottle a few inches from your child's face and tap the bottle with your fingernail, making a clicking sound a couple times to get his attention. Or you might gently touch the bottom of the bottle to his belly or to the sole of his foot, getting his attention in that way. Once you have gotten his attention, bring the bottle closer to his face but don't put the nipple into his mouth yet. Just touch it lightly to his lips, move it away a little and then wait a few seconds. Most likely your child will wake up and notice that his automatic expectation has not been fulfilled. At that point bring the bottle into his line of sight so that he can easily see it. Tap the bottle lightly again with your fingernail and you might even say: "Bottle. Milk. Do you want some?" The moment your child moves his head or his gaze toward the bottle, touch the nipple to his lips, and then slide the nipple into his mouth. Next time you feed your child, begin by tapping on the bottle. See if your child wakes up right away, and is fully aware of the bottle. Is he aware? Does he *know* what he is expecting and is he actively looking for it to happen?

The Power of Asking Questions: Questions are a remarkable tool for awakening your child's awaring powers. A question immediately implies at least two options: yes or no . A question can also be open-ended, implying many options, such as, "What would you like to do today?" "Would you like a sandwich, or an orange, or an apple, or some french fries?" Questions require that we *aware* the options, make a selection, and know that we are choosing one thing over another. Having to make a choice is the opposite of automaticity and lack of awaring. There are infinite numbers of ways and opportunities to awaken and intensify your child's awaring capacities through questions. Look for questions you can ask your child in everyday life that awaken his brain into making choices, bringing the power of his awaring into play.

For example, using a nontoxic marker you can draw the image of a cat on the back of your child's right hand and the image of a dog on the back of his left hand. As you and he are involved in an activity—for example, maybe he is climbing on a play structure in the park—you can ask him, "Is your dog going to grab the bar first, or is your cat?" At that moment he is called to notice his hands and the fact that he can choose one or the other. You might add a duck image to his left foot and a flower image to his right foot. When you are playing catch with him, you can ask, "Who is going to catch the ball? The cat and the dog? Or maybe the duck and the flower?"

If your child is having a tantrum, screaming and hitting the floor with his little fists, remember that no matter how loud and obvious these actions are to you, he is most likely not awaring his behavior at that moment. This is often the nature of tantrumming. At this time you can introduce some questions to see if you can help him awaken his awaring function and give him the ability to get out of his automatic behavior. You may ask: "Are you yelling? I'm not 100 percent sure. Could you be a little louder?" Wait for a few seconds and see if he does get louder. If he does get louder, acknowledge it by saying, "Oh, you are louder. I can hear you better now." His getting louder is an indication that he is awaring. Do not ask him if he is upset. Stay with the concrete and observable and avoid interpreting his behavior.

If he does not get louder, let it go and shift your attention to his fists, which are hitting the floor. You can place a piece of paper near his hands and ask him if he would hit the paper from time to time, with one hand, the other, or with both. See if awaring like that shifts his behavior.

You will be amazed at how your genuine questions, coupled with your observation and your awaring of your child, and your own feelings and actions, can help him access the inner genius of his own Awareness, and catapult him to learn and thrive.

Awaring and making choices about what you are awaring awakens the brain in amazing ways; at such times, differentiation is highly active. It is like turning on a light to reveal and create new possibilities and new combinations in the brain that can lead to remarkable transformations for your child.

13 Beyond Limitations

The limits of the possible can only be defined by going beyond them into the possible.

—ARTHUR C. CLARKE

When I tell parents to "go for it all," to think beyond limitations, I do not mean to imply that limitations aren't real. No matter what, there are always capabilities that are beyond the individual child, whether she has special needs or not. At four months of age we don't lace a pair of roller blades on a child's feet and send her off to skate. And though some children might like to fantasize what it would be like to fly around like Superman, from the movies and comic books, they aren't going to do that. There are obvious limitations involved with being born as a human being. The process of growing and learning is challenging enough in itself when a child is born with no special challenges. That demand is increased exponentially when a child is growing up with special needs. So why do I say go for it all and to think beyond the limitations?

First of all, it is a reminder that the limits are constantly changing, thanks to discoveries in the sciences, to changes in society's view of people with special needs, and to new discoveries by people who dedicate their lives to meeting the challenges of our fellow humans who are born with handicaps. The outer limits for people with special needs are being constantly pushed. And everywhere we turn there are new examples and new heroes guiding the way not just to living with special needs but thriving with them and living fulfilling, even extraordinary lives irrespective of those special needs that make them different.

We have people like Elizabeth, whose story I shared early on in this book. Even today there are experts who say that a condition like hers should have limited her greatly, yet at age thirty she has earned two masters' degrees, is married, runs her own business and, in her own words, has "found her passion." She lives a life that is fulfilling, both for herself and for those around her. So many of the children we have worked with have grown to have a much fuller and more satisfying life than had been believed possible for them.

Elizabeth and all these other children did not get where they are today alone, of course. They had parents who were dedicated to them, who loved them, and refused to accept a limited vision of their child's future and kept hope alive. These children also had the enormous advantage of our working with possibilities rather than focusing on, and being bogged down by, their obvious limitations. This allowed us to help them develop and build on their innate capabilities. The combined work of those who are willing to hold a belief in the endless emergence of new possibilities or limitlessness—parents, scientists, therapists, doctors, health practitioners, caregivers, and the children and adults who have special needs—is constantly pushing beyond the perceived limits.

Limitlessness manifests in many different ways, by individuals as well as by society's constantly changing values. People with missing limbs are able to run, ski, swim, and compete in wheelchair races and various other athletic events. There are everyday heroes and heroines whose accomplishments prove how valuable it can be to think beyond limitations.

There's Kyle Maynard, born without legs or arms, who became a wrestling champion and a popular motivational speaker. There's Stephen Hawking, who at twenty-one discovered he had amyotrophic lateral sclerosis (ALS), a debilitating disease that doctors predicted would kill him within five years, yet today, fifty years after his diagnosis, he is one of the world's most creative physicists, though he has voluntary movement in only one cheek muscle. There's Barb Guerra, born without arms, who is married, has raised her three children, does her own shopping, drives her own car, and runs every day as part of her regular aerobic exercise program. And let's not forget that one of the world's largest athletic events is the Special Olympics, which has drawn more than three million athletes with intellectual disabilities, with over 150 countries participating.

There are doctors, lawyers, scientists, researchers, homemakers, and others, whose lives of limitlessness challenge all the known predictions for their handicaps.

When a child is faced with special challenges, we—parents, therapists, teachers, caregivers, and physicians—are challenged to define what those needs are and to find ways to best help the children we love and care about. Throughout this book I have tried to uncover and to describe ways to access the rich potentials that can almost always be awakened in the child. And I have suggested ways we can all be thinking about what it means to move beyond limitations, to go for it all, and to realize that solutions to problems always lie in what has yet to be created.

In my more than three decades of working with children who have special needs I have seen time and time again how the Nine Essentials described in these pages can provide opportunities to change the way special needs affect our children and help them move beyond limitations.

The Nine Essentials give you the guidelines and the tools to access and awaken the limitless capabilities of your and your child's brain.

At the heart of the Nine Essentials is the miracle of your child's brain and all the many ways that you can help that brain do its job better. This is where limitlessness becomes a reality.

With the Nine Essentials you can provide your child with opportunities that her brain will be able to take advantage of in invaluable ways, to always differentiate further, creating greater refinement of movement, thought, feeling and action. Your child can always become more skillful and continue to grow.

If there is one goal that we all have in mind for our children with special needs, perhaps it is no different from the goal we have for all children: to have a full and meaningful life. In the words of Temple Grandin: "Parents and teachers should look at the child, not the child's label. . . . Be realistic with expectations, but don't overlook the potential for genius that may be quietly hiding inside, just waiting for an opportunity to express itself."

APPENDIX

Frequently Asked Questions

Inevitably, readers have questions that don't fit neatly into the format of a book. I have tried to anticipate what some of these might be, drawing from what parents have asked me during consultations or in workshops. If you have further questions, check out my website, where you will also find videos of actual sessions with parents and children: www.anatbaniel method.com.

What conditions can the Anat Baniel Method (ABM) help?

Because the focus of this method is on the brain and its organizational abilities, the specific diagnosis itself is rarely the deciding factor as to the child's ability to improve and grow. I, along with the practitioners I have worked with, have had success with a wide variety of diagnoses and conditions. We can work with any child as long as we are able to turn on his or her Learning Switch and help the brain begin to form new and more successful patterns of movement and action.

If I use the Nine Essentials, will my child become completely normal?

I wish I could say yes. What I do know is that if you consistently use the Nine Essentials with your child, he or she will begin changing and improving and be able to do more and more.

If I use the Nine Essentials with my child, should he or she also get lessons from an ABM practitioner?

It is always helpful for your child to get some lessons with a practitioner. The practitioner can sharpen and accelerate the process of change in your child, using the specialized knowledge and experience he or she has. You will feel more supported in using the Essentials at home with your child as you and the practitioner become partners in helping your child. Through their practitioners, many families get to know other families who have children with special needs, and this can be a wonderful resource and source of further support.

At what age would you recommend bringing my child to an ABM practitioner?

For thirty years I have recommended starting this work as soon as possible. Now many other professionals advocate the same. We have worked with infants as young as five days old. The child's brain grows and forms at the fastest rate early in life; the sooner we can help the brain organize and function better, the easier it will be for the child later on.

With more research in brain plasticity now suggesting the brain can be rewired at all ages, do you have an opinion about the effectiveness of

ABM for older children? Is there an age at which the ABM stops being effective?

> The brain can change itself at any age. There have been many times when I thought a child was too old to benefit from this work and then was happily proven wrong. Some years ago we worked with an eight-year-old boy with severe athetoid cerebral palsy who couldn't even sit up, yet three months after starting this work he was walking. It is good to keep in mind that the greater the challenges, and the older the child, the more his brain will have formed patterns, including patterns of limitations, and this poses its own unique challenges. We don't know in advance how much a child will improve. We do know that if we don't do anything—or anything different from what he or she has been doing—most likely the child won't get better. *Ultimately, there is the question of quality of life.* A child who uses a wheelchair, even though that child will never walk, can enjoy life more and live a full and satisfying life if he or she can learn to move easier, breathe better, and feel better. ABM helps the child or young adult improve and refine available abilities, and that always improves day-to-day experiences of living.

If I decide to go to an ABM practitioner, how does that work?

> The first session should be an evaluation to see whether there is a fit between your child, the practitioner, and you. If you decide to proceed, we recommend that your child get an intensive series of lessons every few weeks. At our center we usually give the child ten sessions in five days. We have discovered that working this way provides greater breakthroughs and transformations for the child— the brain is able to change in ways that with fewer lessons, or with

lessons spread further apart, it can't. From time to time, when we feel that it would be helpful, we work with the child for a number of weeks straight through, with only weekends off. As the child improves, the frequency of the lessons goes down, until they are not needed any more.

How soon should I expect to see changes?

Most children will have some changes within the first session. I tell parents to take between three to five sessions to see changes and then decide if the changes merit continuing to work with us. Those changes could be that your child is enjoying the session where normally he or she is upset and resistant during therapy; or your child might be eating more or sleeping better. And then there are the obvious changes that you came hoping to get, such as improved movement, better speech, better interpersonal contact and communication, or clearer thinking. Of course you should see changes in your child when you start using the Essentials on your own, as we've discussed in the Essentials chapters.

How do I know when to stop?

Never stop using the Nine Essentials with your child or in your own life for that matter. The Essentials are like food for the brain; they keep nourishing it with new information to continue to grow and evolve throughout life. In most cases, people find that they quickly integrate the Essentials into their everyday lives because they make what they are already doing easier, more productive, and more pleasurable. As far as the private sessions go, when your child is functioning well enough and is able to continue improving by going to school and being in life like other kids, that's a good time to stop. You might find that from time to time your child may need the support of just a few lessons; often this is after a big growth spurt; during puberty; after an illness; or during important life transitions, such as moving to another neighborhood, experiencing a change in the family dynamics, and after a death or birth in the family.

What about other therapy modalities and interventions?

When evaluating a therapy modality, an intervention, or a specific therapist, look for whether that modality or practitioner follows, intentionally or unintentionally, the Nine Essentials. As long as the principles of the Nine Essentials are honored, anything you do with your child is perfectly fine and should be helpful. If the Nine Essentials are not honored, either modify the intervention to follow the Essentials or stop and do something else. Remember that the Nine Essentials answer your child's biological needs, helping provide the brain with what it needs to function well, allowing your child to do his or her best.

I was told I should put my child in braces. Is that okay?

I recommend using the Essentials as the backdrop against which to make the decision about using braces or other devices. Every child and every situation is different. For example, leg braces limit the child's Movement with Attention and Variation in sensation and movement in the feet and lower legs. Braces placed on the hand or the back do the same in those areas. Children who have had braces on their legs for many years lose feeling in the soles of their feet—the brain maps for these areas are mostly gone! Leg braces have also been shown to be responsible for the typical bent knees and hunched over posture of the child with cerebral palsy. On the other hand, there are times when braces are needed, usually temporarily, as after certain surgeries. Also, the braces themselves can be structured to allow more or less movement and to cover more or less of the body of the child. They can be used for short periods of time as an additional Variation. All these factors need to be brought into account as you make decisions about the use of braces. And most important—look at your child's reaction to the brace to make the final decision.

What about assistive devices?

The same thinking regarding braces applies with assistive devices. There are times when an assistive device is necessary, such as a walker or a wheelchair. But you'll also want to consider the different kinds of walkers, for example, as well as when and how often to use a device. These are all questions that need to be thought of in light of the Essentials. For example, I ask parents to not use a back walker, even though they are becoming more and more popular. That is because the child doesn't really stand up when in a back walker, but leans back and sometimes almost sits down. The child uses the power of the arms rather than organizing himself or herself on the legs while using the power of the back to stand up. Many of the Essentials are not followed with a back walker. The child loses Variation of movement and uses too much force rather than Subtlety, and the rigid goal of standing up and walking has been placed ahead of the child's true abilities. As a result, the brain will adopt patterns that ensure that the child will never be able to stand or walk independently. On the other hand, when the child can stand up and get hold of a front walker by himself or herself, then using a walker as a transition toward independent walking is a great idea.

Are there other modalities you recommend doing with the ABM?

Yes! We find the following modalities to be useful and work well together with our method: Hippo therapy, developmental vision therapy, osteopathy, Fast ForWord, homeopathy, music therapy, adaptive marshal arts, and any activity that your child likes and that is in harmony with the Nine Essentials. Discover what works best for your child. We also found that working with a good nutritionist is important. Finding out about possible allergies and eliminating foods that cause symptoms can make a huge difference in your child's life.

What about surgeries and other medical interventions?

We cannot overstate the importance and value of medical intervention. Many of the children we work with would not be alive if it weren't for modern medicine. I strongly recommend getting your child evaluated medically so that you can know as much as it is possible to know about your child's condition or special needs. At the same time, if irreversible interventions, such as surgery, are being recommended, take your time to make a decision, learning all that you can about both short- and long-term impacts on your child. Get the whole picture before going ahead with any surgical procedure. Of course, if the surgery is a matter of life or death, there isn't always time to do all the research you might wish to do but will depend on those who are already helping you make your decision. When making choices about any intervention, be sure to include emotional and social impacts, the pain that your child may experience, and of course, the effect on the brain and how well it brings into account the Nine Essentials.

How do I choose a school for my child?

Look for a school where teachers see the potential and possibility in your child and are not intimidated by his or her challenges. Look for a school and for a teacher with an approach that is compatible with the principles of the Nine Essentials. If your child uses a wheelchair or walker, make sure that the school is equipped to give your child freedom to move in the ways that he or she can. If your child has only limited movement, find out if it will be possible to get your child out of the wheelchair and on the floor for at least some of the time during the day. Look for a school where the best interests of your child come before what's convenient for the school.

Which toys and gadgets are useful?

Think of the Essentials when you choose toys and gadgets for your child. For example, a Johnny Jump Up places the child in sort of a standing position long before he or she has figured out how to stand alone. It restricts the body, limiting the child from doing the Movements with Attention he or she could be doing. It limits Variation, Subtlety, and Slow, denying the brain of the many bits and pieces it needs for forming future skills.

What if my doctor or other professional tells me that my child will never be able to walk, talk, or develop other abilities?

> Your doctor might be right. But he or she might just as well be wrong, very wrong. These kinds of prognoses are based on the degree of limitations that the child is exhibiting at the present time. They often go on the assumption that the present limitations will continue or even get worse as time goes by. What is often missing from these prognoses is an understanding of the brain's remarkable potentials for change, given the right conditions. Further, what is often missing is an appreciation for the unknown and how the limits of human knowledge are constantly changing, always on the verge of new discoveries. Rather than allowing present limitations to dictate what you go for, start with the premise that no one knows for sure. Keep the field of possibilities open and go for it all.

Can the ABM be helpful for normally developing children?

> Yes, absolutely. The Nine Essentials apply to all human brains. The brain of the healthy child can use the optimal conditions that the Nine Essentials provide. Our experience with healthy children is so powerful that parents are asking us to offer the work to all children. But you needn't wait. All that you read in this book applies to the healthy child and will help enhance his or her life physically, cognitively, and emotionally. And, as many parents comment after learning to employ the Nine Essentials in their lives, these are all skills and ways of looking at life that can improve the quality of life for everyone.

ACKNOWLEDGMENTS

First and foremost I want to thank all the parents who brought and are currently bringing their children to us. I am awestruck, over and over again, by the deep love and commitment to their child's well-being and future that propels parents to try something new and beyond the mainstream. I admire the willingness of the parents to learn new ways of thinking and acting with their children, and most of all I'm grateful for the opportunity to make a difference in these children's lives.

I couldn't have been luckier than having Hal Zina Bennett as my co-writer. Ours was a true collaboration to which he brought his enormous talents, experience, and knowledge. But perhaps most important is his deep love for the children and his passion for insisting that I find clear ways to communicate the new knowledge and practices of the Anat Baniel Method to parents, so that they can help their children most effectively.

I would be remiss if I didn't mention my incredible teacher, mentor, and later on, close friend and colleague, Dr. Moshe Feldenkrais. I met Dr. Feldenkrais and began experiencing his work when I was still a young child. Later on, after studying with him for a few years, it was he who saw in me what I didn't see in myself—my ability to connect with children who have great challenges. His complete trust in me gave me the courage to follow what I saw was really happening with the children, to question accepted norms, and to continue to evolve my understanding of what works beyond what he taught me.

I want to thank the teachers who have trained with me and who are now my colleagues. They are remarkable in their dedication to helping children with special challenges, their skill in doing so, and in their commitment to continue learning and evolving as they help the children and their parents do the same. I particularly want to acknowledge my colleague Marcy Lindheimer. Her consistent and unwavering support and encouragement over the years have helped me many a time at moments of questioning, before many others discovered the value in this work. Her dedication to the children and parents she works with is inspiring.

My thanks and gratitude to Dr. Neil Sharp for the countless hours he has put into the scientific notes for this book. He is not only a thorough researcher but a wonderful practitioner of ABM, dedicated to working with the children.

I can't thank enough my fabulous and dedicated staff: Claire Lenyado, who patiently and lovingly manages the office and helps me keep my days straight; Dalit Broner, who is the one scheduling all the sessions and is in ongoing communication with the parents; Jill, who welcomes the children and parents at our center and joyfully deals with the smallest of details.

I am extremely grateful to the highly qualified, collaborative, and supportive teachers who are members of the team working with children at the center: Sylvia Shordike, Neil Sharp, Jan Peterson, and Marcy Lindheimer. Our work together not only gets great results with the children but is a source of encouragement and creative inspiration for us all.

John Duff, my publisher, told me a few years back that he would like to publish a book for parents about my work. I am thrilled to be working with such an exceptional organization, whose books contribute so much to the world. I want to thank my extraordinary editor, Marian Lizzi, for her gentle, yet clear and always to the point suggestions and guidance. My thanks also to all those at Perigee who are making this book possible.

Thanks to my agent, Matthew Carnicelli, for his belief and interest in this work and his help in bringing it out to the world.

The past decade has seen a groundswell of interest in brain research, and research in this area continues to expand. I am grateful to the hundreds of scientists who are working tirelessly to unveil the mysteries and the workings of the brain. Every time their findings validate what I have understood from working with the children, it emboldens me to go further. Each time science uncovers something new and different, it opens up greater richness and opportunities for discovering yet more ways to help the children.

I've been blessed to meet Dr. Michael Merzenich and to discover a brilliant scientist who is dedicated to moving knowledge from the laboratory to practical applications that help make people's daily lives better.

Today, more and more, what was once known as alternative approaches are becoming accepted as an integral part of the mainstream. Helping children with special needs is incredibly challenging and calls for an ever greater creativity and flexibility of mind and heart. I'm grateful for the many remarkable practitioners who are finding new ways to help children. They take the risk of doing things in new ways and creating new bodies of knowledge.

I want to also thank all of the physicians, therapists, and teachers who are helping bring effective alternatives into their mainstream practices.

BIBLIOGRAPHY

Baniel A. 2009. *Move into Life: The Nine Essentials for Lifelong Vitality*. New York: Harmony Books.

Begley S. 2007. *Train Your Mind, Change Your Brain: How a New Science Reveals Our Extraordinary Potential to Transform Ourselves*. New York: Ballantine Books.

Berglund B, Rossi GB, Townsend JT, Pendrill LR. eds. 2011. *Measurements with Persons: Theory, Methods and Implementation Areas*. Abingdon, Oxfordshire, UK: Psychology Press/Taylor & Francis.

Bernstein N. 1996. *On Dexterity and Its Development*. Edited by ML Latash, MT Tuvey; translated by ML Latash. Mahwah, NJ: Lawrence Erlbaum.

Berthoz A. 2000. *The Brain's Sense of Movement*. Translated by G Weiss. Cambridge, MA: Harvard University Press.

Broman SH, Fletcher JM, eds. 1999. *The Changing Nervous System: Neurobehavioral Consequences of Early Brain Disorders*. New York: Oxford University Press.

Bronson P, Merryman A. 2009. *Nurtureshock: New Thinking About Children*. New York: Twelve/Hachette Book Group.

Dawkins R. 1996. *Climbing Mount Improbable*. New York: W. W. Norton.

Doidge N. 2007. *The Brain That Changes Itself*. New York: Viking/Penguin.

Edelman GM, Tononi G. 2000. *A Universe of Consciousness: How Matter Becomes Imagination*. New York: Basic Books

Eliot L. 1999. *What's Going On in There? How the Brain and Mind Develop in the First Five Years of Life*. New York: Bantam.

Feldenkrais, M. 1990. *Awareness Through Movement*. New York: Harper Collins.

Feldenkrais, M. 1994. *Body and Mature Behavior*. Madison, Connecticut: IUP, Inc.

Feldenkrais, M. 1977. *The Case of Nora: Body Awareness as Healing Therapy*. New York: Harper & Row, Publishers, Inc.

Feldenkrais, M. 1992. *The Potent Self: A Guide to Spontaneity*. New York: HarperCollins.

Fogel A. 2009. *The Psychophysiology of Self-Awareness: Rediscovering the Lost Art of Body Sense*. New York: W. W. Norton.

Garber J, Dodge KA, eds. 1991. *The Development of Emotion Regulation and Dysregulation*. Cambridge, UK: Cambridge University Press.

Gerber M, ed. 1979. *The RIE Manual for Parents and Professionals*. Los Angeles: Resources for Infant Educarers.

Gesell A. 1940. *The First Five Years of Life: A Guide to the Study of the Pre-School Child*. New York: Harper & Brothers.

Gopnik A, Meltzoff AN, Kuhl PK. 1999. *The Scientist in the Crib: Minds, Brains and How Children Learn*. New York: William Morrow.

Gould SJ. 1977, rpnt. 2007. *Ever Since Darwin*. New York: W. W. Norton.

Grandin T. 2011. *The Way I See It*. Arlington, TX.: Future Horizons.

Guyton AC. 1981. *Textbook of Medical Physiology*. Philadelphia: Saunders.

Hanson R, Mendius R. 2009. *Buddha's Brain: The Practical Neuroscience of Happiness, Love & Wisdom*. Oakland, CA: New Harbinger.

Hebb DO. 1949. *The Organization of Behavior*. New York: Wiley.

Koch C. 2004. *The Quest for Consciousness: A Neurobiological Approach*. Englewood, CO: Roberts.

Krogman WM. 1972. *Child Growth*. Ann Arbor, MI: University of Michigan Press.

Land G, Jarman B. 1998. *Breakpoint and Beyond: Mastering the Future Today*. Scottsdale, AZ: Leadership 2000.

LeDoux J. 2002. *Synaptic Self: How Our Brains Become Who We Are*. New York: Viking/Penguin.

Lewis MD, Granic I. 2000. *Emotion, Development and Self-Organization: Dynamic Systems Approaches to Emotional Development*. Cambridge, UK: Cambridge University Press.

Llinàs R, Churchland PS, eds. 1996. *The Mind-Brain Continuum*. Cambridge, MA: MIT Press.

Nicolelis M. 2011. *Beyond Boundaries: The New Neuroscience of Connecting Brains with Machines—And How It Will Change Our Lives*. New York: Henry Holt.

Norretranders T. 1998. *The User Illusion: Cutting Consciousness Down to Size*. New York: Viking/Penguin.

Pellegrini A, Smith. PK. 2005. *The Nature of Play: Great Apes and Humans*. New York: Guildford Press.

Pellis SM, Pellis VC. 2010. *The Playful Brain: Venturing to the Limits of Neuroscience*. Oxford: Oneworld.

Pikler E. 1999. *Friedliche Babys, zufriedene Muetter* (Peaceful babies, contented mothers). Freiburg/Breisgau: Herder-Vertlag.

Pikler E. 1988. *Lasst mir Zeit: die sebstaendige Bewegungsentwicklung des Kindes bis zum freien Gehen* (Give me time: The independent movement development of a child up to free walking). Munich: Pflaum-Verlag.

Pikler E. 1997. *Miteinander vertraut werden* (To gain trust with one another). Freiburg/Breisgau: Herder-Vertlag.

Prasad KN. 1980. *Regulation of Differentiation in Mammalian Nerve Cells.* New York: Plenum.

Ratey JJ. 2000. *A User's Guide to the Brain.* New York: Pantheon.

Renninger KA, Hidi S, Krapp A. 1992. *The Role of Interest in Learning and Development.* Hillsdale, NJ: Erlbaum.

Reynolds V. 1967. *The Apes; The Gorilla, Chimpanzee, Orangutan and Gibbon: Their History and Their World.* London: Cassell.

Schaller GB. 1963. *The Mountain Gorilla: Ecology and Behavior.* Chicago: University of Chicago Press.

Schultz AH. 1969. *The Life of Primates.* New York: Universe Books.

Schwartz J, Begley S. 2002. *The Mind and the Brain: Neuroplasticity and the Power of Mental Force.* New York: HarperCollins.

Seligman M. 2006 *Learned Optimism: How to Change Your Mind and Your Life.* New York: Free Press.

Siegel, DJ. 2010. *Mindsight: The New Science of Personal Transformation.* New York: Bantam.

Siegel DJ, Hartzell M. 2003. *Parenting from the Inside Out.* New York: Tarcher/Penguin

Stein N, Leventhal B, Trabasso T, eds. 1990. *Psychological and Biological Processes in the Development of Emotion.* Hillsdale, NJ: Erlbaum.

Thelen E, Smith LB. 1996. *A Dynamic Systems Approach to the Development of Cognition and Action.* Cambridge, MA: MIT Press.

Van Lawick-Goodall J. 1971. *In the Shadow of Man.* Boston: Houghton Mifflin.

Wallechinsky D, Wallace A, Basen I, Farrow J, eds. 2004. *The Book of Lists: The Original Compendium of Curious Information.* Toronto: Knopf Canada.

Watts ES, ed. 1985. *Nonhuman Primate Models for Human Growth and Development.* New York: Alan R. Liss.

Wyer RS, Srull TK. 1984. *Handbook of Social Cognition.* Hillsdale, NJ: Erlbaum.

REFERENCES

1. How It All Began

5   **something was terribly wrong:** Eighteen years later modern diagnostic methods would reveal a third of Elizabeth's cerebellum was missing. Her official diagnosis was cerebral hypoplasia.

2. From Fixing to Connecting

19   **The brain has the ability to figure itself out:** The brain is the ultimate self-organizing system. Thompson E, Varela FJ. 2001. Radical embodiment: Neural dynamics and consciousness. *Trends in Cognitive Sciences* 5: 418–25. Lewis MD, Todd RM. 2005. Getting emotional—A neural perspective on emotion, intention and consciousness. *Journal of Consciousness Studies* 12(8–10): 213–38.

22   **These random experiences . . . are in fact required for every child's brain to form itself as fully as it might:** Coq J-O, Byl N, Merzenich MM. 2004. Effects of sensorimotor restriction and anoxia on gait and motor cortex organization: Implications for a rodent model of cerebral palsy. *Neuroscience* 129(1): 141–56.

23   **to help a child who is unable to crawl, it might seem perfectly logical . . . to assist him in making crawling motions.** What research there is often shows little effect, and part of the reason for this may be a focus on the end result. Damiano DL. 2009. Rehabilitative therapies in cerebral palsy: The good, the not as good, and the possible. *Journal of Child Neurology* 24(9): 1200–04. See also Palmer FB, Shapiro BK, Wachtel RC, et al. 1988. The effects of physical therapy on cerebral palsy. A controlled trial in infants with spastic diplegia. *New England Journal of Medicine* 318(13): 803–08. Butler C, Darrah J. 2001. Effects of neurodevelopmental treatment (NDT) for cerebral palsy: An AACPDM evidence report. *Developmental Medicine & Child Neurology* 43(11): 778–90. Wiart L, Darrah J, Kembhavi G.. 2008. Stretching with children with cerebral palsy: What do we know and where are we going? *Pediatric Physical Therapy* 20(2): 173–78. Dreifus L. 2003. Commentary: Facts, myths and fallacies of stretching. *Journal of Chiropractic Medicine* 2(2): 75–77.

23   **What we know from the science of neuroplasticity:** "[T]he realization that the
      adult brain retains impressive powers . . . to change its structure and function in
      response to experience": Begley S. 2007. How the brain rewires itself. *Time*, January
      19. See also Doidge N. 2007. *The Brain That Changes Itself.* New York: Viking.
25   **all children *learn their experience*:** "Experience coupled with attention leads to
      physical changes in the structure and functioning of the nervous system": Decharms
      RC, Merzenich M. 1996. Neural representations, experience and change. In Llinàs R,
      Churchland PS, eds. *The Mind-Brain Continuum.* Cambridge, MA: MIT Press.
27   **what your child "should" be doing now according to age and known develop-
      mental stages:** Many of the researchers who identified such stages intended them not
      as dogma but as indicators of a developmental process. Gesell A. 1940. *The First Five
      Years of Life: A Guide to the Study of the Pre-School Child.* New York: Harper &
      Brothers.

3. Your Child's Amazing Brain

28   **Our brains . . . create order out of chaos:** Evidence shows that the cerebral cortex
      shows ongoing activity in the absence of a stimulus that is comparable in size to
      stimulus-driven activity. Murphy BK, Miller KD. 2009. Balanced amplification: A
      new mechanism of selective amplification of neural activity patterns. *Neuron* 61: 635–
      48. Lewis MD. 2005. Self-organizing individual differences in brain development.
      Developmental Review 25: 252–77.
29   **After a child is born, she is just beginning to discover that she is a separate
      being in the world:** Evidence suggests neonates have awareness of themselves as
      differentiated and unique entity in the world. Rochat P, Hespos SJ. 1997. Differential
      rooting response by neonates: Evidence for an early sense of self. *Early Development
      and Parenting* 6(2): 150.1–.8. Rochat P. 2003. Five levels of self-awareness as they
      unfold early in life. *Consciousness and Cognition* 12: 717–31.
30   **The child's ability to notice differences . . . is the source of information for
      the brain:** Physiologically, the basis of all sensory perception is contrast. Guyton AC.
      1981. *Textbook of Medical Physiology.* Philadelphia: Saunders.
32   **Recently researchers Michael Merzenich and colleagues:** Merzenich and his
      team at the University of California San Francisco have done experiments to show the
      importance of what he terms *randomized movements.* Coq J-O, Byl N, Merzenich
      MM. 2004. Effects of sensorimotor restriction and anoxia on gait and motor cortex
      organization: Implications for a rodent model of cerebral palsy. *Neuroscience* 129(1):
      141–56.
34   **Kassi's brain was . . . organizing a growing complement of sensations with
      finer and finer differentiation:** As we gain experience we gain control through
      using our muscles in a more refined and precise way. This process has been demon-
      strated in the brain. Jenkins WM, Merzenich MM, Ochs MT, et al. 1990. Functional
      reorganization of primary somatosensory cortex in adult owl monkeys after behavior-

ally controlled tactile stimulation. *Journal of Neurophysiology* 63(1): 82–104. Nudo RJ, Milliken GW, Jenkins WM, Merzenich MM. 1996. Use-dependent alterations of movement representations in primary motor cortex of adult squirrel monkeys. *Journal of Neuroscience* 16(2): 785–807.

35   **The brain uses information it acquires through perceiving differences to create new connections between different brain cells; this capacity is called *differentiation*:** Differentiation is a fundamental process underlying all forms of life. Prasad KN. 1980. *Regulation of differentiation in mammalian nerve cells.* Plenum, NY. Scientists are able to measure and track the process of differentiation as it is taking place in the brain. Hebrew University of Jerusalem. 2007. Scientist observes brain cell development in "Real Time." *ScienceDaily*, May 29. Mizrahi A. 2007. Dendritic development and plasticity of adult-born neurons in the mouse olfactory bulb. *Nature Neuroscience* 10(4): 444–52.

44   **Those connections come together in complex, dynamic, responsive, and continuously evolving patterns:** For research describing development in terms of complex dynamic systems see Smith LB, Thelen E. 2003. Development as a dynamic system. *Trends in Cognitive Sciences* 7(8): 343–48. Thelen E, Smith LB. 1996. *A Dynamic Systems Approach to the Development of Cognition and Action.* Cambridge, MA, MIT Press.

4. Essential One: Movement with Attention

48   **Research shows that movement done automatically creates little or no *new* connections in the brain:** "[T]he variable determining whether or not the brain changes is . . . the attentional state of the animal." Schwartz J, Begley S. 2002, rpnt 2003. *The Mind and the Brain: Neuroplasticity and the Power of Mental Force.* New York: HarperCollins. Recanzone G.H, Merzenich MM, Jenkins WM, et al. 1992. Topographic reorganization of the hand representation in cortical area 3b of owl monkeys trained in a frequency discrimination task. *Journal of Neurophysiology* 67: 1031–56. Nudo RJ, Milliken GW, Jenkins WM, Merzenich MM. 1996 Use-dependent alterations of movement representations in primary motor cortex of adult squirrel monkeys. *Journal of Neuroscience* 16: 785–807. See Doidge N. 2007. *The Brain That Changes Itself.* New York: Viking/Penguin.

48   **when attention is brought to movement, the brain creates new connections and possibilities at an incredibly rapid rate:** My teacher and colleague, Moshe Feldenkrais, used movement to increase awareness, which in turn helped to upgrade people's functioning, often in breakthrough ways; he had his students pay close attention while moving as a way to enhance functioning. However, he did not formulate *Movement with Attention* as an Essential per se, that is, distinct from awareness.

48   **What it does do is reinforce or "groove in" the existing patterns more deeply:** The more often one nerve cell excites another the more likely they are to fire together in the future, or "Cells that fire together wire together." Hebb DO. *The Organization*

of Behavior. New York: Wiley. 1949. McClelland JL. How far can you go with Hebbian learning, and when does it lead you astray? Available at www.psych.stanford.edu/~jlm/papers/McClellandIPHowFar.pdf.

48 **a young child's brain forms 1.8 million new connections per second:** A conservative estimate of the total number of synapses in the adult brain is 100,000,000,000,000, or 100 trillion. The formation of synapses begins in the cerebral cortex—for example, during the 7th week of gestation and continues well into childhood. It is estimated that at its peak each neuron forms an average of 15,000 connections. See Gopnik A., Meltzoff AN, Kuhl PK. 1999. *The Scientist in the Crib: Minds, Brains and How Children Learn.* New York: William Morrow. Eliot L. 1999. *What's Going on in There? How the Brain and Mind Develop in the First Five Years of Life.* New York: Bantam. Ratey JJ. 2000. *A User's Guide to the Brain.* New York: Pantheon. 2000.

48 **a two-month-old infant lies in his crib watching in endless fascination as his own hand moves in space:** See Gerber M, ed. 1979. *The RIE Manual for Parents and Professionals.* Los Angeles: Resources for Infant Educarers. See also Rochat P. 2003. Five levels of self-awareness as they unfold early in life. *Consciousness and Cognition* 12: 717–31.

49 **the little boy has to pay attention to his movements:** When goals are blocked, the emotion they raise and the attention they demand provide a rich set of conditions for learning to occur. Lewis MD, Todd RM. 2005. Getting emotional—A neural perspective on emotion, intention and consciousness. *Journal of Consciousness Studies* 12(-8–10): 213–38.

52 **Think of Movement with Attention as bringing about a virtual explosion of activity in the brain:** Scans showed high levels of activity in the prefrontal cortex during new learning but not once the performance became routine. Jueptner M, Stephan K, Frith CD, et al. 1997. Anatomy of motor learning. I. Frontal Cortex and attention to Action. *Journal of Neurophysiology* 77(3): 1313–24. Johansen-Berg H, Matthews PM. 2002. Attention to movement modulates activity in sensori-motor areas, including primary motor cortex. *Experimental Brain Research* 142(1): 13–24.

53 **At such times, the quality of information that the brain generates is very high, creating order from disorder:** Creating order from disorder is a major focus of the science of chaos theory and complexity. Edelmann G.M, Tononi,G. 2000. *A Universe of Consciousness: How Matter Becomes Imagination.* New York: Basic Books.

53 **brain connections created through one activity can be applied in infinite and predictable and unpredictable ways in developing other skills:** As a child learns, different elements will come together to produce something entirely new and surprising. Levels of constructions of movements. Latash ML, Tuvey MT, eds. *On Dexterity and Its Development.* Translated by ML Latash. Mahwah, NJ: Lawrence Erlbaum. Bernstein NA. 1996b.On exercise and Motor Skill. In Latash ML, Tuvey MT, eds. *On Dexterity and Its Development.* Translated by ML Latash. Mahwah, NJ: Lawrence Erlbaum. See also Thelen E, Smith LB. 1996. *A Dynamic Systems Approach to the Development of Cognition and Action.* Cambridge, MA: MIT Press.

58 **"The practice of intentional, nonjudgmental awareness of moment to moment experience has been practiced since ancient times":** Siegel, D. The science of mindfulness. Available at http://mindful.org/the-science/medicine/the-science-of-mindfulness. Awareness as an action has been practiced and developed for centuries in the Buddhist tradition and is now the subject of intense scientific scrutiny. Barinaga M. 2003. Studying the well-trained mind: Buddhist monks and Western scientists are comparing notes on how the mind works and collaborating to test insights gleaned from meditation. *Science* 302(5642): 44–46. Lutz A, Greischar LL, Rawlings NB, Davidson R. 2004. Long-term meditators self-induce high-amplitude gamma synchrony during mental practice. *Proceedings of the National Academy of Sciences, USA* 16: 16369–73.

58 **"adults and adolescents with attentional problems achieved more executive function improvements (sustaining attention, diminishing distractibility) than are accomplished with medication for this condition."** Siegel DJ. The science of mindful awareness and the human capacity to cultivate mindsight and neural integration. Available at www.instituteofcoaching.org/images/ARticles/Mindful%20Awareness.pdf. Recent scientific findings demonstrate the benefits of practicing mindfulness in many areas of life. See Hanson R, Mendius R. 2009. *Buddha's Brain: The Practical Neuroscience of Happiness, Love & Wisdom.* Oakland, CA: New Harbinger. Siegel D. 2010. *Mindsight: The New Science of Personal Transformation.* New York: Bantam.

58 **In experiments with owl monkeys:** Recanzone, G.H, Merzenich MM, Jenkins WM, et al. 1992. Topographic reorganization of the hand representation in cortical area 3b of owl monkeys trained in a frequency discrimination task. *Journal of Neurophysiology* 67: 1031–56. Nudo RJ, Milliken G.W, Jenkins WM, Merzenich MM. 1996 Use-dependent alterations of movement representations in primary motor cortex of adult squirrel monkeys. *Journal of Neuroscience* 16: 785–807.

59 **"Experience coupled with attention leads to physical changes in the structure and functioning of the nervous system":** Merzenich MM, deCharms RC. 1996. Neural representations, experience and change." In Llinàs R, Churchland PS, eds. *The Mind-Brain Continuum.* Cambridge, MA: MIT Press.

61 **Scientific research demonstrates the importance of playfulness, joy and fun for successful growth and learning:** Play contributes to the growth and development of the brain. Byers JA, Walker C. 1995. Refining the motor training hypothesis for the evolution of play. *American Naturalist* 146(1): 25–40. Play actually shapes the brain. Gordon NS, Burke S, Akil H, Panksepp J. 2003. Socially-induced brain "fertilization": Play promotes brain derived neurotrophic factor in the amygdala and dorsolateral frontal cortex in juvenile rats. *Neuroscience Letters* 341: 17–20. See also Pellis SM, Pellis VC. 2010. *The Playful Brain: Venturing to the Limits of Neuroscience.* Oxford: Oneworld.

61 **These are also manifestations of attentioning that elevate the quality of the functioning of your child's brain:** The novelty that accompanies play sparks exploration and learning. Bunzeck N, Duzel E. 2006. Absolute coding of stimulus novelty

in the human substantia nigra/VTA. *Neuron* 51: 369–79. See also Anonymous. 2006. Pure novelty spurs the brain. *Medical News Today*, August.

61 **are always associated with an increased sense of well-being:** Free, imaginative play is crucial for normal social, emotional, and cognitive development and our well-being. When free play is lacking the results can be disastrous. Wenner M. 2009. The serious need for play. *Scientific American Mind*, February March: 22–29.

65 **Then if you have some inkling about what he's trying to communicate, ask him: "Are you asking about———?":** For thought-provoking research into how speech develops, see Bronson P, Merryman A. 2009. *Nurtureshock: New Thinking About Children*. New York: Twelve/Hachette Book Group.

65 **when touch is lacking, it can have serious consequences for the child's development:** Deprivation of normal social experience or maternal contact has damaging effects in a number of areas, the more deprivation the more disastrous. Harlow HF, Suomi SJ. 1971. Social recovery by isolation-reared monkeys. *Proceedings of the National Academy of Sciences, USA* 68(7): 1534–38.

5. Essential Two: Slow

74 *Fast we can do only what we already know:* See Libet B, Gleason CA, Wright EW, and Pearl DK. 1983. Time of conscious intention to act in relation to onset of cerebral activity (readiness potential): The unconscious intention of a freely voluntary act. *Brain* 106: 623–42.

74 **And it is important to hold off on fast until the brain has formed the necessary connections and patterns for performing that skill:** Then we can speed up successfully and even develop strong intuition in that area. Kahnman D. 2003. A perspective on judgement and choice: Mapping bounded rationality. *American Psychologist* 58: 697–720.

76 *The feeling of what happens is at the core of everything we do:* Emotions are critical in ensuring our survival and allowing us to think. Eakin E. 2003. I feel therefore I am. *New York Times*, April 19. Damasio AR. 1994. Descartes' Error: Emotion, Reason, and the Human Brain. New York: Grosset/Putnam.

76 **When we go fast, the brain has no option but to revert to already existing patterns:** Scientific research shows that we can either react automatically with a short reaction time of 0.25 second or less or act consciously with a delayed reaction time of 0.5 second or more. See Norretranders T. 1998. *The User Illusion: Cutting Consciousness Down to Size*. New York: Viking/Penguin. Norretranders's writings are based on an interview with Libet that took place on March 26–27, 1991, in San Francisco. See Libet B, Gleason CA, Wright EW, and Pearl DK. 1983. Time of conscious intention to act in relation to onset of cerebral activity (readiness potential): The unconscious intention of a freely voluntary act. *Brain* 106: 623–42.

77 **Slow is a great tool for getting there:** The learning of any skill involves putting together elements that have been formed by learning to do something else previously.

Going slowly allows the brain to figure out what in its existing repertoire may be useful, allowing the new skill to emerge. Bernstein NA. 1996. On exercise and motor skill, In Latash ML, Tuvey MT, eds. *On Dexterity and Its Development*. Translated by ML Latash. Mahwah, NJ: Lawrence Erlbaum. See also Thelen E, Smith LB. 1996. *A Dynamic Systems Approach to the Development of Cognition and Action*. Cambridge, MA: MIT Press.

79   **Current brain science confirms . . . the critical importance of Slow:** When developing his Fast ForWord program, Michael Merzenich saw the underlying problem of children with language and learning impairment as one of signal and noise— that is, the inability to filter out or generate meaningful information from background stimuli rather than a lack of stimulation per se. Merzenich MM, Tallal P, Miller SL, et al.1996. Language comprehension in language-learning impaired children improved with acoustically modified speech. *Science* 271(5245): 81–84.

83   **Parents are told to place infants as young as two weeks old on their bellies— what is called "tummy time":** Despite the fact that many infants are distressed by it, the advice to put young infants on their belly while awake arose after the findings of the connection between children sleeping on their bellies and sudden infant death syndrome (SIDS). Anonymous. 1992. Positioning and SIDS AAP Task Force on Infant Positioning and SIDS. *Pediatrics* 89: 1120–26. Anonymous. 1996. Positioning and sudden infant death Ssndrome (SIDS): Update—Task Force on Infant Positioning and SIDS. *Pediatrics* 98:1216–18. Davis BE, Moon RY, Sachs HC, and Ottolini MC. 1998. Effects of sleep position on infant motor development. *Pediatrics* 102(5): 1135–40.

83   **"Man has absolutely the most protracted period of infancy, childhood and juvenility of all forms of life":** Nearly 30 percent of a human's life is devoted to growing. Quoted in Gould SJ. 2007. *Ever Since Darwin*. Rev. ed. New York: W. W. Norton. See also, Krogman WM. 1972. *Child Growth*. Ann Arbor. MI: University of Michigan Press.

83   **When we compare the speed at which humans reach developmental milestones with that of chimpanzees:** Sources consulted during the composition of this passage include the following: Chevalier-Skolnikoff S. 1983. Sensorimotor development in orangutans and other primates. *Journal of Human Evolution* 12: 545–61. Domingo Balcells C, Veà Baró JJ. 2009. Developmental stages in the howler monkey, subspecies *Alouatta palliata mexicana*: A new classification using age-sex categories. *Neotropical Primates* 16(1): 1–8. Gerber M, ed. 1979. *The RIE Manual for Parents and Professionals*. Los Angeles: Resources for Infant Educarers. Gesell A. 1940. *The First Five Years of Life: A Guide to the Study of the Pre-School Child*. New York: Harper & Brothers. Eisenberg A, Murkoff H, Hathaway S. 1989. *What to Expect the First Year*. New York: Workman. Reynolds V. 1967. *The Apes: The Gorilla, Chimpanzee, Orangutan and Gibbon: Their History and Their World*. London: Cassell. Schaller GB. 1963. *The Mountain Gorilla; Ecology and Behavior*. Chicago: University of Chicago Press. Schultz AH. 1969. *The Life of Primates*. New York: Universe Books. Van Lawick-Goodall J. 1971. *In the Shadow of Man*. Boston: Houghton Mifflin. Watts ES. 1985. Adolescent growth and development of monkeys, apes and humans. In

Watts ES, ed. *Nonhuman Primate Models for Human Growth and Development.* New York: Alan R. Liss.

86 **Stephen Jay Gould writes: "Human babies are born as embryos":** Gould SJ. 1977. *Ever Since Darwin.* New York: W. W. Norton.

87 **What does matter is the underlying process that leads the child to accomplish that milestone:** "Do not look for linear increases in a single . . . function but for progressive patterns of maturity. Nor should we look for static absolutes. Nothing *is.* Everything is *becoming.*" Gesell A. 1940. *The First Five Years of Life: A Guide to the Study of the Pre-School Child.* New York: Harper & Brothers.

89 **Merzenich, using the principle of slowing the child and the process down, developed a software program called Fast ForWord;** Merzenich MM, Tallal P, Miller SL, et al. 1996. Language comprehension in language-learning impaired children improved with acoustically modified speech. *Science* 271(5245): 81–84.

89 **children with autism were showing improvements in listening, attention, and focus; in handwriting; and in general mental processing, indicating that their brains improved as a whole:** One study showed that Fast ForWord quickly moved autistic children from severe language impairment to the normal range. Merzenich MM, Saunders G, Jenkins WM, et al. 1999. Pervasive developmental disorders: Listening training and language possibilities. In Broman SH, Fletcher JM, eds. *The Changing Nervous System: Neurobehavioral Consequences of Early Brain Disorders.* New York: Oxford University Press. Another pilot study of 100 autistic children showed that Fast ForWord had a significant impact on their autistic symptoms. Melzer M, Poglitsch G. November 1998. Functional changes reported after Fast ForWord training for 100 children with autistic spectrum disorders. Paper presentation to the American Speech Language and Hearing Association, San Francisco. See also Tallal P, Merzenich M, Miller S, Jenkins W. 1998. Language learning impairment: Integrating research and remediation. *Scandinavian Journal of Psychology* 39: 197–99. Rubenstein JL, Merzenich MM, et al. 2003. Model of autism: Increased ratio of excitation/inhibition in key neural systems. *Genes, Brain and Behavior* 2: 255–67.

6. Essential Three: Variation

95 **In the first three years of life, the brain grows fourfold, reaching 80 percent of its adult weight:** Gould SJ. 1977. *Ever Since Darwin.* New York: W. W. Norton..

96 **The brain itself creates variation all the time:** "Thus, and this is the most important note that we are going to make, the motor skill involved in even a very simple and monotonous movement cannot be a movement formula. . . . It is the ability to find a solution across a range of variations." Bernstein NA. 1996. On exercise and motor skill. In Latash ML, Tuvey MT, eds. *On Dexterity and Its Development.* Translated by M L Latash. Mahwah, NJ: Lawrence Erlbaum. Furthermore, no one learns a skill directly through practicing that skill: "A human starts learning a movement because he cannot do it. . . . The essence and objective of exercise is to improve the move-

ments, that is, to change them. Therefore, correct exercise is in fact a repetition without repetition." Ibid.

96 **If we eliminated all variation in our environment we would actually be unable to function:** Eliminating variation has such a powerful effect on us that paranoid psychosis has been reported in prisoners in solitary confinement, in communication-deprived refugees, and in the hard of hearing. Ziskind E. 1964. A second look at sensory deprivation. *Journal of Nervous and Mental Disease* 138:223–32. Recent research has shown that as little as 15 minutes of near complete deprivation of sight and sound leads to increases in several aspects of psychotic-like experience. Mason O, Brady F. 2009. The psychotomimetic effects of short-term sensory deprivation. *Journal of Nervous and Mental Disease* 197(10): 783–85.

97 **known as developmental dysplasia of the hip (DDH):** For more information about this condition and its surgical treatment, visit the Lucile Packard Children's Hospital at Stanford website, www.lpch.org.

99 **I was very aware of his phantom cast; for Michael, even though the cast was no longer there, it was real:** The phenomenon known as *phantom limb* is felt by amputees, who sense that missing arm or leg is still present and in many cases can even feel pain. It is relatively easy to generate such illusions in otherwise normal individuals, and experiments suggest that inanimate objects may be assimilated into a person's own body image. Ramachandran VS, Hirstein W. 1998. The perception of phantom limbs. *Brain* 121: 1603–30.

101 **In 1990 a group of brain scientists set up a very interesting research project with four separate groups of adult rats:** Black JE, Isaacs KR, Anderson BJ, et al. 1990. Learning causes synaptogenesis, whereas motor activity causes angiogenesis, in cerebellar cortex of adult rats. *Proceedings of the National Academy of Sciences, USA* 87: 5568–72.

103 **Researcher Melissa A. Schilling and colleagues state:** Schilling, MA, Vidal P, Ployhart RE, Marangoni A. 2003. Learning by doing something else: Variation, relatedness, and the learning curve. *Management Science* 49(1): 39–56.

7. Essential Four: Subtlety

114 **what Ernst Heinrich Weber, a psychophysiologist, discovered more than a century ago:** The Weber-Fechner law emphasizes that the greater the intensity of the background sensory stimulus, the harder it is to perceive a change. See Uppsala University. 2004. The Weber Fechner law. Available at www.neuro.uu.se/fysiologi/gu/nbb/lectures/WebFech.html. Guyton AC. 1981. *Textbook of Medical Physiology.* Philadelphia: Saunders.

123 **"Thinking is the same fundamental process in the brain as organizing movement."** Merzenich M. April 2009. Lecture on brain plasticity to students in the Anat Baniel Method Professional Training Program. Anat Baniel Method Center, San Rafael, CA.

127 **Researchers have found that babies' ability to recognize differences followed the same Weber-Fechner law:** Infants as young as six month olds perceive differences in number in accordance with the Weber-Fechner law. Lipton JS, Spelke ES. 2003. Origins of number sense: Large-number discrimination in human infants. *Psychological Science* 14(5): 396–401. Subsequent research suggests that all information that can be conceptualized in ordinal (more vs. less) terms may share representational mechanisms in the brain, including number, space, and time; among other possible candidate dimensions are speed, loudness, luminance, and even less obvious sources of magnitude information, such as emotional expression. Lourenco SF, Longo MR. 2010. General magnitude representation in human infants. *Psychological Science* 21(6): 873–81.

8. Essential Five: Enthusiasm

133 **Think of enthusiasm as a skill:** Enthusiasm amplifies our experience, and amplification is a characteristic of many biological systems. Guyton AC. 1981. *Textbook of Medical Physiology.* Philadelphia: Saunders. Murphy BK, Miller KD. 2009. Balanced amplification: A new mechanism of selective amplification of neural activity patterns. *Neuron* 61: 635–48. Lewis MD. 2005. Self-organizing individual differences in brain development. *Developmental Review* 25: 252–77.

134 **In 1996 Giacomo Rizzolatti, a neuroscientist at the University of Parma, discovered the activity of mirror neurons in the brain:** As early as the 1980s Rizzolatti and his colleagues identified a type of brain cell that fires when observing the actions of another. Rizzolatti G, Fadiga L, Gallese V, Fogassi, L. 1996. Premotor cortex and the recognition of motor actions. *Cognitive Brain Research* 3: 131–41. Recent research suggests the mirror neuron system to be key in the learning of language, empathy, and emotions. Craighero L, Metta G., Sandini G., Fadiga L. 2007. The mirror-neurons system: Data and models. *Progress in Brain Research* 164(3): 39–59. However, the exact level of involvement and indeed the involvement of other as yet unknown mechanisms are still matters for debate. Debes R. 2009. Which empathy? Limitations in the mirrored "understanding" of emotion. *Synthese* 175(2): 219–39. Oberman LM, Ramachandran VS. 2007. The simulating social mind: The role of the mirror neuron system and simulation in the social and communicative deficits of autism spectrum disorders. *Psychology Bulletin* 133: 310–27. Singer T, Seymour B, O'Doherty J, et al. 2004. Empathy for pain involves the affective but not the sensory components of pain. *Science* 303(5661): 1157–62. Singer T. 2006. The neuronal basis and ontogeny of empathy and mind reading. *Neuroscience and Biobehavioral Reviews* 30(6): 855–63. Niedenthal P. 2007. Embodying emotion. *Science* 316(5827): 1002–05. Gallagher H, Frith C. 2003. Functional imaging of "theory of mind." *Trends in Cognitive Sciences* 7: 77–83. See Hanson R, Mendius R. 2009. *Buddha's Brain: The Practical Neuroscience of Happiness, Love & Wisdom.* Oakland, CA: New Harbinger.

134 **"The human brain has multiple mirror neuron systems":** Blakeslee S. Cells that read minds. 2006. *New York Times*, January 10.

139 **His experience itself is the reinforcement:** The spontaneous excitement of doing something new essentially gets his brain to select the relevant connections that are being formed. LeDoux J. 2002. *Synaptic Self: How Our Brains Become Who We Are.* New York: Viking/Penguin. The emotional arousal facilitates learning by increasing neural excitation and consolidating synaptic change. Lewis MD. 2005. Self-organizing individual differences in brain development. *Developmental Review* 25: 252–77.

141 **I have also observed that when pressure was placed on a child to repeat his performance of a newly acquired skill, this new skill often seems to disappear:** See Siegel D. 2003. *Parenting from the Inside Out.* New York: Tarcher/Penguin.

143 **Others' emotions as well as our own can affect us, even when we are not consciously aware of it:** The way people behave around us has a direct influence on us without requiring our full attention or requiring that the visual stimulus be consciously seen. Sinke CBA, Kret ME, de Gelder B. 2011. Body language: Embodied perception of emotion. In Berglund B, Rossi GB, Townsend JT, Pendrill LR, eds.. *Measurements with Persons: Theory, Methods and Implementation Areas.* Abingdon, Oxfordshire, UK: Psychology Press/Taylor & Francis. Kret ME, Sinke CBA, de Gelder B. 2011. Emotion perception and health. In Nyklicek I, Vingerhoets A, Zeelenberg M, eds. *Emotion Regulation and Well-Being.* New York: Springer.

143 **And these emotions can initiate synaptic changes, activating new neural connections:** Current research and theory point ever more clearly to the link between our emotions and our brain's ability and tendency to learn. Ikemoto S, Panksepp J. 1999. The role of nucleus accumbens dopamine in motivated behavior: A unifying interpretation with special reference to reward-seeking. *Brain Research Reviews* 31(1): 6–41.

143 **it is easy for him to acquire feelings of learned helplessness:** See Seligman M. 2006. *Learned Optimism: How to Change Your Mind and Your Life.* New York: Free Press.

143 **A fearful face is fast-tracked to the amygdala:** Yang E, Zald DH, Blake R. 2007. Fearful expressions gain preferential access to awareness during continuous flash suppression. *Emotion* 7(4): 882–86.

143 **Studies have shown that even when researchers made fearful faces that were invisible to conscious awareness:** Jiang Y, He S. 2006, Cortical responses to invisible faces: Dissociating subsystems for facial-information processing. *Current Biology* 16: 2023–29.

143 **places the child's brain in a "motive state," coordinating information processing in the brain:** LeDoux J. 2002. *Synaptic Self: How Our Brains Become Who We Are.* New York: Viking/Penguin.

144 **These emotions are generally manifest as stress:** Too much cortisol can damage receptors in the hypothalamus, amygdala, and prefrontal cortex, affecting mood and memory and leading to hyperreactivity to stress. Fogel A. 2009. *The Psychophysiology of Self-Awareness: Rediscovering the Lost Art of Body Sense.* New York: W. W. Norton. Lewis MD. 2005. Self-organizing individual differences in brain development. *Developmental Review* 25: 252–77.

147 **Focusing on these feelings increases the release of dopamine:** Dopamine and oxytocin (the bonding hormone) mediate strong pleasant, rewarding situations like falling in love and cause the human brain to expand its neural model of the self. Nicolelis M. 2011. *Beyond Boundaries: The New Neuroscience of Connecting Brains with Machines—And How It Will Change Our Lives.* New York: Times Books. Young L. 2009. Being human; Love; Neuroscience reveals all. *Nature* 457(7226): 148. Young L, Zuoxin W. 2004. The neurobiology of pair bonding. *Nature Neuroscience* 7(10): 1048–54.

149 **recalling, strengthening, and accessing feelings in this way . . . has been shown to lead to measurable changes in neural structures in our brains:** The longer something is held in awareness and the more emotionally stimulating it is, the more neurons that fire and thus wire together, and the stronger the trace in the memory. Lewis MD. 2005. Self-organizing individual differences in brain development. *Developmental Review* 25(3–4): 252–77. Hanson R, Mendius R. 2009. *Buddha's Brain: The Practical Neuroscience of Happiness, Love & Wisdom.* Oakland, CA: New Harbinger.

151 **"Moment by moment we choose and sculpt how our ever changing minds will work":** Merzenich MM, deCharms RC. 1996. Neural representations, experience and change. In Llinàs R, Churchland PS, eds. *The Mind-Brain Continuum.* Cambridge, MA: MIT Press.

9. Essential Six: Flexible Goals

154 **Baboons in the Kalahari Desert have excellent caches of water:** This story is presented in the 1975 documentary film *Animals Are Beautiful People,* written, produced, and directed by J. Uys.

161 **ways for her brain to differentiate and produce small changes at the edges of what she was already able to do:** Thanks to science and technology, we can now see and hear this process of a young child learning speech in action. Deb Roy: The birth of a word [TED]. Available at www.youtube.com/watch?v=VwgkT34g6lw.

163 **Play It as It Lays:** Didion J. 1970. *Play It as It Lays.* New York: Farrar Straus & Giroux.

164 **One example of imposing a rigid goal is the practice called tummy time:** It is true that babies who are subject to such efforts do tend to reach some of the earlier milestones a bit sooner. Dudek-Shriber L, Zelazny S. 2007. The effects of prone positioning on the quality and acquisition of developmental milestones in four-month-old infants. Research report. *Pediatric Physical Therapy* 19(1): 48–55.

164 **A number of followup studies:** Kuo YL, Liao HF, Chen PC, et al. 2008. The influence of wakeful prone positioning on motor development during the early life. *Journal of Developmental and Behavioral Pediatrics* 29(5): 367–76. See also Davis BE, Moon RY, Sachs HC, Ottolini MC. 1998. Effects of sleep position on infant motor development. *Pediatrics* 102(5): 1135–40.

165 **One of the studies of tummy time focused on infants with low birth weight:** Monterosso L, Kristjanson L, Cole J. 2002. Neuromotor development and the physiologic effects of positioning in very low birth weight infants. *Journal of Obstetric Gynecologic and Neonatal Nursing* 31(2): 138–46.

165 **"parents and other persons engaged in childcare":** Strassburg HM, Bretthauer Y, Kustermann W. 2006. Continuous documentation of the development of infants by means of a questionnaire for the parents. *Early Child Development and Care* 176(5): 493–504. See also Pikler E. 1988. *Lasst mir Zeit: die sebstaendige Bewegungsentwicklung des Kindes bis zum freien Gehen* (Give me time: The independent movement development of a child up to free walking). Munich: Pflaum-Verlag. Pikler E. 1997. *Miteinander vertraut werden* (To gain trust with one another). Freiburg/Breisgau: Herder-Vertlag. Pikler E. 1999. *Friedliche Babys, zufriedene Muetter* (Peaceful babies, contented mothers). Freiburg/Breisgau: Herder-Vertlag.

166 **"Not only did the children learn to sit stand and walk by themselves":** Pikler E. 1968. Some contributions to the study of gross motor development of children. *Journal of Genetic Psychology* 113: 27–39.

166 **"We regard the secure and well balanced movements of the children reared in our institute as significant":** Pikler E. 1972. Data on gross motor development on the infant. *Early Child Development and Care* 1: 297–310.

166 **among the fourteen hundred children who were raised in her institute:** Pikler E 1968. Some contributions to the study of gross motor development of children. *Journal of Genetic Psychology* 113: 27–39. Strassburg HM, Bretthauer Y, Kustermann W. 2006. Continuous documentation of the development of infants by means of a questionnaire for the parents. *Early Child Development and Care* 176(5): 493–504.

10. Essential Seven: The Learning Switch

171 **It is an actual change in the way your brain is working:** "We all know that the brain can be in a learning mode or a non-learning mode; we just don't fully understand what that mechanism is." Mark Latash, personal communication, 2007. Latash is the author of *Neurophysiological Basis of Human Movement* (Champaign, IL: Human Kinetics, 1998) and distinguished professor of kinesiology at the Pennsylvania State University.

172 **Using an electroencephalogram to measure brain waves:** Certain patterns characteristic of childhood become less common in adulthood but are seen in dreaming, in creative states, and during meditation. Oken B, Salinsky M. 1992. Alertness and attention: Basic science and electrophysiologic correlates. *Journal of Clinical Neurophysiology* 9(4): 480–94.

172 **When it is turned on, the brain is receptive:** Anticipation can affect perception. By directing our attention we can alter what we perceive of our environment. Kanwisher N, Downing P. 1998. Separating the wheat from the chaff. *Science* 282(5386): 57–58.

176 **in areas that are not directly or obviously connected to the known problems:**
The Fast ForWord program designed to help with language learning has been shown
to provide general improvements in mental processing. Merzenich MM, Saunders G,
Jenkins WM, et al. 1999. Pervasive developmental disorders: Listening training and
language possibilities. In Broman SH, Fletcher JM, eds. *The Changing Nervous System: Neurobehavioral Consequences of Early Brain Disorders.* New York: Oxford
University Press. Fast ForWord has also had a significant impact on autistic symptoms.
Melzer M, Poglitsch G. November 1998. Functional changes reported after Fast For-
Word training for 100 children with autistic spectrum disorders. Paper presented to
the American Speech Language and Hearing Association, San Francisco. See Doidge
N. 2007. *The Brain That Changes Itself.* New York: Viking/Penguin.

179 **While the term** *Learning Switch* **does not describe a mechanical device in the
brain:** When arousal is sufficient, the brain is responsive to stimuli and learning can
take place. LeDoux J. 2002. *Synaptic Self: How Our Brains Become Who We Are.*
New York: Viking/Penguin. Emotional arousal facilitates learning by increasing neural excitation and consolidating synaptic change. Lewis MD. 2005. Self-organizing
individual differences in brain development. *Developmental Review* 25: 252–77.
Forebrain arousal and motivational controls have been shown to modulate reorganization of the auditory cortex in response to new learning experiences. Kilgard MP, Merzenich MM. 1998. Cortical map reorganization enabled by nucleus basalis activity.
Science n.s. 279(5357): 1714–18; Research findings suggest that events that are not
emotionally significant may not maintain arousal or attention long enough for learning
to take place. Lewis MD. 2005. Bridging emotion theory and neurobiology through
dynamic systems modeling. *Behavioral and Brain Sciences* 28: 169–245.

179 **there are chemicals in the brain, called neuromodulators:** Neuromodulators
are neurotransmitters and neuropeptides manufactured in the brainstem and hypothalamus that are released in large volumes, at many synapses simultaneously, far
from their sites of origin. Izquierdo I. 1997. The biochemistry of memory formation
and its regulation by hormones and neuromodulators. *Psychobiology* 25: 1–9. The
effects of neuromodulators are global rather than local, providing a key mechanism by
which motivational concerns influence cognitive and perceptual processes and hence
learning. Lewis MD. 2005. Bridging emotion theory and neurobiology through
dynamic systems modeling. *Behavioral and Brain Sciences* 28: 169–245.

180 **Emotions, most brain researchers agree, also guide our attention, which is
necessary for any new learning to occur:** Cognition in general and attention in
particular are assumed to be guided by emotional relevance. Isen AM. 1984. Toward
understanding the role of affect in cognition. In Wyer, RS, Srull TK, eds. *Handbook
of Social Cognition.* Hillsdale, NJ: Erlbaum. Dodge KA. 1991. Emotion and social
information processing. In Garber J, Dodge KA, eds. *The Development of Emotion
Regulation and Dysregulation.* Cambridge, UK: Cambridge University Press. Renninger KA, Hidi S, Krapp A. 1992. *The Role of Interest in Learning and Development.*
Hillsdale, NJ: Erlbaum. See Lewis MD, Todd RM. 2005. Getting emotional—A neu-

ral perspective on emotion, intention and consciousness. *Journal of Consciousness Studies* 12(8–10): 213–38.

180 **"The ability to respond to threat and to seek safety is the most important job of our nervous system":** Fogel A. 2009. *The Psychophysiology of Self-Awareness: Rediscovering the Lost Art of Body Sense.* New York: W. W. Norton.

180 A **prolonged stress response to threat (perceived or real) is particularly damaging:** The stress response to threat is mediated by cortisol, which can damage receptors in the brain and affect mood, memory, and hyperreactivity to stress. Fogel A. 2009. *The Psychophysiology of Self-Awareness: Rediscovering the Lost Art of Body Sense.* New York: W. W. Norton. Lewis MD. 2005. Self-organizing individual differences in brain development. *Developmental Review* 25: 252–77.

180 **Safety, connection with the parent, playfulness, joy, comfort, acceptance, and love:** Isen AM. 1990. The influence of positive and negative affect on cognitive organization: Some implications for development. In Stein N, Leventhal B, Trabasso T, eds. *Psychological and Biological Processes in the Development of Emotion.* Hillsdale, NJ: Erlbaum. Conversely, anxiety narrows attention to specific themes or perceptions. Mathews A. 1990. Why worry? The cognitive function of anxiety. *Behavior Research and Therapy* 28: 455–68.

183 **Researchers have discovered that the ideal span of time for learning is no more than twenty minutes:** The study assessed student's recall of chemistry information following a lecture. Ralph A. May 22–25, 1985. Information impact and factors affecting recall. Paper presented at the Seventh Annual National Conference on Teaching Excellence and Conference of Administrators, Austin, TX.

11. Essential Eight: Imagination and Dreams

190 **Research shows that adults who practiced playing the piano in their imagination:** "mental practice alone led to the same plastic changes in the motor system as those occurring with the acquisition of the skill by repeated physical practice.... Mental practice alone seems to be sufficient to promote the modulation of neural circuits involved in the early stages of motor skill learning." Pascual-Leone A, Nguyet D, Cohen LG, et al. 1995. Modulation of muscle responses evoked by transcranial magnetic stimulation during the acquisition of new fine motor skills. *Journal of Neurophysiology* 74: 1037–45. See also Pascual-Leone A, Amedi A, Fregni, F, Merabet LB. 2005. The plastic human brain cortex. *Annual Review of Neuroscience* 28: 377–401.

191 **George Land tested 1,500 children between the ages of three and five:** Land conducted the study beginning in the late 1960s. It employed repeated administrations of eight tests that had been used by NASA to measure the potential for creative work by its engineers and scientists. Land G, Jarman, B. 1998. *Breakpoint and Beyond: Mastering the Future Today.* Scottsdale, AZ: Leadership 2000.

193 **all physical activity is organized in the brain by images of the person moving through space:** Alain Berthoz discusses how the development of perception critically depends on movement and the information that movement provides. Decety J, Jeannerod M, Prablanc C. 1989. The timing of mentally represented actions. *Behavioral Brain Research* 34: 35–42. Berthoz A. t2000. *The Brain's Sense of Movement.* Translated by G Weiss. Cambridge, MA: Harvard University Press.

194 **That three-dimensional movie . . . contains information from all of our senses:** A stable internal model of the self is constructed from fragments of information resulting from multiple sensory systems—vision, proprioception, hearing, etc. Ramachandran VS, Hirstein W. 1998. The perception of phantom limbs. *Brain* 121: 1603–30. Dawkins, R. 1996. *Climbing Mount Improbable.* New York: W. W. Norton.

194 **A child who was raised with wolves:** In May 1972, a boy aged about four was discovered in the forest of Musafirkhana, about twenty miles from Sultanpur, India. The boy was playing with wolf cubs. Wallechinsky D, Wallace A, Basen I, Farrow J, eds. 2004. *The Book of Lists: The Original Compendium of Curious Information.* Toronto: Knopf Canada.

195 **Research shows just the opposite is the case:** Researchers observed activity within the brains of people engaged in tasks that required high levels of mental concentration, then compared those results to brain activity when the people were daydreaming. Mason MF, Norton MI, Van Horn JD, et al. 2007. Wandering minds: The default network and stimulus-independent thought. *Science* 315(5810): 393–95. Jones H. 2007. Daydreaming improves thinking. *Cosmos Online,* January 19.

196 **Steven Jay Lynn and Judith Rhue, both psychologists, studied six thousand men and women:** Lynn SJ, Rhue JW. 1988.Fantasy proneness. Hypnosis, developmental antecedents, and psychopathology. *American Psychologist* 43(1): 35–44.

196 **But it's not only in mental or cognitive functions that Imagination and Dreams make a Difference:** Crum AJ, Langer EJ. 2007. Mind-set matters: Exercise and the placebo effect. *Psychological Science* 18(2): 165–71.

197 **Children begin participating in pretend play, or make believe by their second year of life:** Pretend play is typical between fifteen months and six years of age. Piaget J. 1951. *Play, Dreams and Imitation in Childhood.* London: Heinemann. Smith PK. 2005. Social and pretend play in children. In Pellegrini A, Smith PK, eds. 2005. *The Nature of Play: Great Apes and Humans.* New York: Guildford Press.

12. Essential Nine: Awareness

209 **Philosophers have also referred to this capacity as "meta- consciousness" or "meta-awareness":** Meta-awareness is a concept that points to the possibility of taking awareness itself as an object of attention. Schooler JW. 2001. Discovering memories in the light of meta-awareness. *Journal of Aggression, Maltreatment and Trauma* 4: 105–36. Studies in mind wandering show that it is not the mind wandering per se that interferes with the ability to process knowledge and information and learning but

the lack of awareness of the mind wandering. Winkielman P, Schooler JW. 2011. Splitting consciousness: Unconscious, conscious, and metaconscious processes in social cognition. *European Review of Social Psychology* 22(1): 1–35.

210 **researchers are finding out that infants as young as seven months old demonstrate at least some capabilities of awaring:** Kovács ÁM, Téglás E, Endress AD. 2010. The social sense: Susceptibly to others' beliefs in human infants and adults. *Science* 330(6012): 1830–34. Bryner J. 2010. 7-month-old babies show awareness of others' viewpoints. Available at www.livescience.com/10924-7-month-babies-show-awareness-viewpoints.html.

210 **Scientists at MIT have shown that twelve-month-old babies can use knowledge to form surprisingly sophisticated expectations of how novel situations will unfold:** If no relevant past experience is available results suggest that infants reason by mentally simulating possible scenarios and figuring out which outcome is most likely, based on a few physical principles. Téglás E, Vul E, Girotto V, et al. 2011. Pure reasoning in 12-month-old infants as probabilistic inference. *Science* 332(6033): 1054–59.

13. Beyond Limitations

220 **"Parents and teachers should look at the child, not the child's label":** Grandin T. 2011. *The Way I See It*. Arlington, TX: Future Horizons.

INDEX

ABOUT THE AUTHOR

© Carl Studna

ANAT BANIEL, born and raised in Israel, has established a worldwide reputation for her work with special needs children. The results of her more than thirty years of experience working with thousands of children and parents, and training hundreds of practitioners, and her ongoing search and revolutionary discoveries have led to the creation of the Anat Baniel Method. She has been called a miracle worker for her ability to bring new life and vitality to the children she has been working with.

A dancer and clinical psychologist, with a degree in statistics, she became interested in the functioning of the human brain, which led, in her early twenties, to her close association with Dr. Moshe Feldenkrais, arguably the greatest movement scientist of the twentieth century. This opened a path for her to discover breakthrough ways to communicate with the child's brain, helping him or her to change for the better. She has never been stopped by currently limiting beliefs about what is possible for the child.

Her focus on improving the functioning of the child's brain, and approaching the child as a whole, unified, moving, feeling, and thinking human being, allows her and the practitioners she has trained to work with a wide range of children. This includes children on the autism spectrum as well as those with cerebral palsy, genetic disorders, ADD, ADHD, feeding challenges, brachial plexus injury, torticollis, and undiagnosed developmental conditions. Her work is endorsed by medical professionals and scientists throughout the world.

At the Anat Baniel Method Center in Marin County, California, she and her team of teachers train new practitioners in her method and work with private clients from all over the world. She travels extensively, giving public presentations and teaching workshops for parents and professionals. Visit her website at www.anatbanielmethod.com.